Behavioral Economics

Fabrizio Ghisellini • Beryl Y. Chang

Behavioral Economics

Moving Forward

palgrave
macmillan

Fabrizio Ghisellini
Center for Monetary and Financial Studies
LUISS University
Rome, Italy

Beryl Y. Chang
New York University
New York, NY, USA

ISBN 978-3-030-09170-5 ISBN 978-3-319-75205-1 (eBook)
https://doi.org/10.1007/978-3-319-75205-1

Cover illustration: natbasil / Alamy Stock Vector

Printed on acid-free paper

This Palgrave Macmillan imprint is published by the registered company Springer International Publishing AG part of Springer Nature.
The registered company address is: Gewerbestrasse 11, 6330 Cham, Switzerland

Preface

"Oh no! Yet another book on behavioral economics? Do we really need it?"

This could plausibly be the knee-jerk reaction of a potential reader after picking up this book from the shelf of a bookshop. And on the surface, this impulsive reaction would be justified. In the last few years there has been a growing supply of books on the subject or referencing to it. Try inputting the keywords "behavioral economics" in the Amazon advanced book search tool, and you will get a clear upward publishing trend: 136 books in 2013, 181 in 2014, 200 in 2015, and 293 in 2016. So the burden of proof is on us. We have got to demonstrate that this book is not just one more of the same, but is different.

In order to do so, let's turn for a second to the mainstream contents that dominate the editorial supply. This is an important issue, as behavioral economics, being interdisciplinary and at the crossroad of economics and psychology, is an incredibly wide subject. Consider the best sellers first. The all-time top three books are the following:

Thinking, Fast and Slow by Daniel Kahneman
Predictably Irrational: The Hidden Forces That Shape Our decisions by Dan Ariely
Nudge: Improving Decisions about Health, Wealth, and Happiness by Richard H. Thaler and Cass R. Sunstein

On the surface, these three brilliant books look diverse. The core of Kahneman's book is the description of the two different systems governing mind processes (System I, quick and intuitive; System II, slow and analytical). Ariely focuses on the systematic nature of human mistakes. Thaler and Sunstein explain why it is appropriate and useful that institutions and governments gently push citizens toward specific choices deemed to be in their best self-interest.

There is a strict conceptual link that ties together these three brilliant books, however, and it has to do with the rather negative view of the way in which humans form their deliberations. Humans are depicted as prone to all sorts of cognitive distortions and biases, and this leads to inaccurate judgments and decisions. In many cases, people are judged to be simply irrational.[1]

This is indeed the dominating mantra in behavioral economics.

If you had been sitting in front of your PC on August 1, 2017, googling "What is behavioral economics?" and just zapped across the first page results, you would have found definitions such as:

- *The field of behavioral economics blends insights of psychology and economics, and provides some valuable insights that individuals are not behaving in their own best interests. Behavioral economics provides a framework to understand when and how people make errors.*
- *Behavioral economics (BE) uses psychological experimentation to develop theories about human decision making and has identified a range of biases as a result of the way people think and feel.*
- *Behavioral economists.... aim to develop models which account for the facts that people procrastinate, are impatient, aren't always good decision-makers when decisions are hard (and sometimes even avoid making decisions altogether), go out of their way to avoid what feels like a loss, care about things like fairness in addition to economic gain, are subject to psychological biases which make them interpret information in biased ways, and so on.*

The common gist of all these definitions is therefore that behavioral economics studies the how and the why people make errors, most of the times as a result of biases (i.e. cognitive distortions). As we will see later on, these definitions can be questionable. But are they at least meaningful? They would be only if we were in a position to rely on an authentic interpretation of what an "error" is or what a "bias" is. But to define a decision as an "error", you do need a consensus view on what instead a "correct" decision is. And this consensus view can emerge only if we agree beforehand on what the "benchmark" economic decision-making model is. That's exactly the problem. It is as if a fish-based diet were defined "wrong" simply because the specific reference diet one has in mind contains just steaks and sausages. In the case of these definitions, the steaks and sausages diet is conventional economics, based on the theory of rational choice and on a set of axioms regarding preferences that univocally defines the conventional definition of rationality; it does not matter whether alternative economic theories can describe better real-world decision-making. Everything that is outside the realm of steaks and sausages is therefore by definition "wrong", and leads to "errors".

This is why the dominant conceptual framework regulating the relationship between conventional and behavioral economics can be sketched as follows:

- the benchmark model is conventional economics, based on axiomatic rationality and markets equilibrium, that depicts the world as it should be.
- Behavioral economics is a subordinated discipline that can help in identifying the circumstances and the reasons why people deviate from rationality and do not act in their best interest.

But is this really all that it is to behavioral economics? The fundamental message of this book—and what makes it different from the hundreds of behavioral economics books aiming at showing just how irrational we are—is that behavioral economics should not be taken just as a subordinated discipline. How can that be? The picklock stands in the definition of rationality.

The conventional definition of rationality prescribes that an individual has clear preferences that are stable over time, complete, and transitive (if I prefer A to B and B to C, then I also prefer A to C). So if you, generally speaking, prefer spaghetti to hamburgers, you are bound to always choose spaghetti to hamburgers for the whole of your lifetime. Try to just relax that definition in favor of the one put forward by Nobel laureate Herbert Simon: "*Behaviour is rational in so far as it selects alternatives that are conducive to the achievement of the previously selected goals*". So what counts is whether behavior works, not how it works. Then much of the alleged irrationality portrayed in the three bestsellers above disappears. And the definition of behavioral economics becomes simply that of a method of economic analysis that applies psychological insights to enrich the explanation of economic decision-making. Should this discipline be subordinated to conventional economics or rather…replace it? We think it could, but not just as yet. As House (2014) writes:

> *Today, it seems like behavioural economics has slowed down somewhat. For whatever reason, the flood of behavioural economists we were anticipating 10 years ago never really materialised… Behavioural economics won't get very far if it ends up being just a pile of quirks.*[2]

In order to move forward, behavioral economics needs therefore to go through a streamlining process, in which gaps are filled and questions at least begin to be answered. This is what the book is about, and this is why it is not "yet another book on behavioral economics".

Rome, Italy
New York, USA

Fabrizio Ghisellini
Beryl Y. Chang

Notes

1. Daniel Kahneman might have a communication problem in that respect. In the book he states that "*I often cringe when my work with Amos is credited with demonstrating that human choices are irrational, when in fact our research only showed that Humans are not well described by the rational-agent model*". But he then adds, "*Although Humans are not irrational, they often need help to make more accurate judgments and better decisions, and in some cases policies and institutions can provide that help*", which implies that institutions are more rational than citizens and therefore do not really help to shed clarity on whether people are rational at all.
2. Chris House. "Is Behavioral Economics the Past or the Future?" *Orderstatistic*, February 28, 2014 <https://orderstatistic.wordpress.com/2014/02/28/is-behavioral-economics-the-past-or-the-future/>.

Contents

List of Figures

List of Tables

Part I

How did we get here?

1

Introduction to Part I

How to begin?

Before we plunge into the "unfinished businesses" in behavioral economics, it is appropriate to give a refreshing overview of "how we got here", that is, the process by which behavioral economics has become a serious competitor to what we call "conventional economics" (CE). And this is what we deal with in Part I.

To start with, Chap. 2 gives a concise but complete report on the rise and fall of conventional economics. We identify contemporary conventional economics with New Classical Economics, led by people such as Nobel laureate Robert J. Lucas and Thomas Sargent, which has been mainstream throughout the last three decades of the last century and beyond. In this section, we present:

- the conceptual pillars of decision-making in conventional economics (i.e. expected discounted utility, rational choice, and rational expectations)
- an example of the decision-making process for the leading character of conventional economics, the *homo economicus*, who has wealth maximization as the sole target, is characterized by consistent preferences

F. Ghisellini, B. Y. Chang, *Behavioral Economics*,
https://doi.org/10.1007/978-3-319-75205-1_1

and linear time discounting, acts in splendid isolation, and is endowed with complete information and advanced computing capabilities. In particular, after introducing the efficient market hypothesis (EMH), we show the way in which the *homo economicus* would be supposed to elaborate and implement an asset allocation strategy

- analytical evidence of the inadequacy of conventional economics, including EMH, to fit reality, using as a litmus test what happened during the global financial crisis begun in 2007

Chapter 3 is devoted to an overview of the behavioral economics revolution.

We first present the reasons for the emergence and the success of behavioral economics. We then proceed to highlight the features of the behavioral "versions" of utility and rationality. Utility is no longer just egotistic wealth maximization, but a much wider and complex concept which can also be a function of drivers related to fairness and altruism.

Similarly, behavioral economics questions the conventional view of rationality (based on consistency and coherence). So to start with, we review the seminal contribution of Nobel Prize winner Herbert Simon, who 60 years ago introduced the concepts of bounded rationality and "satisficing" choices. Then, after giving an account of the major breakthrough implied by the prospect theory developed by Daniel Kahneman and Amos Tversky, we compare the different tenets of the "American" and the "German" schools: for the former, people who use heuristics (mental shortcuts) are plagued by biases and therefore make irrational choices; for the latter, which has its most influential advocate in Gerd Gigerenzer, heuristics are in fact "ecologically rational", that is, optimal if environmental factors are taken into account in the decision-making. After describing the way in which real-world people take decisions, we investigate the extent to which the psychological insights introduced by behavioral economics fit reality, using again the global financial crisis as a test bed.

So with Part I of the book, a (hopefully) complete and clear account of how we got here is given.

2

Does Conventional Economics Fit Reality?

2.1 The Rise of New Classical Economics

As it is often the case in history, what is now considered conventional started off as a revolution. Economics is no exception. The revolution began in the early 1970s, especially in the work of Robert Lucas (Nobel Prize winner in 1995) at the University of Chicago, and its name was New Classical Economics.

Given that this book is mainly about behavioral economics and decision-making, in what follows we only give a brief account of the main innovations and tenets of the New Classical paradigm as regards macroeconomics, and focus instead on its basic microeconomic pillars (e.g. utility and rationality).

The name "New Classical" was meant to suggest a revival of the Classical Economics, against the then prevailing Keynesian school of thought. In Keynes' view, the macroeconomic framework was especially prone to the possible shortage of aggregate demand (the sum of consumption, investment, government expenditure, and net exports), and recessions would in that case readily ensue. In particular, the sequence of events could begin with a fall in private investments. With firms produc-

F. Ghisellini, B. Y. Chang, *Behavioral Economics*,
https://doi.org/10.1007/978-3-319-75205-1_2

ing less and, given wage stickiness, unable in the short term to cut wages to a level which would be in any case acceptable for workers, the net result is the appearance of "involuntary unemployment". In such a situation, an increase in public expenditure is key to boost aggregate demand and bring the system back to equilibrium.

This account of reality seemed quite inconceivable to Lucas and his fellow New Classicals (including famous economists such as Thomas Sargent, Robert J. Barro, and Edward Prescott), as for them price changes would ensure that markets always tend to equilibrium and agents always optimize. If for whatever occasional reasons private investments fell, firms would promptly cut wages to restore profits and workers would accept the best option available (i.e. lower wages) rather than facing unemployment. So, very much as it was the case for the "old" Classicals, equilibrium is almost always there.

Almost always. Fluctuations in output can indeed occur, and they can be large and/or persistent. In the latter case, the explanation given by New Classicals is structural, as it has to do with productivity/technology changes, which require the entire system to adapt, and of course that may take some time. What is perhaps even more interesting is, however, the interpretation given to non-structural shocks.

As a matter of fact, in order for the New Classicals' macroeconomic policies (fiscal and monetary policies) to have any effects on real output, they are subject to one condition—they must be unanticipated by economic agents. Why? In order to give a satisfactory answer to this question, we should take a step back to what was one of the most successful concepts until the New Classicals showed up on the macroeconomic scene: the Phillips curve.

In 1958, A. W. H. Phillips published in the *Economica* magazine the results of his study of wage inflation and unemployment in the United Kingdom from 1861 to 1957, which highlighted an inverse relationship between the two variables, as visualized in Fig. 2.1.

During the 1960s, this led many to believe that, through the use of monetary policy, governments could choose the combination of inflation and unemployment which was deemed more suitable in any specific circumstance. Unfortunately, that turned out to be not the case. In the US, during the 1970s, the average inflation rate rose by about 4.5% vis-à-vis

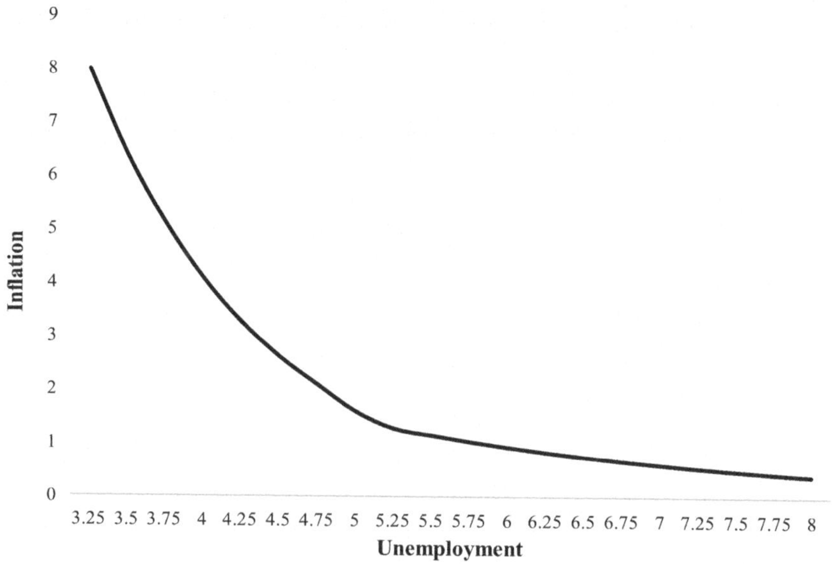

Fig. 2.1 Basic Phillips Curve

the previous decade, and the response of the unemployment rate was not a reduction, but an *increase* of more than 2%.

From a theoretical point of view, the first (big) nail on the coffin of the simplest version of the Phillips curve was placed by important economists like Milton Friedman and Edmund Phelps. They stressed that the key adjustment variable for equating labor demand and supply is the real wage, rather than the nominal one. Given that there is just one equilibrium real wage, there is also only one long-run unemployment rate, the natural rate of unemployment. While in the short run monetary policy may produce real effects while people recalculate the level of real wages, in the long run the Phillips curve is therefore vertical (i.e. no exploitable trade-off between inflation and unemployment).

There would be much more to write about the Phillips curve issue and related variations on the theme (like, for example, the "expectations augmented Phillips curve"), but for our purposes we just needed to introduce the basic concept as it represents an outstanding example of "interventionist" policies on the part of the state at the moment in which Robert Lucas began to work on what came to represent his most influential piece of research: the Lucas' (1976) critique.

Focusing on econometric models, what Lucas argued was that the "simulations made using these models can, in principle, provide no useful information as to the actual consequences of alternative economic policies". The reason for this is identified by Lucas in the fact that after a policy change is introduced, households and firms "recalculate" the parameters governing the structural dynamics of the economy and optimize accordingly. So, using the simulations for the effect of a policy change parameter that is estimated *before* the policy change actually occurs is essentially deprived of any significance. And no simulation can forecast accurately the effects of "interventionist" policies.

Almost simultaneously with the Lucas' critique, the inadequacy of active macroeconomic policies was also forcefully highlighted by Robert J. Barro (1974) with special reference to fiscal policy and government debt. Say that a government wants to run a deficit in order to boost aggregate demand, and the deficit is financed by bond issuance. Barro argues that rational households would know that government debt shall have to be repaid by their descendants via higher taxes. Given intergenerational altruism, bequests will have to be robust enough to accommodate this, which in turn implies an immediate increase in savings. As a consequence (this is the "Ricardian equivalence" effect), fiscal deficits will have no expansionary effect at all.

So, should we forsake macroeconomic policies? Lucas' answer is that in order to survive, the nature of policies has to change. What government and central bank policies should do is just create the best possible environment for economic agents, that is, minimize intertemporal distortions. And to do that, policy rules are bound to be very simple, very credible, and very transparent. The new framework should therefore have as essential components:

- an intertemporal general equilibrium with markets that clear continuously,
- markets populated by optimizing agents, and
- economic agents who use rational expectations (i.e. they make the best possible use of available information).

Of these three essential components, the first and the second are not new, as they are exactly the same of the "old" Classical Economics. What about the third? Was it the third to make the difference and to grant New Classical Economics such a resounding success, not only over Keynesian theories but also over monetarism?

Let's proceed in an orderly fashion, and consider first the actual historical circumstances. As a matter of fact, Keynesianism in the 1970s suffered a series of reputational blows. In particular, the stagflationary process following the "oil shock" was taken as a proof that the Phillips curve simply didn't work.

In this context, the mathematical beauty and the apparently stringent logic of the new models gained quite an audience, especially among the younger generations.

But how to explain the speed with which New Classical Economics took over mainstream macroeconomics to become the standard (this is why today we can equate it with "conventional" economics)?

Many would agree that the crucial reason had to do with the fact that the new doctrine filled one main conceptual gap in Keynesian macroeconomics: microfoundations.

In many Keynesian models, the individual was not a leading and active character, but rather just another material input, very much like commodities. In contrast, the revolutionary concept introduced by New Classicals was that there was no longer any distinction between micro- and macroeconomics. The New Classicals not only brought back at the center of the scene the way in which the individual takes his decisions, but also argued that such decisions are highly efficient, as they optimize expected utility and, above all, are based on full-blown rationality.

In the next two sections we examine in more detail the pillars of what was New Classical and is now conventional economics: agents' maximization of expected utility AND rational expectations.

2.2 The First Pillar of Conventional Economics: Maximization of Utility

What is utility in economic terms? Why and how do we want to measure it? In simple terms, utility is a function or ability that creates value or effectiveness which benefits us in whatever we strive to accomplish in life.

Similarly, and in economic terms, utility is something that is useful or a means, such as money, of meeting our needs and wants of daily life necessities mostly in the form of consumption, such as buying foods and clothing. From a different perspective, utility can also be experiences that satisfy our aspirations or give us certain kind of fulfillment and gratification beyond the daily mundane essentials, for example, traveling to Rome or visiting La Scala in Milan. Since the subject of utility interacts with the most fundamental concept of the quality of human lives and well-beings, the topic is among one of the most popular and intensely studied areas in the field of economics. Understanding how utility works among people is also paramount to a nation's economy. If we know pasta is recognized to be the most utility-enhancing of all grains in the local grocery market, the price of pasta in the store may be the highest. This leads us to the question of how we measure utility and whether we could measure all types of utilities.

For centuries economists have come up with theories of how we should measure utility and how an economic agent is expected to behave if he is to be considered "rational". In standard utility analysis, which has been put into practice for at least a few hundred years, a "rational" economic agent is supposed to be able to make decisions now about the utility that he will benefit in the future based totally on the final outcome of his calculations. In other words, his calculation should disregard the context or a particular situation he is in and therefore the reference point of the outcome that he may care about. Suppose there is a combination of a stock and a bond position that you are considering taking for your portfolio. One year from now, you expect to have equal probability of gaining or losing \$1000. Would you take the chance of investing in these positions? To sum up the probability with 50% chance of gaining and 50% chance of losing, ignoring the time value of money for now, the expected utility in the conventional theory looks something like $(0.5 \times 1000) - (0.5 \times 1000) = 0$.

Since the result is neither a gain nor a loss, as a "rational" agent, you should be indifferent about whether to invest in these positions. Or it does not matter if you decide to sway one way or the other following the practice of the expected utility function. Is this how we actually behave and make decisions?

The expected utility theory (EUT) was originally proposed by the Swiss mathematician Daniel Bernoulli around 1738. The story went like this: in trying to find a reasonable price for a gamble using coin flipping and payoff as an estimate, say you receive a payoff of \$ $(2 \times n)$, where n is the number of throws with the head and the game ends when the tail first appears. People were exasperated by the fact that as they could get the head of the coin for infinite number of throws, the price would have an unlimited growth and no one would be willing to pay for the end result. This is a paradox since the expected value generated from getting the head of a coin by random throw could be infinite while people are only willing to pay some small amounts. Bernoulli then came up with an idea and believed that most people would only be willing to pay a small amount to enter the gamble or the "utility" on monetary outcomes and the value of a gamble would be the expectation of these utilities. However, having no means to establish a uniformed utility function in precise numeric terms from a disparity of subjective utility expectations among different individuals, Bernoulli had to make assumptions of some arbitrary sorts. To achieve small amounts that gamblers are willing to pay for, one of the assumptions he made was that of the diminishing marginal utility. In this case, one's utility decreases as the next round of payoff from the gamble increases on a per unit basis, continuing with greater amounts for subsequent units. So in calculating expected utility values, utility does not increase proportionally to the increase of payoffs or wealth. Since the proposal by Bernoulli was published in St. Petersburg in Russia, a city where he resided at one time, the problem is named as the St. Petersburg Paradox.

From this simple example on whether to invest in a stock and a bond position in your portfolio, you may want to poke a little deeper to see what a choice based on expected utility implies. There are several assumptions in the function. First, the "rational" agent is supposed to not only have the cognitive ability to do the calculations, as we just showed, but also know precisely the weight of the probability of gains and losses one year from now. In other words, the agent has perfect information and knowledge about exactly what will occur due to the choice he makes net of any unforeseeable market variations occurring in the meantime. Moreover, since expected utility theory is prescribed for "rational" agents and independent from any reference points, the behavior of the agent is only "rational" if he gives symmetrical responses to gain and to loss prospects. In addition, even if utility in some form is considered to be a means and not an end, the agent pursues further along the same path without looking back to see whether it indeed created value that truly benefits him, or whether there are other important factors to consider in choosing the appropriate course of action for boosting his well-being.

To see how the reference-independent axiom works in the expected utility theory, here is an illustration: suppose the value of your portfolio went down from $5M to $4M and your sister's went up from $1M to $1.5M within the last month. According to expected utility theory, your utility is considered higher, as the final outcome of $4M in your portfolio is higher than $1.5M in your sister's portfolio. Clearly, expected utility theory does not take into account the specific as well as relative situations of investors, the reference points, at a particular point in time. But in reality, our satisfaction or utility in life is derived mostly from our relative position. In 1937, Paul Samuelson introduced the concept of discounted utility in gauging intertemporal choices and therefore differentiate the effective levels of utility as a result of the timing of goods consumed. However, there are several restrictions and assumptions in the model: (1) an individual's tastes do not vary throughout time, (2) the prices of all goods remain constant during the same period, (3) the rate of discount for future utilities is constant for all time periods, and (4) the discount rate is the same for all types of goods and all categories of intertemporal decisions. So for a specific time period t of consumption c, the individual maximizes and integrates all future utilities V with the first derivative dt: $J = \int_0^T V(c, t)\,dt$ where future utility J is maximized to the end of the period T and individual's future utilities are discounted as $V(c, t) = U(c)e^{-\beta t}$. And β bears the relationship to the rate of discount (positive or negative) p, which is assumed to be constant $\beta = \log e(I + p)$. So at any moment in time, an individual maximizes a stream of all future utilities of consumption discounted with constant rate: $J = \int_0^T U(c)e^{-\beta t}\,dt$.

The assumptions in the discounted utility model lead to few implications. With the discount rate for a lifetime consumption stream from t to T being constant, future consumptions are reprimanded given higher power in t with deeper discounts for time periods further away from today, and the premium factor required for postponing consumption is not discussed or considered in the model. The constant discount rate also ignores any time preferences during the long stream of consumptions in one's life time and therefore assumes that utility generated from all consumptions is independent of any personal time preferences. Similarly, the discount rate for all types of goods and all categories of intertemporal decisions being the same as in Samuelson's model implies, for example, that half a dozen drinks you consumed last night at a party will have no impact on your behavior or craving for the number of drinks you will have today, or similarly, the food you had in an Italian restaurant yesterday will have no role in the kind of food you would like to have today. The assumption disregards time preferences that often occur among consumers and consequently implies that utility from consumption is independent of any particular time preferences given actual situations. The model also says that utility of consumption $U(c)$ in each period is constant over time, so all utilities created through various consumptions are the same for every period. Considering the spontaneous and capricious nature of human life, these features in the model would be unrealistic most of the time.

In conventional (New Classical) economics, an agent's rational choice depends only on his own monetary payoff. However, studies in various experiments show otherwise. In most cases, people don't pay attention solely to material gains or losses. These developments in the study of utility functions demonstrate the heterogeneous nature in human rationality in the process of decision-making. Throughout human history, at least some categories of utility are considered to be personal or subjective experiences or views, and therefore may not be passed on across all humans with different beliefs, tastes, and values. While attending a concert could give one individual tremendous pleasure and therefore a high level of utility, such experience may be considered tiresome by others. On the other hand, a good soccer game may generate high level of utility for a large group of people worldwide. So in many cases and depending on the nature of the function or the experience, whether a prescribed utility for a "rational" agent in theory actually creates value for him is a subjective matter that cannot be uniformly calculated in homogeneous terms. In the following section, we will discuss more on aprioristic notions of rationality or what it means to be rational for CE.

In order to fit what is in the model discussed earlier, we cannot really have our favorite piece of clothing or hair dresser, a scenario that rarely occurs in a capitalist system that promotes competition on the supply side. In addition, with the integration of a stream of lifetime consumption strategies, it means that buying a Stradivarius violin is not a decision in isolation but must be preceded by an evaluation of its impact on consumptions in all future periods. In other words, one must be able to calculate and predict her future consumption expenditures in order to make up for the high cost of the music instrument to even out the consumption stream in the future. In reality, this may be too difficult to do—a person may not have well-formed plans about future consumption stream, or be able (or willing) to recompute the new optimal plan every time she makes an intertemporal choice.

Clearly, the discounted utility model has many unrealistic assumptions or restrictions. As an illustration, consider how expected utility, in the case of making choices, is generated under some form of probability estimation. As you may recall, a probability set, say P, is derived from the gambling game of coin flipping and stanched out of the St. Petersburg Paradox by Daniel Bernoulli in the eighteenth century. So there is a finite set of outcomes or prizes from tossing the coin, say a set of O ranging from \$20 to \$200, which generates payoffs of real money values *v*. All probability distributions of O, \$20, \$30, \$50, and so forth, are represented in the set P. Since the coin has two sides with head H and tail T, where each has distinctive values assigned, there are two probability distributions H and T in set O. The expected utility or preference is decided based on the expected value *v*, say H is preferred to T when $Ehv > Etv$. Note that in the expected utility theory—albeit the method is meant to solve problems in an uncertain world with an open system—it assumes finite outcomes from two probability streams as well as some level of stationarity in the probability distribution. In other words, it applies the existing or known finite values in predicting the likelihood of future outcomes, therefore assuming a closed system.

2.3 The Second Pillar of Conventional Economics: Rationality and Expectations

We are looking to buy a used car for our oldest son, who is turning 18 in three months and cannot wait to get hold of his first car. We are no car experts ourselves, but given our budget, at the same time we want to get the best deal that money can buy. What do we do in practice to solve this problem?

Well, first of all we remind ourselves that in the last few months (when we were already thinking about this gift) a series of newspaper articles reported that brands A and B were very hot with teenagers. Brands C and D, which were in general very popular as well, were not mentioned. Then we proceed to check specialized websites just to have an idea of how much used A and B cars cost. Finally, we visit a few nearby car showrooms, and as soon as we find an A or a B car with a price in line with the average one resulting from our web exploration, we buy it. All in all, we devoted 3 half days and a couple of evenings to get through the challenge. Not bad. We thought it was going to be much harder!

All is well that ends well, then? Not exactly, as, according to conventional economics, this situation—which is very frequent in real life—cannot exist.

As a matter of fact, in conventional economics, decisions such as the used car one, are based on rational choice theory. The rational choice approach to this problem is based on the fundamental premise that *people do their best to achieve their objectives, given all relevant factors that are beyond control.*

What is meant, exactly, by "do their best" in our case? Well, probably that we should have spent much more time in acquiring:

- information on different cars' performances and quality (we should have read specialized magazines and maybe conducted road tests),

- information on prices (a few websites are not enough, maybe on eBay we would have found better prices), and
- car expertise (how can we choose if we don't really know how an engine works?).

Only after all that information/knowledge retrieval, we would have been in a situation compatible with the respect of the following rational choice axioms:

1. The agent faces a known set of alternative choices.
2. For any pair of alternatives (A and B, say), the agent either prefers A to B, prefers B to A, or is indifferent between A and B. This is the axiom of *completeness*.
3. These preferences are *transitive*. That is, if an agent prefers A to B and B to C, then she necessarily prefers A to C. If she is indifferent between A and B, and indifferent between B and C, then she is necessarily indifferent between A and C.
4. The agent will choose the most preferred alternative.

Rational choice theories usually represent preferences within a *utility function*. This is a mathematical function that assigns a numerical value to each possible alternative facing the decision-maker. The function U(·,·) is normally assumed to have certain properties. First, it is generally assumed that *more is preferred to less*—so that U rises with increases in x and with increases in y. Another way of saying this is that marginal utility is positive—where the term "marginal utility" is the change in utility associated with a small increase in the quantity of a good consumed. The second property of U(·,·) is that of *diminishing marginal utility*, which means that the (positive) marginal utility of each good gets smaller and smaller the more the good is being consumed in the first place.

Another important element of the choice process is the presence of *constraints*. The presence of constraints makes choice necessary, and one virtue of rational choice theory is that it makes the trade-offs between alternative choices very explicit. A typical constraint in a simple one-period consumer choice problem is the *budget constraint*, which says that the consumer cannot spend more than her income. That is, an agent is assumed to make the feasible choice (feasible in a sense that it is not prohibited by constraints) that results in the highest possible value of his or her utility function.

This concludes the discussion of the first component of a rational choice: choosing the best means to realize one's desires, given one's beliefs. Clearly, this is only a necessary condition for rationality, not a sufficient one. Rational beliefs are those that are shaped by processing the available evidence using procedures that, in the long run and on average, are most likely to yield true beliefs. Suppose we want to form a belief about the probability of buying a good condition used car (brand A or B) for less than 5000 dollars (our budget constraint).

This process of belief revision is often called Bayesian learning (named after the eighteenth-century Presbyterian minister Thomas Bayes). Assume that we have an initial ("prior") subjective probability distribution and that the prior distribution is derived from past observations, for example, the rough percentage of newspaper ads in the last month in which the sale price of the car was not higher than 5000 dollars. On the basis of intuition, we might assign, for instance, probability 60% to a price above 5000 dollars and 40% to a lower price.

We then observe what happens right now. And what happens is a jump in the price of gasoline, caused by terrorist attacks in Arabic countries, which may hit the demand for cars and reduce prices. So in the last week or so we notice that on CARSFORALL, an influential website for car sales, some A and B cars are beginning to be offered at about 4500 dollars, well below our budget constraint. But are CARSFORALL's prices really representative of trends in average market prices?

In rational decision theory, Bayes's rule shows how we can update our initial probability (called *prior*), given the new accruing observations.

The sample space is defined by two events—in three months' time, the market price of used A and B cars is above or below 5000 dollars. Additionally, a third event occurs when in new ads on CARSFORALL, used A and B cars are priced below 5000 dollars. Notation for these events is as follows:

- Event A1. Future market prices are below 5000 dollars.
- Event A2. Future market prices are above 5000 dollars.
- Event B. CARSFORALL prices are below 5000 dollars.

In terms of probabilities, from all the observations we have, we know the following:

- P(A1) = 10/100 = 0.1 [prices below 5000 dollars have been observed only in 10 cases out of 100]
- P(A2) = 90/100 = 0.9 [prices above 5000 dollars have been observed in 90 cases out of 100]
- P(B | A1) = 0.8 [when prices fall, CARSFORALL anticipated it 80% of the time]
- P(B | A2) = 0.2 [when prices do not fall, CARSFORALL anticipated a price fall 20% of the time]

We want to know P(A1 | B), the probability prices will fall below 5000 dollars, given new lower prices by CARSFORALL. The answer can be determined from Bayes' theorem, as shown here.

$$P(A1|B) = \frac{P(A1)P(B|A1)}{P(A1)P(B|A1) + P(A2)P(B|A2)}$$

As compared to our prior of 0.1, the updated probability rises to P(A1 | B) = 0.3.

Rational choice theory and rational learning stand at the core of the most revolutionary concept introduced by New Classical Economics: the rational expectations hypothesis (REH). The outstanding feature of the REH, which made it just perfect for New Classical Economics, is simply that the REH appeared as the only expectation mechanism characterized by a priori consistency with a theoretical framework populated by utility maximizing agents.

The concept was originally introduced by John Muth in 1961. Muth argued that people, who are rational and also correct their forecasts taking into account previous mistakes, would readily discover the "true" model of the economy and revise their expectations accordingly. "Expectations of businesses" or, more generally, the subjective probability distribution of outcomes tend to be distributed, for the same information set, about the prediction of the theory (or the "objective" probability distributions of outcomes). The ineffectiveness of government policies is nothing but the logical conclusion of this line of reasoning, as Abraham Lincoln put it:

> *You can fool some of the people all of the time, and all of the people some of the time, but you cannot fool all of the people all of the time.*

For example, in figuring the expectations of investors on a specific stock, the REH assumes that investors will use available information about the company under investigation. The model presumes that, on average, expectations of future outcomes from individuals at the aggregation on a particular phenomenon based on the available information, ex ante, should not deviate systematically from the actual value, ex post. It focuses on the internal consistency of the assumed variables and the optimization of their relations of the model. A simple version of REH in equation terms looks like: $P = P^* + e$ and $E(P) = P^*$, where P^* is the rational expectation and e is a random error term, which has an expected value of zero and is independent of P^*. For finance, REH is the building block for the EMH, which assumes stock prices reflect all available information. The very close relationship between the REH and the EMH is perfectly illustrated by Lucas, when in his *Professional memoir*, he states that "*if your theory reveals profit opportunities, you have the wrong theory*".

REH model building is supposed to involve knowledge in economic modeling and techniques of the stochastic processes as it evolves with new information. If these requirements cannot be met, individuals will not be likely to form rational expectations. More significantly, because REH concerns with expectations at the aggregate level, the process assumes that every market participant has the same amount of information and will interpret the information in the same way: a representative agent who thinks just like everyone else; their beliefs are correct, and in fact the "true" probability distribution, which in turn is the distribution of states that is determined by their actions. REH is considered an endogenous model based purely on incoming information. To be fair, it is also important to note that Muth specified that it is only the average of economic agents′ forecasts (not the individual forecast) that will be in line with the values predicted by the "true" model.

With all of these assumptions and since REH is an ex ante model, which means it attempts to come up with estimations using available information for future events, the REH does not apply to the non-routine change component of the market. "*In cases of uncertainty, economic reasoning will be of no value… Insofar as business cycles can be viewed as repeated instances of essentially similar events, it will be reasonable to treat agents as reacting to cyclical changes as 'risk', or to assume their expectations are rational*" (Lucas 1977). Precisely in order to support the development of "stable" environments, policies should be as simple and clear as possible. This is the only context in which rational expectations can be developed in a cumulative fashion: "*Economics has tended to focus on situations in which the agent can be expected to 'know' or to have learned the consequences of different actions so that his observed choices reveal stable features of his underlying preferences… Technically, I think of economics as studying decision rules that are steady states of some adaptive process, decision rules that are found to work over a range of situations and hence are no longer revised appreciably as more experience accumulates*" (Lucas 1986). But is this realistic? Volz and Gigerenzer (2012) claim that "*decision making under uncertainty is what our brain does most of the time, while situations of known risk are relatively rare*". If this were true, then the actual relevance of the REH would shrink significantly. But we will come back to this problem later.

2.4 How the *Homo Economicus* Takes His Decisions

But how does the *homo economicus* operate in practice? Perhaps the best way to illustrate the concept is by means of a concrete example.

You are John Smith, a 40-ish executive, married with two children, earning a decent salary but with limited financial wealth, and the whole of it is placed in your local bank account. Then the massive inheritance of a forgotten old aunt arrives. We are talking about 1 (one) million dollars!

What shall you do? Conceptually, it's simple. Among infinite choices or actions, you shall opt for the one which maximizes your personal utility. Of course, utility is not directly observable, so the assumption made in CE is (almost tautologically) that choices reveal both preferences and utility. If you risk your life climbing the Everest, you could still be maximizing your utility, because the value of the probability of a longer life for you would not be worth the cost of giving up climbing. And you maximize utility even when you make what may seem pure altruistic choices: the decision of having children, for example, implies a cost which is perceived smaller than the related return (e.g. children supporting you when you are old). So what action on the inheritance would maximize your personal utility? You could as well spend it all following George Best's example ("I spent a lot of money on booze, birds and fast cars. The rest I just squandered"). But given that you are already married and with children, chances are that your utility is more traditional, and has to do with the achievement of a higher level of wealth in the medium-long term. But you are also risk-averse. And in conventional finance, risk is identified with volatility, that is, the extent to which the prices of a specific asset fluctuate over time around their mean. In statistical terms, this is measured by the variance (or its square root transformation, the standard deviation). So utility (wealth) maximization is subject to the constraint that the standard deviation of your financial wealth (i.e. your portfolio of assets) cannot be higher than a predetermined value. In conventional finance, this is called mean-variance optimization. In general terms, you are supposed to maximize a function of form $a = e^{-v/t}$, where a represents the appeal of the portfolio for the investor, e is the portfolio's expected return, v is its variance of return, and t is the investor's risk tolerance.

Therefore, for any given risk tolerance, a mean/variance optimization requires the following inputs: (1) forecasts of asset return standard deviations, (2) forecasts of correlations among asset returns, and (3) expected asset returns. The individual must consequently form conditional expectations or forecasts of the future, but on what basis?

For all the inputs, the simplest assumption would be that expected values coincide with historical values. The slightly more sophisticated approach generated by adaptive expectations provides for a role to be assigned to a so-called adjustment factor reflecting the gap between past realized values and forecasts. But, of course, the strong form of the rational expectations hypothesis prevailing in the second half of last century goes beyond that, as it postulates that you are fully informed at all times, and at no cost, not only about historical values and statistics (e.g. variances and correlations) but also of whatever news that may be relevant to predict the future. To be sure, less extreme rational expectations model also factors incomplete information and the incurrence of information costs, with optimal level of information retrieval also subject to rational cost-benefit calculation.

As a *homo economicus*, in one way or the other you have now the optimal amount of information which is needed to make your forecasts. But, of course, that is not enough. You are bound to be a skilled statistician. For each asset, you need to be able to calculate volatility, that is, variance and standard deviation. You first calculate the mean of the series of numbers. Then for each number, subtract the mean and square the result. The average of those squared differences will be the variance (and its square root the standard deviation).

And correlations?

In principle, you should be first concerned about covariances.

But given that covariance numbers cover a wide range, you normalize them into correlations, ranging from −1 for a perfectly negative correlation to +1 for a perfectly positive correlation. An uncorrelated investment pair would have a correlation coefficient close to zero, yet a negative correlation could form risk hedging. That could be the least risky choice for your portfolio, that is, the choice which minimizes volatility.

Assume you have the time series of two variables 1 and 2.

Subtract the mean of 1 from every number in the 1 series, and call the obtained series X. Do the same for 2, and call the series Y. Calculate X*Y, X^2, and Y^2 for all numbers in the series. Sum all X*Y, X^2, and Y^2. Divide the sum of X*Y by the square root of [(sum of X^2) × (sum of Y^2)] and you have the correlation between 1 and 2.

That is for the statistics you need. But then, how would you choose your ideal portfolio?

Of course, your behavior is bound to be entirely rational. In other words, you will follow the prescriptions of rational choice; that is, in trying to achieve your targets with the minimum allocation of resources, your actions would fulfill the necessary requirements of consistency and coherence. Only after full information/knowledge retrieval and statistical elaboration is completed for each asset, you would be in a situation to which you can apply the usual rational choice axioms already discussed.

On that basis, you will choose the most preferred alternative.

But what are the available alternatives? In conventional finance, the *efficient frontier* represents the best combinations of assets (i.e. portfolios), those that produce the maximum expected return for a given level of risk. Portfolios below the frontier are irrational, because you could get higher return with less risk (see Fig. 2.2).

So, which portfolio on this frontier should you choose? A popular approach in conventional finance is that of using the so-called capital market line which provides for the incorporation of a risk-free asset in the portfolio. Assume, for example, that you have a Treasury bill (proxy for the risk-free asset) yielding 2%. If you draw a straight line from 2% on the *Y*-axis so that it is tangent to a point on the efficient frontier, that point will identify the tangency portfolio, that is, the portfolio with the highest return for unit of risk on the efficient frontier[1] (see Fig. 2.3).

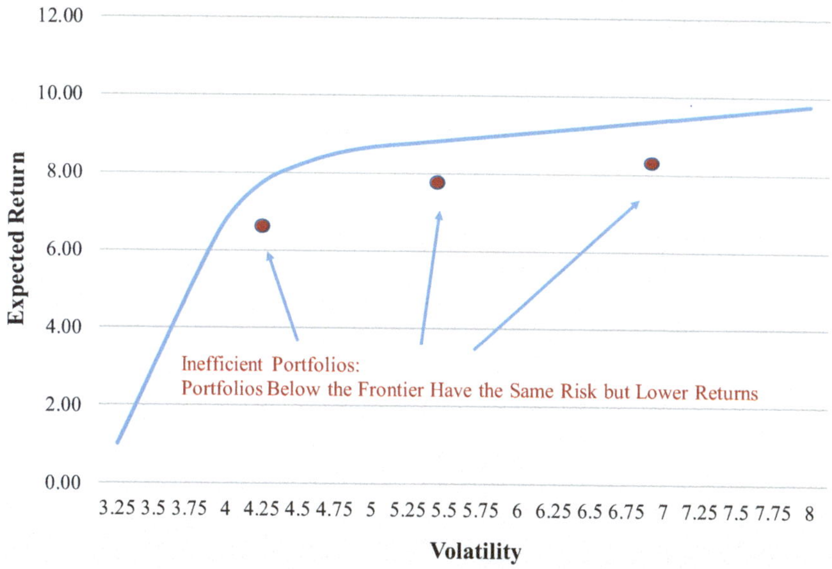

Fig. 2.2 Efficient Frontier

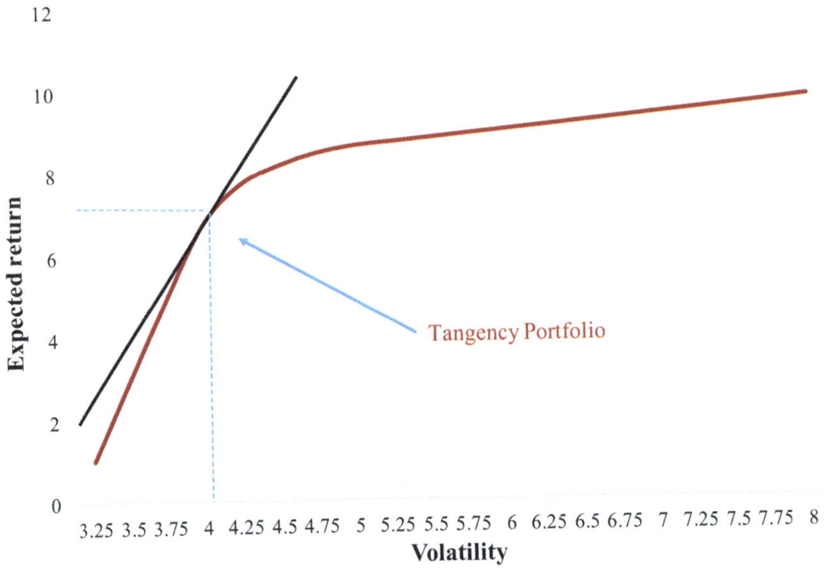

Fig. 2.3 Tangent Portfolio

Now assume that you can invest in two risky assets 1 and 2

Asset 1: Expected return $E(r_1) = 0.02$ Standard deviation $\sigma_1 = 0.2$
Asset 2: Expected return $E(r_2) = 0.06$ Standard deviation $\sigma_2 = 0.6$

Risk-free asset return $(r_f) = 0.01$

If you now want to build a tangency portfolio, as a good *homo economicus*, you have got to make sure that the following condition linking returns and covariances applies (don't ask for a detailed explanation, it would take three pages):

$$\frac{E(r_1)-r_f}{\text{cov}(r_1,r_f)} = \frac{E(r_2)-r_f}{\text{cov}(r_2,r_f)}$$

If the weight to assign to asset 1 in the portfolio is w (with $0 < w < 1$), and the weight to assign to asset 2 in the portfolio is $(1 - w)$, for you the aforementioned condition may be rewritten as

$$0.01\left[w\,\mathrm{cov}(r_1,r_2)+(1-w)\sigma_2^2\right]=0.05\left[w\sigma_1^2+(1-w)\mathrm{cov}(r_1,r_2)\right]$$

Given this, and after a further round of substitutions/calculations, the optimal portfolio turns out to be one assigning a weight of 58% to asset 1 and 42% to asset 2.

It was quite a slog, wasn't it John?

Axioms, probabilities, statistics. The (obvious) question at this stage is: how much of all this enters the real-world behavior (and decisions)?

According to the Nobel Prize winner and master of rational choice theory Milton Friedman, although individuals do not possess the formal tools with which to calculate the optimum adequately, they behave as if they do—like bicycle riders who keep themselves in dynamic equilibrium even though they are unaware of the complex equations of the dynamics of motion.

Friedman expressed skepticism about the possibility of discovering how business decisions are made just through observation of behaviors, suggesting that individuals might not actually be aware of the mental processes involved in their actions. This observation was related to the idea that a part of relevant knowledge may be tacit, and it led Friedman to the extreme of prescribing that the individual expression of preferences must be disregarded.

In line with the prescription of the Chicago school, the "as if" hypothesis was then supplemented with the further assertion that individual preferences are not observable, and indeed that they are irrelevant to proving the validity of an economic theory (Friedman 1953).

According to these assumptions, the theory of rational choice is normative (what you should do), rather than positive (what you actually do), as it indicates to economic agents how best they can achieve their goals, and it is explicitly assumed by Milton Friedman that those who fail to conform are gradually excluded by a process of selection which permits only "rational" operators to survive. But then it could be argued that the theory translates into a positive one, describing actual behavior!

Unfortunately (for Milton Friedman), so far this prophecy has failed to materialize. Although dominant for many decades, the theory neither succeeded in explaining reality nor showed any normative power. And the ultimate acid test for the theory and the CE apparatus behind it was the global financial crisis of 2008.

2.5 The Reality Test

> *A new scientific truth does not triumph by convincing its opponents and making them see the light, but rather because its opponents eventually die, and a new generation grows up that is familiar with it.*
> —Max Planck, *Scientific Autobiography and Other Papers.*

For at least the three decades preceding the end of the last century, New Classical Economics and the efficient market hypothesis reigned undisturbed, in spite of the criticism of many economists with regard to the unrealistic nature of many of its core assumptions, such as that of changes in returns on assets having a Gaussian distribution (Markowitz's portfolio theory, 1952) or asset prices following a lognormal process (Black-Scholes option pricing theory, 1973). Critics were often marginalized and even ridiculed as people who hadn't a robust enough mathematical background.

But then came the first blow, the burst of the *dot.com* bubble just at the beginning of the new century. The bubble was macroscopic, price/earnings ratios grossly out of line for years for all to see. Yet, leading economists kept congratulating themselves and showed great self-confidence, as did Robert Lucas, who in his 2003 presidential address to the American Economic Association proclaimed solemnly that the "central problem of depression-prevention has been solved".

And in 2008, seconds before the global financial system melted down, Olivier Blanchard (then at the MIT, now with the IMF) stated that "the state of macro (economics) is good". How could it not be a good framework in which rational agents populate perfectly and always clear the markets? And the same framework was also so beautiful and elegant, as described by immaculate mathematical setups!

In what follows we use the global financial crisis as a test bed for economic theory. The reason is that the best evaluation of the robustness of a theory is not the steady state, but rather a situation in which the economy is hit by a systemic shock. And what shock was more systemic than the one materializing in 2008?

Of course, "unforeseeable" crises are a regular feature of the world economy. From the great depression in the 1920s to the "Asian flu" of the 1990s, every two or three decades a new crisis hits, with (ex post) experts' explanations typically pointing to a limited number of factors triggering the crisis itself. First, loose money: when interest rates are historically low, people come out with all sorts of (risky) inventions to lure investors' appetite. Second, the absence of sufficiently rigorous regulation. Third, greed and carelessness on the part of financial professionals. If you take all these three ingredients and shake them well, more often than not you get a crisis.

But it is only when this cocktail is prepared in a bubble environment that you get a real BIG crisis. Roughly speaking, an asset price bubble occurs whenever the price of an asset deviates significantly and for a long enough period from its underlying or intrinsic value (i.e. the value that fully expresses fundamental or expected returns and risk for that asset looking forward for a given level of uncertainty). To begin with, the very occurrence of bubbles is hardly consistent with conventional economics and in particular with the EMH, by which at any point in time asset prices are in line with intrinsic values (while intrinsic values may be defined in static terms here). So, bubbles should not exist in the first place.

Unfortunately for conventional economics, however, it is well known that the 2008 global financial crisis (GFC) was triggered by the burst of the US real estate market bubble. For most of the previous five years, the unprecedented credit expansion in the housing sector was generated by the combination of historically low interest rates and the growing financialization of the economy. The latter factor played a crucial role, especially as far as derivatives were concerned. Originally conceived as a risk hedging instrument, derivatives were more and more used for speculative purposes, and this was crucial in generating a market which, at times, was 10 times bigger than the markets for underlying assets. In the context of continued money expansion, the creativity of traders and portfolio managers knew no limit, and so with the beginning of the century, a spectacular success was granted to a couple of new financial products: the so-called credit risk swaps (CRS) and, above all, collateralized debt obligations (CDOs). The latter were essentially securitized bonds representing a "basket" of mortgage loans, and, given the internal diversification, were considered safe assets, especially after slicing and dicing the product into tranches of risk grades in order to suit the preferences of investors in terms of their varied levels of risk tolerance.

Thanks to the issuance of CDOs, it became increasingly easy (and cheap) for banks to borrow and to expand their lending targets to socio-economic areas never touched before for their riskiness in mortgage lending. In particular, the possibility offered by CDOs to "smooth out" credit risk and the existence of instruments such as CRS capable on paper to hedge against financial risks made banks willing to extend house mortgages to people who could not demonstrate permanent employment, regular income, or any material assets. These people were referred to as NINJAs (No Income, No Job or Assets). For a while, it seemed like heaven. But when interest rates began to rise, a growing number of NINJAs experienced severe problems in making mortgage payments on schedule. With increasing defaults and property prices beginning to fall, the value of bank assets like CDOs was also reduced. In order to rebalance their financial positions at that point, banks were forced to increase their reserves. However, this only option implied borrowing further, an increasingly expensive exercise in an environment of higher interest rates and deteriorating creditworthiness. The global financial crisis officially stepped in when banks which were deemed "too big to fail" like Lehman Brothers had to declare bankruptcy. After that, a burst of spiraling panic brought down a number of banks and worked as the starting point for what was about to be the worst global economic crisis ever.

* * *

When looking at the mess, the first obvious question is: could someone have predicted all this? To be sure, some economists (including Robert Shiller) did raise doubts, but only to be scoffed by the overwhelming majority of New Classical economists. Not surprisingly, the impact of all of the above has been particularly significant in financial markets. Shiller compared actual stock prices and the hypothetical "efficient market" prices (i.e. prices that would prevail in an efficient market when investors

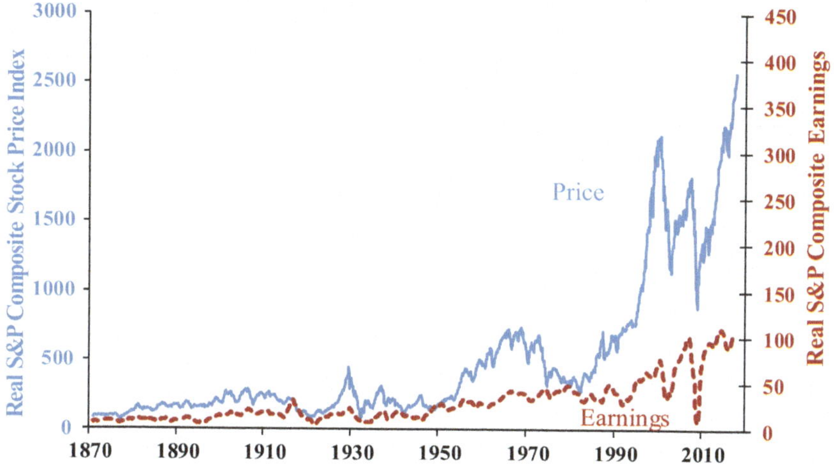

Fig. 2.4 Real S&P Composite Stock Price Index and Earnings

have perfect foresight about future dividend cash flows) and found a complete disconnection of the two prices emerging at the turn of the century. More simply, as shown in Fig. 2.4, a historical break emerged even in the correlation between prices and earnings.

In a 2007 interview, Eugene Fama, the father of the EMH, declared that "*the word 'bubble' drives me nuts*" and went on to explain why we should have trusted the housing market: "*Housing markets are less liquid, but people are very careful when they buy houses. It's typically the biggest investment they're going to make, so they look around very carefully and they compare prices. The bidding process is very detailed*". Of course, this doesn't tell us anything on whether the overall housing price level is distorted or not. It is just ketchup economics, by which if a one-liter bottle of ketchup costs as much as the sum of two half-liter bottles of ketchup, then the price of ketchup is right!

The second question that comes to mind is: how different was investors' and borrowers' behavior from the one associated by conventional economics to the *homo economicus*? It was very different. Consider, for instance, information. The *homo economicus* is supposed to have access to all the information which is needed to take a rational decision. In the case of CDOs, information was apparently available, but in reality the "cost" of retrieving it was so high that it was hardly retrievable. In order to properly evaluate the CDOs which were being acquired, institutional investors would have needed to read more than 30,000 pages of prospectuses. So the choice of most investors was simply to stick to rating agencies' recommendations; unfortunately, for the same reasons, in many cases rating agencies in turn relied on the originator banks' analyses.

Also, the *homo economicus* decision-making is not impacted by what others do. So how would a *homo economicus* behave when faced with a bubble (which, of course, should not exist in the first place)? Of course, he would retain his composure and not buy any asset which is (inconceivably) overvalued. But that was not the case for financial instruments linked to the US real estate market. People were sucked in by bubbles after watching others become wealthier by the day. They took the train to prosperity even if they were aware that there was a chance that the train could derail before reaching the next station.

On the borrowers' side, it seems clear that the NINJAs were not able to calculate and estimate properly the sensitivity to higher interest rates of their future consumption within a discounted utility framework. This is why first year defaults on subprime mortgages reached an unprecedented value of 8% in 2007.

But what about institutions?

Again, an information problem was crucial in determining the final disaster. The fact is that many institutions, in order to reduce risk, entered into bilateral credit default swaps (CDS) with other institutions.[2] And the latter did the same. So eventually in the pass-the-hot-potato game, no one was in a situation to assess the net risk position of anyone else.

In this chaotic context, how well could the most significant expression of CE, that is, the efficient market hypothesis, fare?

In fact, excessive reliance on EMH itself can be considered as one of the factors at the origin of the crisis. During the first seven years of this century, the relaxed attitude of regulators, policymakers, and financial institutions alike largely came as the result of unconditional faith in the following tenets of EMH:

- Asset prices are by definition in equilibrium, as they reflect all the risks and the rewards estimated on the basis of relevant available information.

- The same applies to innovative financial instruments such as CDOs, which can be traded in liquid markets and distributed to a varied investor base with different return goals and risk tolerance levels.
- The simultaneous workings of market forces and internal risk models will allow for a natural selection of market instruments, which would only clear those instruments that are efficient in terms of return and sustainable from a risk perspective.

And it was precisely that relaxed attitude that made things worse, as people discovered themselves at a loss to understand the cascade of failures throughout the whole chain of financial activity, or the sudden appearance of panic selling, with each bank desperately trying to liquidate its positions just a second before other banks did exactly the same. As Ben Bernanke (2010), chairman of the Federal Reserve, noted in one of his speeches:

> *During the worst phase of the financial crisis, many economic actors—including investors, employers, and consumers—metaphorically threw up their hands and admitted that, given the extreme and, in some ways, unprecedented nature of the crisis, they did not know what they did not know. The profound uncertainty associated with the "unknown unknowns" during the crisis resulted in panicky selling by investors, sharp cuts in payrolls by employers, and significant increases in households' precautionary saving.*

For the New Classical economists, since 2007, world markets on the one hand were simply not behaving as they should have. In the world according to conventional economics, recessions are not contemplated so they cannot be forecast; all that is there are the unexpected shocks portrayed in the dynamic stochastic general equilibrium models. Of course, this implies that there are no policy recommendations to handle recessions and restore growth.

On the other hand, the crisis also revealed to New Classical economists that the overall setup of world markets was different from the one they imagined. In the New Classical world, disturbances always originate in the real economy, whereas the crisis was largely driven by a financial sector which had never been so big and autonomous (see Fig. 2.5).

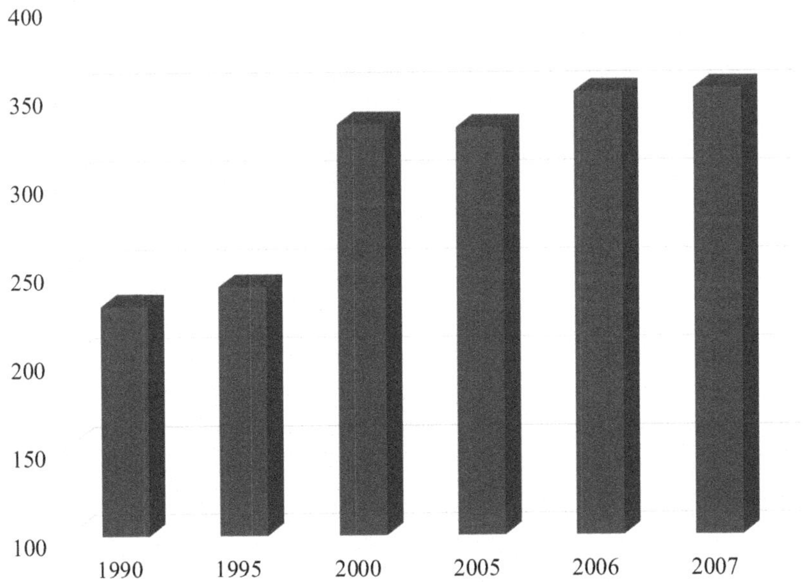

Fig. 2.5 Global Financial Assets as a Percentage of Global GDP. Source: *Elaboration on "Mapping the world's financial markets", Deutsche Bank, 2011*

So it is not just the markets being inefficient. Conventional economics got it entirely wrong, as the world simply turned out to be completely different from the one beautifully depicted in New Classical math-filled exercises on general equilibrium.

And here lies the original sin of New Classical Economics. Brasser-Pereira (2009) describes well the problem. He distinguishes between two kind of sciences: methodological sciences such as mathematics and statistics, which do not have an object but are instrumental to reasoning, and substantive sciences such as natural and social sciences (including economics), which have a clear object to analyze. The latter are typically supposed to adopt the historical-deductive method, by which hypotheses are formulated starting from the observations of realities and have as a truth criterion predictive capacity. In contrast, methodological sciences are based on the hypothetic-deductive method, by which the scientific character of a theory is assessed not with reference to reality, but to its mathematical validity.

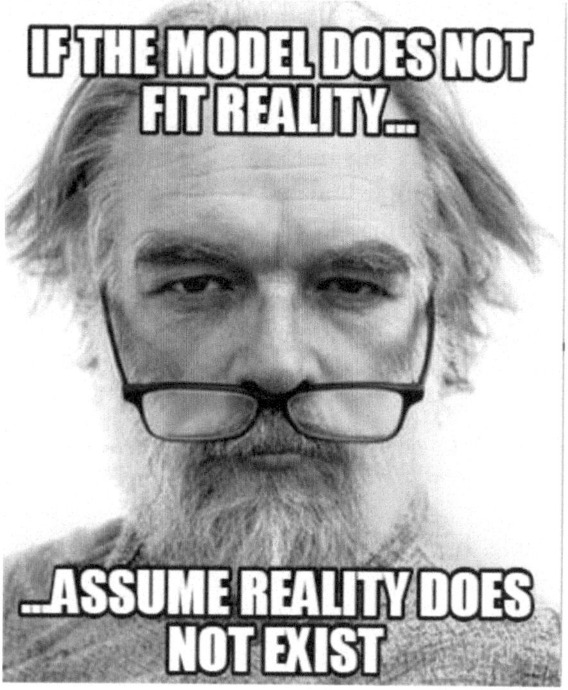

What New Classical economists did was using the "wrong" method (the hypothetical-deductive method) to build models that had no correspondence to reality, but were useful to claim that such models were scientific and could fully support hypotheses such as market efficiency. Unfortunately, science and mathematical formalization are NOT the same thing.

But apparently, the New Classical economists didn't care much about this detail. A common phrase was that "*All models are wrong, but some are useful*". Basically, in order to avoid taking into account the complexities of real-world decision-making (including bubbles, biases, social constraints, altruism, etc.), they preferred to be elegantly wrong rather than trying to be roughly right. What can be the utility of using simplified—but beautiful!—models with only one consumer in the economy or a world where people have perfect information? Should we examine the world as it really is and can be, or the world as we wish it were?

Take, for example, the case of the Capital Asset Pricing Model (CAPM), which for decades was thought of as the best illustration of how financial markets work. This conviction also stemmed from the results of econometric research conducted by Fama and MacBeth (1973) on a sample running until 1965. It was only unfortunate that the results generated by the same model over a sample updated to include two additional decades were such that they led Fama (1991) to conclude that CAPM could be considered "*atrocious as an empirical model*".

That presumably came as no surprise to Nobel Prize winner William Sharpe, who, in his interview in July 1980 by the Institutional Investor, plainly stated that

> *[i]t's almost true that if you don't like an empirical result, if you can wait until somebody uses a different [time] period… you'll get a different answer.*

It took a while, but the almost complete uselessness of many New Classical models was eventually acknowledged by many, maybe too late as the crisis was already looming at the horizon.

In this context, the way in which Robert Solow (2010) summarized the issue in front of the US Congress is enlightening:

> *Under pressure from skeptics and from the need to deal with actual data, DSGE (Dynamic stochastic General Equilibrium) modelers have worked hard to allow for various market frictions and imperfections like rigid prices and wages, asymmetries of information, time lags and so on. This is all to the good, and they have done very good work. But the basic story always treats the whole economy as if it were like a person trying consciously and rationally to do the best it can on behalf of the representative agent, given its circumstances. This cannot be an adequate description of a national economy, which is pretty conspicuously not pursuing a consistent goal. A thoughtful person faced with that economic policy based on that kind of idea might reasonably wonder what planet he or she is on.*

But perhaps the most striking demonstration of the empirical failure of conventional economics/finance is paradoxically associated with the financial choices of one of the founding fathers of conventional portfolio theory, Harry Markowitz. In his models, Markowitz described a process of portfolio allocation based on sophisticated mean-variance optimization and the reduction of risk via the choice of assets characterized by low correlations. As reported by Shefrin (2000), however, when Markowitz as a new pensioner had to decide on the composition of his own personal portfolio, all he did was to apply the so-called $1/n$ rule. In other words, he just allocated equal amounts of money to the n available assets! What a *Homo Economicus*!

Notes

1. Building on the minimum variance approach, in the theory developed by Markowitz, the investor maximizes a utility function, which is given by expected return, variance, and a new parameter, measuring absolute risk aversion. The parameter of absolute risk aversion is assumed to be positive, because all investors are assumed to be risk-averse. A negative value would imply that an investor is risk-loving.
2. In a CDS, flows are similar to those implied by insurance contracts. Counterparty A pays to Counterparty B on a regular basis an amount X. In case the credit entity of interest defaults, Counterparty B pays to Counterparty A a predetermined lump sum and the swap ends.

References

Barro, R.J. 1974. Are Government Bonds Net Wealth? *Journal of Political Economy 82* (6): 1095–1117.

Bernanke, B. 2010. Speech at the Conference Co-sponsored by the Center for Economic Policy Studies and the Bendheim Center for Finance, Princeton University, Princeton, NJ.

Branas-Pereira, L.C. 2009. The Two Methods and the Hard Core of Economics. *Journal of Post-Keynesian Economics 31* (3): 493–522.

Fama, E. 1991. Efficient Capital Markets: II. *The Journal of Finance 46* (5): 1575–1617.

Fama, E., and J.D. MacBeth. 1973. Risk, Return and Equilibrium: Empirical Tests. *Journal of Political Economy 81* (3): 607–636.

Friedman, M. 1953. The Methodology of Positive Economics. In *Essays in Positive Economics*, ed. M. Friedman. Chicago: University of Chicago Press.
Lucas, R.E. 1976. Econometric Policy Evaluation: A Critique. In *The Phillips Curve and Labor Markets*, ed. K. Brunner and A. Meltzer. Carnegie-Rochester Conference Series on Public Policy, American Elsevier.
———. 1977. Understanding Business Cycles. In *Carnegie-Rochester Conference Series on Public Policy, Vol. 5, Stabilization of the Domestic and International Economy*, ed. K. Brunner and A. H. Meltzer. Amsterdam, North Holland.
———. 1986. Adaptive Behaviour and Economic Theory. In *Rational Choice: The Contrast between Economics and Psychology*, ed. R.M. Hogarth and M.W. Reder, 217–242. Chicago and London: University of Chicago Press.
Shefrin, H. 2000. *Beyond Greed and Fear; Understanding Behavioral Finance and the Psychology of Investing*. Harvard Business School Press.
Solow, R. 2010. Building a Science of Economics for the Real World. In *Hearing before the Subcommittee on Investigations and Oversight Committee on Science and Technology*. House of Representatives.
Volz, K.G., and G. Gigerenzer. 2012. Cognitive Processes in Decisions Under Risk are not the Same as in Decisions Under Uncertainty. *Frontiers in Neuroscience 6*: 105.

3

The Behavioral Alternative

3.1 The Behavioral Revolution: From Normative to Positive Economics

As just argued, New Classical Economics (the twenty-first-century conventional economics) did not pass the reality test represented by the global economic crisis. Conventional economics, which does not contemplate the possibility of bubbles and/or recessions, was intrinsically incapable of predicting the crisis, nor was it able to make sense of it on an ex post basis, and to acknowledge that the "irrational" behavior of borrowers, investors, and institutions was hardly consistent with the concept of *homo economicus*. But why was conventional economics so successful, in spite of its lack of explanatory power?

Incredible as it may sound, the main reason was simply that CE, through its oversimplifications, made economics look as if it had eventually achieved the dignity of an exact science. Especially so in view of the increasingly sophisticated mathematical tools used to build economic models in the second half of the twentieth century. In turn, the domination of math-filled models and the neglect of psychological factors received a decisive justification from what Camerer (1999) calls the "F twist" (after its main theorist Milton Friedman). According to the F twist,

F. Ghisellini, B. Y. Chang, *Behavioral Economics*,
https://doi.org/10.1007/978-3-319-75205-1_3

the forecasting accuracy of a model is all that counts, irrespective of whether its basic assumptions are realistic, or at least plausible. Given that there is no guarantee that more realistic models would yield superior forecasts, why should then one "corrupt" the mathematical beauty of general equilibrium models with such mundane features as loss aversion or mental accounting? So in the twentieth century, psychology was simply left behind, in part because of its "vagueness" and also because all its nuances impeded the self-contained definition of perfect theoretical models.

What follows is a page from a research paper written in the 1980s on rational expectations equilibrium (Blume and Easley 1984), which describes how, according to the then prevailing finance theory, traders' utility functions are perturbed (see Fig. 3.1).

We wonder whether traders knew how nasty their utility perturbations are!

And precisely the gap between prevailing elegant models and harsh reality propelled many to question the validity of the F twist (can you really get satisfactory forecasts from an improbable model?) and an economic theory which had completely expunged psychology from the determinants of human decisions.

But psychology was there in earlier times. Adam Smith, who is best known for the concept of the "invisible hand" and *The Wealth of Nations*, wrote a less well-known book, *The Theory of Moral Sentiments*, which laid out psychological principles of individual behavior that are arguably as profound as his economic observations. The book is bursting with insights about human psychology, many of which presage current developments in behavioral economics. For example, Adam Smith (1792) commented that

> *we suffer more… when we fall from a better to a worse situation, than we ever enjoy when we rise from a worse to a better.*

Loss aversion!

This is just one of many possible proofs that behavioral economics has always existed, at least since the beginning of capitalism conceivably in more uttered forms.

The revenge of psychology began already in the 1950s. In the following, we examine a few examples that truly define behavioral economics as a positive discipline studying the world as it really is.

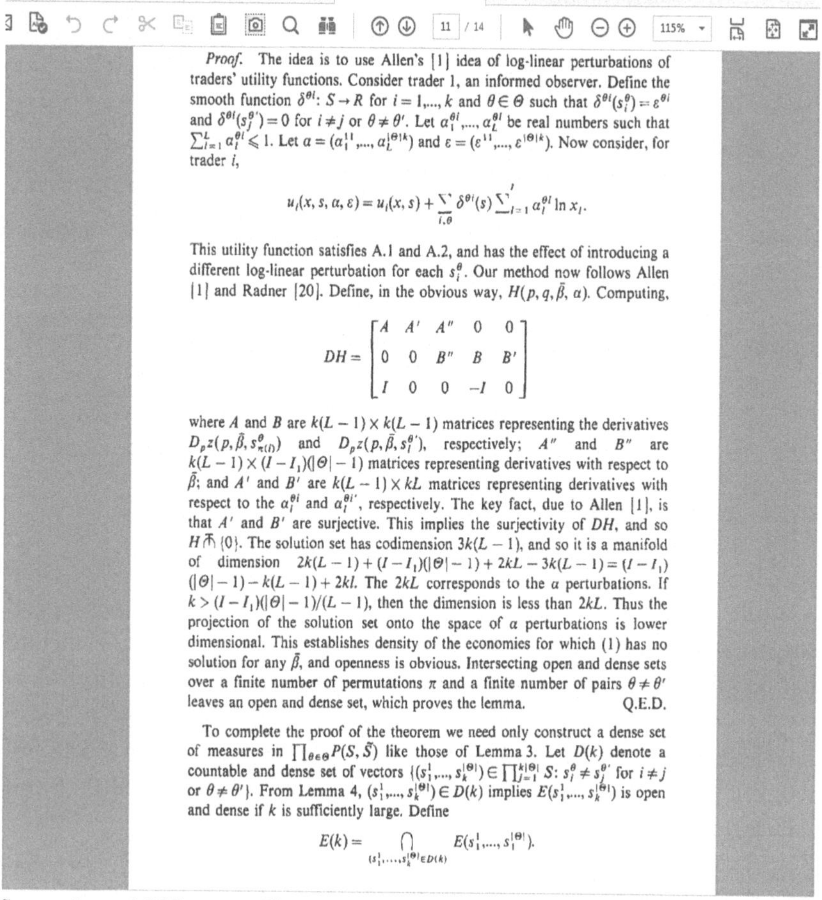

Proof. The idea is to use Allen's [1] idea of log-linear perturbations of traders' utility functions. Consider trader 1, an informed observer. Define the smooth function $\delta^{\theta l}: S \to R$ for $i = 1, \ldots, k$ and $\theta \in \Theta$ such that $\delta^{\theta i}(s_i^\theta) = \varepsilon^{\theta i}$ and $\delta^{\theta l}(s_j^{\theta'}) = 0$ for $i \neq j$ or $\theta \neq \theta'$. Let $\alpha_1^{\theta l}, \ldots, \alpha_L^{\theta l}$ be real numbers such that $\sum_{l=1}^{L} \alpha_l^{\theta l} \leqslant 1$. Let $\alpha = (\alpha_1^{11}, \ldots, \alpha_L^{|\Theta|k})$ and $\varepsilon = (\varepsilon^{11}, \ldots, \varepsilon^{|\Theta|k})$. Now consider, for trader i,

$$u_i(x, s, \alpha, \varepsilon) = u_i(x, s) + \sum_{i,\theta} \delta^{\theta i}(s) \sum_{l=1}^{l} \alpha_l^{\theta l} \ln x_l.$$

This utility function satisfies A.1 and A.2, and has the effect of introducing a different log-linear perturbation for each s_i^θ. Our method now follows Allen [1] and Radner [20]. Define, in the obvious way, $H(p, q, \bar{\beta}, \alpha)$. Computing,

$$DH = \begin{bmatrix} A & A' & A'' & 0 & 0 \\ 0 & 0 & B'' & B & B' \\ I & 0 & 0 & -I & 0 \end{bmatrix}$$

where A and B are $k(L-1) \times k(L-1)$ matrices representing the derivatives $D_p z(p, \bar{\beta}, s_{\pi(l)}^\theta)$ and $D_p z(p, \bar{\beta}, s_l^{\theta'})$, respectively; A'' and B'' are $k(L-1) \times (I - I_1)(|\Theta| - 1)$ matrices representing derivatives with respect to $\bar{\beta}$; and A' and B' are $k(L-1) \times kL$ matrices representing derivatives with respect to the $\alpha_l^{\theta i}$ and $\alpha_l^{\theta i'}$, respectively. The key fact, due to Allen [1], is that A' and B' are surjective. This implies the surjectivity of DH, and so $H \pitchfork \{0\}$. The solution set has codimension $3k(L-1)$, and so it is a manifold of dimension $2k(L-1) + (I - I_1)(|\Theta| - 1) + 2kL - 3k(L-1) = (I - I_1)(|\Theta| - 1) - k(L-1) + 2kl$. The $2kL$ corresponds to the α perturbations. If $k > (I - I_1)(|\Theta| - 1)/(L-1)$, then the dimension is less than $2kL$. Thus the projection of the solution set onto the space of α perturbations is lower dimensional. This establishes density of the economies for which (1) has no solution for any $\bar{\beta}$, and openness is obvious. Intersecting open and dense sets over a finite number of permutations π and a finite number of pairs $\theta \neq \theta'$ leaves an open and dense set, which proves the lemma. Q.E.D.

To complete the proof of the theorem we need only construct a dense set of measures in $\prod_{\theta \in \Theta} P(S, \tilde{S})$ like those of Lemma 3. Let $D(k)$ denote a countable and dense set of vectors $\{(s_1^1, \ldots, s_k^{|\Theta|}) \in \prod_{j=1}^{k|\Theta|} S: s_i^\theta \neq s_j^{\theta'}$ for $i \neq j$ or $\theta \neq \theta'\}$. From Lemma 4, $(s_1^1, \ldots, s_k^{|\Theta|}) \in D(k)$ implies $E(s_1^1, \ldots, s_k^{|\Theta|})$ is open and dense if k is sufficiently large. Define

$$E(k) = \bigcap_{(s_1^1, \ldots, s_k^{|\Theta|}) \in D(k)} E(s_1^1, \ldots, s_1^{|\Theta|}).$$

*Source: Journal Of Economic Theory (1984) Rational Expectations Equilibrium: An Alternative Approach * Lawrence E. Blume And David Easley*

Fig. 3.1 Is this really the way in which traders'utility function is perturbed?

Seminal papers by Allais (1953) and others pointed out anomalous implications of expected and subjective expected utility.

In particular, the Nobel Prize–winning economist Maurice Allais carried out an experiment which revealed subjects' preferences or how they made decisions and whether these decisions would lead to the same or consistent outcome or level of utility, say the utility of winning the following gambles (see Table 3.1).

Table 3.1 The Allais Paradox

Experiment 1				Experiment 2			
Gamble 1A		Gamble 1B		Gamble 2A		Gamble 2B	
Winnings	Chance	Winnings	Chance	Winnings	Chance	Winnings	Chance
$25,000	100%	$30,000	95%	Nothing	66%	Nothing	67%
		Nothing	5%	$25,000	34%	$30,000	33%

While most people prefer 1A to 1B, and 2B to 2A, it becomes a problem when they prefer 1A and 2B at the same time, since EUT dictates that people can't simultaneously have (P = probability, U = utility):

- U($25,000) for certain > 0.95P U($30,000) + 0.05P U($0) ≈ $28,500
- 0.33P U($30,000) + 0.67P U($0) ≈ $9900 > 0.34P U($25,000) + 0.66P U($0) ≈ $8500

As the two equations are inconsistent in formal numeric logic but preferred as real-life choices based on personal or subjective reasoning (the difference between various levels of chance and certainty in this case), the conclusion is that people don't have a utility function to apply uniformly over all outcomes.

This is known as the Allais paradox, and it demonstrates that in the real world, people tend to give extra values to total absence of uncertainty (1A preferred to 1B) and use expected utility only when differences in probabilities are small.

Allais' experiment was considered a paradox because results from the experiment were in contradiction with what was stipulated as the independent axiom in the Expected utility Theory (EUT). So instead of blaming poor reasoning on the human part, studies show that it is the proposition in the EUT that incorporates inadequate assessments of human rational actions. Specifically, EUT assumes that the description of a choice in quantitative logic, which does not consider diverse standings of its recipients or its qualitative reasoning, does not vary and is independent from decision-making processes. This is a critical variable in a free-market environment that has been disregarded in almost all cases in modeling a "rational" agent because of the conviction on the validity of axioms in the EUT.

EUT is also considered to be symmetrical. So if you are risk-averse, you are always unlikely to take bets, irrespective of whether you are facing a gain or a loss. Unfortunately for EUT, what really drives most of our choices is loss aversion. Unlike the standard risk measures that assume similar magnitude of either satisfaction or dissatisfaction when people face monetary gains or losses, loss aversion predicates that people suffer twice or more from loss in utility than rejoice in gain of the same amount. It is subjective or personal as utility loss varies across different individuals even with the same or relatively similar amount. One explanation for this outcome is associated with the *endowment effect* when people put higher value on an item they own than on another same item they do not own, and conversely, they suffer more from utility loss when they no longer have what they used to own. From neural science perspective, findings show that loss aversion is associated with the activities and the construct of a particular area of the human brain, and the difference in the degree of loss aversion among individuals is therefore determined by the idiosyncrasies of our respective brains.

Standard economics also assumes that money is fungible. This means that people should be flexible in maneuvering between the sources and uses of their income in meeting daily expenditures as well as long-term investments. In reality, however, people categorize and organize income sources so that each income source is associated with a different expenditure account—the mental accounting.

Since mental accounting divides as well as combines certain categories of money accounts that could affect decision-making, it is associated with the concept of "choice bracketing". There are few corollaries in the practice of mental accounting because of choice bracketing that relates to the EUT in terms of individual utility. Depending on how the accounts are divided or combined, decisions made according to the particular setup of these accounts could be either too restrictive or too extensive in reward or utility seeking. In the former case, one's utility may be lowered due to a too conservative long-term investment account with a lower interest rate than a shorter-term savings' account. In the latter case, and because people tend to perceive lower risk when evaluating risks in combination, for example, taking two similar risky investments while foregoing one risky position, one may take too much risk in this case and therefore lose utility.

Finally, conventional economic theory is based on an exponential time discounting function. So if we were a *homo economicus*, the difference in utility of having our favorite dish, such as aubergine parmigiana, today rather than tomorrow is the same as having it in 10 days rather than in 11 days.

Since human lives are not immortal and there are noticeable and predictable limits on what one could think s/he could do at an old age, lives are lived in mostly present terms or transitory periods relating to consumption needs and aspirations. In this case, it is only natural that people value more or perceive higher level of utility for something that they could get hold of today rather than tomorrow, while, given uncertainty and distance in time however, it doesn't really matter if that something is achieved in 11 days rather than in 10 days. This is the effect of hyperbolical discounting developed within behavioral economics: subjects have a tendency to choose earlier, smaller rewards over later, larger rewards when the earlier reward offers immediate utility.

Many other examples of how people actually behave and make decisions in the real world could be shown, and we will proceed to do that later in the book. For the moment, here is what Daniel Kahneman (2003a) thinks about how real-world people make choices:

> *Utility cannot be divorced from emotion, and emotions are triggered by changes. A theory of choice that completely ignores feelings such as the pain of losses and the regret of mistakes is not only descriptively unrealistic, but also leads to prescriptions that do not maximize the utility of outcomes as they are actually experienced. When a choice is to be made, the option that is associated with the higher remembered utility (more liked) is chosen. This mode of choice is likely to yield choices that do not maximize the utility that will actually be experienced.*

But if these are the main components of real-world decision-making, is there a simple and uncontroversial definition of what behavioral economics really is?

It is fair to say that there is no consensus on what behavioral economics really is. Nor have the "fathers" of behavioral economics provided us with their definition. In this respect, the only available quote from them is an implicit one, as it refers to the "delta" between conventional and behavioral economics:

> *The standard economic model of human behavior includes three unrealistic traits—unbounded rationality, unbounded willpower, and unbounded selfishness—all of which behavioral economics modifies.* (Mullainathan and Thaler 2001)

If we reverse the concept from negative (what is wrong with standard models) to positive and make it more general, we could say that BE is the learning of how humans behave in the real world in the context of economic and financial systems. So unlike CE, which is normative (illustrates how people should behave), BE is positive (studies the world as it is or it can be). It goes beyond the straightforward numeric techniques or the "rational" mean in the Gaussian normal distribution that we learned in classrooms for economics and finance. Instead, BE investigates human behaviors in real-world situations.

3.2 The Behavioral Revolution: Is Utility Just a Function of Wealth?

Already in the nineteenth century, English philosopher Jeremy Bentham (1789) formalized a definition of utility which was only apparently simplistic. "By utility is meant that property in an object, whereby it tends to produce benefit, advantage, pleasure, good, or happiness (all of this in the present case comes to the same thing), or (what comes again to the same thing) to prevent the happening of mischief, pain, evil, or unhappiness to the party whose interest is considered." So, according to Bentham, it is not material property in itself that generates utility. Property can generate utility, but only if it is instrumental to happiness. This is why Ebenezer Scrooge, the main character in Dickens' *A Christmas*

Carol, is extremely wealthy, but being avaricious and insensitive, is a very unhappy man (at least until he rediscovers the true meaning of the Christmas spirit and the happiness coming from giving). John Stuart Mill (Utilitarianism, 1864) went beyond Bentham's definition of utility, to say that "*it is better to be a human being dissatisfied than a pig satisfied; better to be Socrates dissatisfied than a fool satisfied*". So utility was not just coming from seeking of pleasure and avoidance of pain, but rather from belonging to a species longing for knowledge and overall sense.

Once again, conventional economics cut it short, and took on board only the intermediate objective described by Bentham (property), irrespective of whether the achievement of the intermediate objective was conducive to the attainment of the ultimate objective (happiness). In CE, the concept of utility is therefore typically equated to wealth maximization. The more you own, the greater your utility, and that's about all.

There are three major issues with the conventional setup. The first one has to do with the way in which wealth enters the utility function.

According to conventional economics, individuals estimate their utility just in terms of levels of wealth (additive utility functions), which are subject to diminishing returns. The first issue relates to the intertemporal dynamics of wealth flows. As demonstrated in Scitovsky's *The Joyless Economy* (1976), a positive income change is necessary for happiness. If, in contrast, people develop a habituation to a specific level of income for a long enough period, they first experience just comfort, then boredom, and eventually unhappiness.

The second and perhaps most important issue was raised by Kahneman and Tversky in 1979 with their prospect theory (examined in detail in Chap. 3). Under prospect theory, what counts in generating utility are not specific levels of wealth, but rather deviations of actual wealth levels from a reference point. Empirical evidence does support the hypothesis, as shown by a famous experiment. You first put your right hand in cold water and your left hand in hot water. After a while, you take out your hands and put them in a bowl of lukewarm water. Given a different "reference" (cold for the right hand and hot for the left hand), the right hand will feel warm and the left hand will feel cold.

Also, in prospect theory, positive utility is NOT the mirror image of negative utility. In other words, gains and losses do not impact symmetrically on utility. People are loss-averse, meaning that loss weighs more than gains (it is estimated that in order to compensate for the disutility of a loss, a gain will have to be of an amount 200–250% bigger).

The third issue about the conventional relationship between wealth and utility has to do with relational and expectational factors. In order to illustrate this point, a well-known salary increase example can be useful. According to CE , if you receive a salary increase of 5%, this will translate into higher wealth levels and a corresponding increase in utility. But is this always the case? As a matter of fact, your utility can actually decrease if either:

- you discover that a coworker doing exactly the same things you do has simultaneously been granted a 10% salary increase (relational factors) or
- you were expecting a 10% increase (expectational factors).

Obviously, you will be the unhappiest of men if both circumstances materialize at the same time!

All in all, the way in which wealth enters the utility function according to conventional economics can indeed be considered too simplistic.

Let us now turn to the second major problem in the conventional setup.

It relates to the neglect of important causal variables in the determination of utility.

As already highlighted, in conventional economics wealth was often identified as the sole determinant of utility. That approach sounded increasingly inadequate as the level of individual wealth grew significantly over the last decades, and still this did not equate with increased happiness. Easterlin (1974) showed that happiness does not increase in line with income in affluent societies such as the US.

So, many economists began to ponder on what really counts most for us and for most of us, what contributes to our overall well-being as living humans, or enduring satisfaction, therefore commendable utility, that would genuinely make us happy or content.

In a Gallup study on more than 150 countries around the globe representing almost all cultures, ethnic groups, and more than 98% of the world's population, questions concerning health, wealth, relationships, jobs, and communities were presented as measures of social norm and common elements of human well-being, as well as in distinguishing a thriving life from one spent suffering. There are five elements that emerged as broad categories associated with the overall human well-being, happiness, or life satisfaction, hence utility: (1) career, (2) social, (3) financial, (4) health, and (5) community well-beings. While these five elements seem to have an order of importance, deficiencies in any one of them would lead to struggles in us, short- or long term, and cause damage to our well-being. And contrary to other beliefs in the capitalist system which assume that utility only comes from monetary rewards, this empirical study demonstrates that one may not have lived one's life to the fullest unless one lives virtually in all five of them.

In reality, an individual may have a multidimensional goal system that is much richer than that of a narrow-minded *homo economicus*. So, making the choices that would maximize wealth will not only be inconsistent with the maximization of true utility but also can in fact be at odds with it.

The neglect of negative linkages between the individual's multiple utility components has been defined "internality" by Frank (1999).

And what is most interesting is that some of the potential components of the multi-goal utility function are not only different from wealth accumulation, but are in some cases apparently conflicting with the model of a selfish egotistic maximizer.

There is an economic experiment called ultimatum game where two players enter the game. The first player, who has some amounts of money allocated for the game, makes decisions on how the money should be divided. And the second player, though does not have direct control on how the money should be divided, has the decision-making power to either accept or reject his share of money at the end of the game and the latter option will make both players empty-handed. When the ultimatum game was played out among various social groups in different countries, results show that offers less than 30% to the second player are usually rejected. The results from the ultimatum game played repeatedly around the world are robust and prove clearly that the behavior of a real-world economic agent works at odds with the assumption of a *homo economicus* who should choose something rather than nothing in maximizing his utility. Here again, and on the path of dehumanizing for purposes of pure theory and particular ideologies, rational models had considered human decisions based purely on monetary or material terms, thus neglected and were regarded as independent of other objectives, drivers, or principles in humans.

There are several messages we get from the game when the offer is rejected by the second player. One, the act of the second player, which seems to be a decision against his best interest from a rationalist point of view, is a protest against an unfair offer that takes priority over an act that is supposed to suit his interest. Second, the opportunity cost for the first player is even larger since he not only loses the chance to gain a larger portion from the game but also gets nothing, so the two are actually on a leveled playing field. Third, as the first player learns his lesson, he may behave differently next time with a more generous offer. Lastly, and perhaps most importantly, the act of rejecting the offer could simply be a manifestation of altruism.

What is altruism or the motivation behind it? And speaking of utility, what kind of utility or value does an altruistic act generate? From the dictionary, altruism is defined as a traditional virtue across all cultures. It is a feeling and behavior that show a desire to help other people and a principle or practice of unselfish concern or devotion to the welfare of others. Here, the quality of one's unselfishness and concerns for others may incur costs to oneself while not necessarily expect or seek reciprocity. This innate trait in human is also shared by other species in the animal kingdom in the evolutionary process. A warning bird cry that reveals the location of the caller to a predator can at the same time alert the rest of the bird community. In CE, however, one of the key assumptions is that all acts and human behaviors are motivated by selfishness. Is the assumption completely wrong? As conventional economists define utilities mostly in terms of material values, they neglect the utilities associated with non-material or psychological values such as the individual's share in the collective pursuit of higher-level goals like justice, truth, freedom, and love.

Psychologically based altruism may be associated with utilities such as experienced utility, emotional utility, belief- or ideology-based utility, social, moral, or spiritual-based utilities. Take the case of donations and monetary support to students in the fields of music and art. Every year, thousands of patrons, either as an individual or as an entity, pour millions of dollars to support the efforts of young artists in pursuit of art and music in conservatories, art institutions, and universities without knowing whether these students would become true artists later in life. While the sacrifices and opportunity costs behind these generous bequests may well exceed any quantifiable utilities they receive at the time or in the unknown future in material terms, the psychological utility apparently dominates and supersedes the more measurable monetary utility in these outcomes.

While the act of altruism may be considered a cost to an individual and works at odds with utility theory that deems selfishness as the basic motivation in human behavior in pure material terms, we witness altruistic acts beyond material measures almost on a daily basis, in a society that connects many dots with invisible hands for the long-term well-beings and utilities of humans as an individual and as a genus. On a different kind of non-material-based utility or altruism, there are empirical examples of health benefits from volunteerism as a form of altruism.

One study examined the physical health of mothers who volunteered over a 30-year period and found that 52% of those who did not belong to a volunteer organization experienced a major illness while only 36% of those who did volunteer experienced one. A study on adults aged more than 55 found that during the four-year study period, people who volunteered for two or more organizations had a 63% lower likelihood of dying. After controlling for prior health status, it was determined that volunteerism accounted for a 44% reduction in mortality (Moen et al. 1993).

It is fair to say that the purely altruistic interpretation of ultimatum game schemes characterized by generous offers has been on occasion questioned. In particular, some would consider the generosity of the offer as a move by selfish proposers to strategically avoid rejection (Eckel and Grossman 1996). More generally, especially when self-sacrifice is not anonymous, what looks as altruism could actually be accounted for as a form of "indirect egotism", which could, in theory, be consistent with a revisited version of utility as defined by CE. For example, altruism could emerge when reciprocity is expected. Or donating to charities could be an option to enhance potential wealth via an improvement in reputation and social status.

But there are (very frequent) cases in which even the broadest and most indirect selfish interpretation cannot apply—if you are alone in the street and give a dollar to an unknown beggar, for example. Or if you make donations to charities on an anonymous basis; or if you, with no colleagues and friends around, tip in a restaurant where you are not likely to return.

Even if you stretch the concept of conventional utility, you cannot account for these behaviors. So, the definition of utility has to be much more complex. Andreoni (1990) defines this missing explanatory variable of utility as the "warm-glow" effect, by which you make material self-sacrifices when these sacrifices simply make you feel good about yourself. Full circle and back to Bentham: no utility without happiness.

To illustrate the concept, consider this excerpt from an interview given by Nobel laureate Robert Shiller to Nigel Warburton[1]:

> *Nigel Warburton: One that I know you've discussed is this notion of fairness that might trump the economic rationality.*
>
> *Robert Shiller: A sense of fairness is a fundamental human universal. It's been found in some recent studies that it even goes beyond humans, that higher primates do have some vestigial or limited understanding of fairness and equity. In terms of how the market responds to crises, economists assume that everything is done purely out of self-interest. And yet non-economists when we ask them about how things work, they have a totally different view. In one of my questionnaire surveys we asked something like this: if the economy were to improve what would your employer do?*
>
> (a) *nothing—why should he help me just because the economy goes up?*
> (b) *well, the economy improves means the market for my services improves so my employer would realise out of self-interest that he would have to raise my wage in order to keep me.*
> (c) *my employer is a nice person and he would recognise that he should share the benefits with his employees. I gave this question to both economists and non-economists. The economists all picked B, or most of them picked B! They think that market forces dominate. Whereas very few of the non-economists did: they thought either their employer was a bad guy which is A, or their employer is a nice guy, that's C. So there's a different worldview and I think that if people think that fairness is such an important thing in labour contracts then modelling the world as if it's of total insignificance is wrong.*

Nigel Warburton: So doesn't this just make everything much, much more complicated because you can't reduce individuals then to some kind of cipher where they are simply maximising their self-interest in terms of economic benefits?

Robert Shiller: That's why a lot of economists don't like this. Maybe with some justification they'll say that there's too many details in this theory, you can explain anything with it. But I'm un-persuaded by that criticism because, first of all, we can work on this and study people more and understand what psychological principle is relevant. And secondly, it doesn't help to have a theory based on wrong assumptions.

3.3 The Behavioral Revolution and the Concept of Rationality

> *If you look at economics textbooks, you will learn that homo economicus can think like Albert Einstein, store as much memory as IBM's Big Blue, and exercise the willpower of Mahatma Gandhi. Real people have trouble with long division if they don't have a calculator, sometimes forget their spouse's birthday, and have a hangover on New Year's Day. They are not homo economicus; they are homo sapiens.* (Sunstein and Thaler 2008)

A recent study (Gilboa 2014) usefully surveys the way in which the definition of rationality in CE has changed over time:

> Philosophers of the 18th and 19th century did not shy away from making statements about the substantive meaning of rationality. They expressed views about what "Rational Man" should think and do, on issues that are often a matter of value judgment. The rise of mathematical Neoclassical Economics in the early 20th century, influenced by logical positivism, could be viewed as taking a step back, and reducing the concept of rationality to consistency. Rationality started to be defined as behaving in a way that is sufficiently coherence to allow certain formal representation, such as utility maximization, expected utility maximization, and the like. No longer did rationality say what the utility function should be; rather, rationality was taken to be tantamount to having such a utility function, with, at most, minor restrictions such as monotonicity or concavity. In a sense, rationality ceased to be a matter of content, and became a matter of form.

In turn, such a formal definition of rationality was bound to imply certain minimum requirements for the information set of individuals. In particular, proper expected utility maximization would require the correct utilization of mathematical and statistical tools. The further implication was therefore that whenever a decision was found not to be based on correct mathematical/statistical reasoning, it had to be considered "irrational".

How do we define rationality, and what types of human behaviors should be considered as rational in the context of making choices? In Werner and Kliemt's words:

> *the rational choice assumption that all choices are made intentionally and strictly opportunistically, in view of the expected consequences of each choice taken separately, seems off the mark empirically. Individuals choose according to rules or dispositions of a general nature rather than in a case-by-case manner. Because of either the limits of their rational faculties or their ability to follow rules intentionally they do not behave in an opportunistically rational way, at least not completely so.* (Werner and Kliemt 1998)

A major breakthrough in the analysis of different concepts of rationality came from the work of Herbert Simon.

Simon won the Nobel Prize in Economics in 1978 for his *"pioneering research into the decision-making process within economic organizations"*. So you would have expected him to be recognized as the polar star in economic research on decision-making and become an undisputed reference personality, as it happened to people like Milton Friedman or Robert Lucas. But perhaps for the first time in the history of Nobel Prize winners, nothing of that sort happened.

In fact, the reaction of the academic world was to progressively marginalize the Nobel laureate and his ideas, and it was only symptomatic that Simon eventually had to leave the Graduate School of Industrial Administration at Carnegie Mellon University and join the psychology department. In his autobiography (1991), Simon wrote: *"My economist friends have long since given up on me, consigning me to psychology or some other distant wasteland"*. As clearly shown by the previous excerpt of a research paper on rational expectations equilibria, economics in the final part of the twentieth century was striving hard to gain legitimacy as an exact science, very much like engineering or physics. Simon came and upset this plan. So, with the benefit of hindsight we could slightly amend Simon's statement, as what the "economist friends" really meant to do was to reconsign the alien Simon to where he, in their judgment, belonged, that is, the "non-scientific" social disciplines. But what were the "mortal sins" committed by Simon in the eye of his "friends"? At least two, and correlated. The first one was a real blasphemy, as it was a direct attack against the star of conventional economics and finance: the *homo economicus*, endowed with real-time information and capable of complex mathematical calculations.

In a 1955 paper on decision-making, Simon (1955) first describes the computations implied by the alleged optimization process of the *homo economicus* only to conclude that "my first empirical proposition is that there is a complete lack of evidence that, in actual human choice situations of any complexity, these computations can be, or are in fact, performed".

For many "economists", it was the end of the world. All the years spent in building increasingly sophisticated mathematical models, with people choosing whether to buy a bond or a stock only after having solved complex systems of differential equations! Who was this "psychologist" to challenge such formally beautiful constructs?

But luckily enough for the concerned cohorts of white lab coat "economists", the second mortal sin of Simon was there to provide them with a way out of embarrassment. As a matter of fact, Simon stated that the *homo economicus* did not exist, but without giving a formal proof (no differential equations!) of his statement. This made extremely easy for mainstream economists to just ignore the substance of Simon's point. The whole episode is, of course, paradoxical in many ways. On the one hand, because Simon was no *homo economicus* himself and so could not use any complex formal apparatus to prove his point. On the other hand, because the requirement of formally proving the nonexistence of something can at times become impossible to satisfy. Can you PROVE that ghosts do not exist? This situation has similarities with the story reported by Robert Lucas (1981). In the story, the archeologist Heinrich Schliemann, the discoverer of Troy, becomes convinced that a particular skull unearthed in a later excavation is the head of Agamemnon. To the frustration of this creative and productive scientist, his associates confront him with one commonsense argument after another. Exhausted, Schliemann thrusts the skull in the faces of his unconstructive critics: "*Alright then, if he is not Agamemnon, who is he?*" If you want to convince me that the *homo economicus* doesn't exist, would have said conventional economists, give me a formal proof of it!

But if the *homo economicus* doesn't exist, then we can legitimately ask Herbert Simon not whose skull it is that we are looking at, but at least how real-world decision-making works. To explain that, Simon (1959) chose to use molasses:

> *Suppose we are pouring some viscous liquid molasses into a bowl of very irregular shape.... How much would we have to know about the properties of molasses to predict its behavior under the circumstances? If the bowl were held motionless, and if we wanted only to predict behavior in equilibrium, we would have to know little, indeed, about molasses. The single essential assumption would be that the molasses, under the force of gravity, would minimize the height of its center of gravity. With this assumption, which would apply as well to any other liquid, and a complete knowledge of the environment, in this case the shape of the bowl, the equilibrium is completely determined. Just so, the equilibrium behavior of a perfectly adapting organism depends only on its goal and its environment; it is otherwise completely independent of the internal properties of the organism. If the bowl into which we are pouring the molasses were jiggled rapidly, or if we wanted to know about the behavior before equilibrium was reached, prediction would require much more information. It would require, in particular, more information about the properties of molasses: its viscosity, the rapidity with which it "adapted" itself to the containing vessel and moved towards its "goal" of lowering its center of gravity. Likewise, to predict the short run behavior of an adaptive organism, or its behavior in a complex and rapidly changing environment, it is not enough to know its goals. We must know also a great deal about its internal structure and particularly its mechanisms of adaptation.*

We are all molasses, aren't we? Simon's point is that in theory, when situations are simple with not much information required and when there are no time constraints, the decision-maker could be an optimizer in the sense defined by conventional economics. Pity that most situations are not simple; they are changing: a lot of information should be retrieved and time limits are binding. Thus the "normal" (most common) state of the world is not equilibrium (the realm of "normative" disciplines like conventional economics), but turbulence, to which human beings have to adapt continuously.

And in Simon's view, they do so in a way that has nothing to do with the processes described in conventional economics. In order to describe the way in which humans make their choices in an ever changing environment, Simon used different terms in a series of important papers published between 1953 and 1957. The most famous (and perhaps the most misleading) is "bounded rationality", but he also referred to "limited rationality" and perhaps unsatisfied with the negative bias implied by these definitions, he eventually described human behavior as "intendedly rational".

More than definitions, however, what is important is the content of Simon's view of decision-making. His idea is that humans decide using SOME information and decision rules (heuristics) without any recourse to probability weighting of future events and/or mathematical algorithms.

People have limited time for processing data, and information retrieval and computational processes are costly in terms of time and effort. So mental shortcuts or simple rule of thumbs (heuristics) are used, the more so if they worked reasonably well in the past.

In short, human beings have bounded capabilities, resources, and willingness to always find procedures to reach the best alternative, even if they can abstractly define it, given changing environment, time constraints, and the lack or cost of information. They would stop their search for a solution as soon as a possible choice can deliver a good enough result—a satisficing (satisfactory-sufficing) result. People do not optimize, not even among heuristics.

Therefore, Simon's "bounded rationality" is not just "optimization under constraints". If it were, decision-making would follow a path by which the search for an optimal solution would be carried on until the "costs"—direct and opportunity costs—would outweigh the gain for further search. That would be the optimal stopping point, at which the best option materialized so far is chosen. But in Simon's view, the acceptance of such an approach would imply the same implausible assumptions (omniscience) associated with unconstrained optimization: as a matter of fact, in order to calculate the optimal stopping point, people should have all the information needed to estimate the marginal utility and the additional costs of continuing the search (Simon 1947, 1956).[2]

But if there are constraints and we cannot optimize, what do we do? When is it that our behavior is "satisficing"? In order to answer this question, it is useful to first clarify what the term "bounded rationality" truly means. Let's start from what it does not mean. "Bounded" should not simply be taken to mean "incomplete" or "insufficient". It has rather to do with the interactions between two bounds that were traditionally considered separate and unrelated: the mind and the environment.

The two bounds interact continuously. In particular, the cognitive processes of the human mind (and the specific decision rules adopted) keep adapting to an environment which may dynamically change over time.

As Simon (1990) put it, "*Human rational behavior…is shaped by a [pair of] scissors whose two blades are the structure of the task environments and the computational capabilities of the actor*". These two blades—the two sources of bounds on our rationality—must fit together closely for rationality to cut. And a strategy is "rational" or "irrational" only with respect to a particular (physical or social) environment. Here are the scissors' blades (see Fig. 3.2).

The first blade of Simon's scissors is meant to reflect the fact that humans "must use approximate methods to handle most tasks" (Simon 1990: 6). These methods include heuristics that guide search and simple decision rules that make use of the information found. As we will see shortly, there is a strand of behavioral economics that focuses only on the first blade, and evaluates it (the workings of the mind) with laws of probability and logic, rather than situational factors, thus often reaching the conclusion that people are simply irrational.

But one blade alone does not work as well as two; by introducing a properly fit second blade (crucial aspects of environment structure), humans can be shown to exhibit ecological rationality (Gigerenzer et al. 2000), which is there when people make good decisions with mental mechanisms whose internal structure can exploit the information structures available in the environment.

The word "satisficing" comes from the combination of "satisfy" and "suffice". The decision-maker settles for a choice that is "good enough"

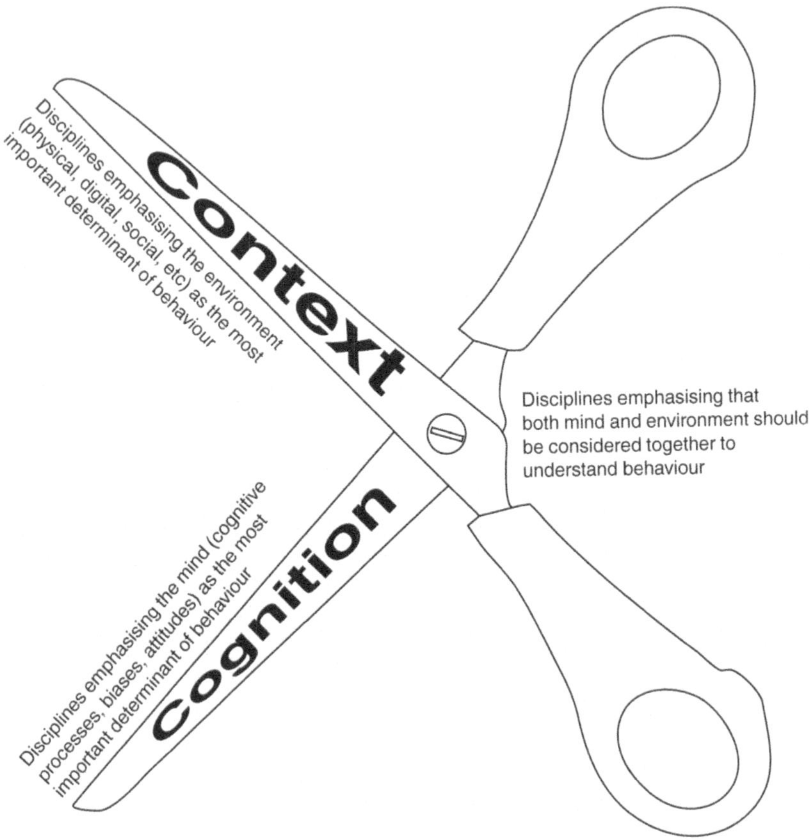

Source: Lockton, D (2012), 'Simon's scissors and ecological psychology in design for behavior change'

Fig. 3.2 Simon's Scissors

for the purpose at a particular time given resource constraints instead of maximizing expected utility, which may involve an indefinite search effort (because of lack of information) or feasibility issues, or incur greater current costs or future uncertainties. Considering the constraints an individual faces in the decision-making process involving costs of time and mental and physical efforts, along with other internal resources required, yet with varying external resources such as information, the satisficing method is not only more rational and realistic but also a happier experience for the decision-maker. Let's take a closer look at the difference between "maximizing" and "satisficing" approaches in utility seeking.

As we know, the utility maximization model is consistent with and a derivative of the conventional definition of human rationality, as discussed previously. So, the assumptions include the one by which the individual decision-maker is (1) rational, albeit rationality is thinly defined; (2) able to do all the calculations needed with complete information; (3) going after the option that has the highest calculated material value, even if it may not be the best, taking into account other criteria; and (4) willing and able to take on exhaustive search for all options with unlimited time and effort. Apparently, this process does not consider that some components in the options may change before the decision-maker makes up his mind and a particular option could vary afterward, so the best choice as the highest material value at the time may not be so in the unforeseeable future. In an example of decision-making for college selection, studies show that maximizers often focus on external sources as the sole criteria in the evaluation process for expected utility maximization. So instead of contemplating on whether they would truly benefit the choice they make, their choice is more likely based on the college's reputation, social status, or how it is perceived by others in general. This "rational" yet impersonal choice could very well end up with unhappy or even disastrous, outcomes. In other cases, maximizers opt for choices that are determined by calculable and material-based utilities without reflecting on causes such as fairness. In the ultimatum game, the maximizer would choose something rather than nothing in maximizing his utility even if the payoff is severely iniquitous in the context.

For satisficers, however, what is more important is whether the choice would meet their specific needs and aspirations and is really "the best" for them personally. Good examples are Bill Gates, the founder of Microsoft, and Mark Zuckerberg, the founder of Facebook. While attending a college such as Harvard has the highest appeal to many, it apparently had none to either of these two. These personal decision choices were in line with Schwartz's argument (2015) that the value of decision outcomes cannot be assessed independent of the decision contexts that give rise to them and that the relation between the magnitude of an outcome and its value is often non-monotonic. He argued that the honorific "rational" should be based on the substantive and not the formal properties of decisions, in a way that enable people to live good, meaningful, and satisfying lives.

More specifically, and as Simon describes, it is neither rational nor realistic nor economical to examine all available options, or an optimal solution may not be determined under certain circumstances. Simon insisted that problems in reality are characterized by lack of information and remarked in his Nobel Prize speech that "*decision-makers can satisfice either by finding optimum solutions for a simplified world, or by finding satisfactory solutions for a more realistic world*". As an individual, the satisficer is not only well aware of his mental, physical, informational, economic, and other personal-related resource constraints, but also susceptible to unknown future developments that any options available to him could lead to. So the satisficer considers different types of costs, material, non-material, explicit and implicit, in different time horizons. In some cases, and while maybe suboptimal, the satisficing approach is more balanced, thoughtful, and therefore rational, taking all factors into account.

Important conceptual factors behind the satisficing approach could be defined not only by satisfactory level or acceptability of all costs, which include but are not limited to mental efforts, but also by time, security, availability of information, and analytical tools. Here is a good example to illustrate the contrast ideas of satisficing vs. maximizing in making a decision to buy a professional-level violin. With the modern technology and information available for exchange knowledge in the creation of the art of making a superb instrument, there are hundreds of luthiers around the world cultivating on the complex process to look for not only specific sounds but also certain forms and shapes of the instrument. For a satisficer, she has a sound, color, and general model and style of a violin in mind that she is looking for within a certain price range, and she tries out in shops in New York or other well-known cities where there are good luthiers such as in Cremona, Italy, or in Montpellier, France. For a maximizer, the process is much costlier and longer if it can be determined. He may visit dozens of shops around the world, seeking what is the most popular sound at present time, combined with the best craftsmanship and affordable price. Every instrument has its unique sound and characteristics yet the final result also varies from one player to another, as the sound of the instrument is shaped by the player with hands that exert a certain amount of pressure and different ways of generating a sound. So the true maximizer may never find the instrument that would make him completely happy.

The next important question is what the impact will be on the decision-maker in terms of satisfactory outcomes if one has the inclination to be a maximizer rather than a satisficer. Using regret and maximizing scales, Schwartz et al. (2002) studied how the satisficing vs. maximizing approach in decision-making impacts our well-being. Some of the scaled scenarios look like the following:

- Whenever I make a choice, I try to get information about how the other alternatives turned out.
- If I make a choice and it turns out well, I still feel like something of a failure if I find out that another choice would have turned out better.
- No matter how satisfied I am with my job, it's only right for me to be on the lookout for better opportunities.
- I often fantasize about living in ways that are quite different from my actual life.

From seven samples of correlated scores on a maximization scale with established measures of well-being, the study revealed that maximizers reported significantly less life satisfaction, happiness, optimism, and self-esteem, and significantly more regret and depression, than did satisficers. The study also showed that maximizers were less satisfied than non-maximizers or satisficers with consumer decisions, and more likely to engage in social comparison. To see why there are negative correlations between maximizers and their social well-being and how the mental structure and process actually work for maximizers, Schwartz et al. explained that the freedom to choose and the abundant options in modern economics pose problems for maximizers. One needs to examine all the alternatives in order to maximize choice, but when examining all the alternatives is infeasible, the maximizer is forced to finally choose; therefore, there is a lingering doubt and potential regret that she or he could have done better with more searching. So, as alternatives increase, the likelihood of successful maximization goes down as she or he keeps looking for better and better options, which cannot be determined in reality, while in the meantime may have passed up the best or a better option since not all opportunities are available at all times in some cases.

Not understanding that there are time and information-processing constraints in making a choice in terms of the options available at the time as well as the reality that there are almost always other options, maximizers often have regrets because they would question themselves, "Is this the best choice I've made?" or "Could I've done better?" and in turn, they would look how others made their choices as an ex post assessment. This leads to various types of social- and consumption-related comparisons, and social and product comparisons stimulated counterfactual thoughts, which then engendered regret. These psychological setbacks, however, are not a problem for satisficers who only look for "good enough" options or know what is acceptable to them. As they understand the limits of time and knowledge when the choice was made, a better option that shows up later will not have much impact on them—they may simply ignore them or are unlikely to experience regret.

If we use the criteria of conventional economics as normative measures, maximizers would be rated higher than satisficers in terms of objective measures, and in some cases in outcomes, as they input more efforts and exhaustive searches with almost unbounded expectations as they continuously seek better options. However, strategies used by maximizers often generate worse subjective utility outcomes than those for satisficers. And from the findings on the effect of maximizing strategy vs. those of satisficing and the perspective of human well-being, the former is apparently psychologically counterproductive. So if the main purpose of making a decision is to increase utility, a process which cannot escape the element of subjectivity, the satisficing strategy wins, since it leaves the decision-maker much better off mentally, emotionally, and most likely in material and economic terms. In Schwartz's words:

> *In many cases in which people decide among alternatives, it is the* <u>*subjective*</u> *rather than the* <u>*objective*</u> *consequences of the decision that should be the standard for assessing the rationality of the decision* (underline added).

An example of satisficing maximization applied to career decision-making could be the following:

$$\text{MAX}\,Wealth\left(\text{Income from Work / Career}\right)$$

Subject to a minimum acceptable level X of H (happiness), where

$H = H_{t-i} + \alpha\, G + \eta$
H_{t-i} = a particular memorable happy year in career
$G = G_{t-i} + \beta FT$ (freetime) + γ SS (social and family popularity)
G_{t-i} = a year in the past with satisfying personal and social gratification, *at subjective level X*
η = any new aspirations

But how would you empirically test it and get results of general relevance?

In light of this question, it is not difficult to understand why Simon's intuitions enjoyed a limited appeal not only among "conventional" economists but also in more receptive quarters. The central point is that, as realistic as Simon's telling of human behavior may be, its "satisficing" theoretical framework is hard to use in practical terms, especially as far as the "second blade" (environment) is concerned. That's a factor which presumably led people like Daniel Kahneman and Amos Tversky to focus on the first blade: the human mind. Nonetheless, with the principles of ecological rationality in today's information technology and market structure, and the understanding of a yet imperfect knowledge economy, a topic that we will introduce shortly, does "bounded rationality" interpreted in conventional terms still serve any purposes?

* * *

On June 23, 2016, the referendum held in the UK on whether Britain should remain in the European Union or leave it was won with a narrow margin by the "leave" supporters. That was a shock, even for the savvy community of UK bookmakers, whose forecasts were completely different (see Fig. 3.3).

Source: https://www.smartbets.com/

Fig. 3.3 The Goof of UK Bookmakers

But it didn't come as a surprise for Daniel Kahneman, who was interviewed on June 6, by the *Daily Telegraph*:

> *"British voters are succumbing to impulsive gut feelings and irrational reflexes in the Brexit campaign with little regard for the enormous consequences down the road, the world's most influential psychologist". Daniel Kahneman, the Israeli Nobel laureate and father of behavioural economics, said the referendum debate is being driven by a destructive psychological process, one that could lead to a grave misjudgment and a downward spiral for British society. "The major impression one gets observing the debate is that the reasons for exit are clearly emotional," he said. "The arguments look odd: they look short-term and based on irritation and anger. These seem to be powerful enough that they may lead to Brexit."*

Fourteen years before Brexit, in 2002, Daniel Kahneman was awarded the Nobel Prize in economics. He was the second psychologist to win the prize (the first was Herbert Simon). In previous years, he worked in close association with Amos Tversky, who died in 1996 at the age of 59. Had Tversky lived, he would certainly have shared the Nobel with Kahneman.

As shown by his Brexit forecast, human "irrationality" is Kahneman's cup of tea.

His research work can be divided into three sequential stages (the first two together with Tversky).

In the first one he explored 20 or so "cognitive biases"—unconscious errors of reasoning that distort our judgment of the world and are often the product of the usage of "heuristics", mental shortcuts used to assess probabilities (Kahneman and Tversky 1974). An example? We can use what is perhaps the most famous heuristic, the representativeness heuristic, by which "probabilities are evaluated by the degree to which A is representative of B, that is, by the degree to which A resembles B".

Linda is 31 years old, single, outspoken, and very bright. She majored in philosophy. As a student, she was deeply concerned with the issue of discrimination and social justice, and also participated in antinuclear demonstrations. Which of the following is more probable: (1) Linda is a bank teller (T); (2) Linda is a bank teller and is active in the feminist movement (T and B). Most people chose answer 2, although it is obvious that a conjunction can never be more likely than any of its constituents alone (see Fig. 3.4).

An additional example of how representativeness works? Imagine you receive a call interrupting your dinner, with an offer for a contract with company X granting lower heating charges. There are many chances that you would simply put down the phone without listening further if the

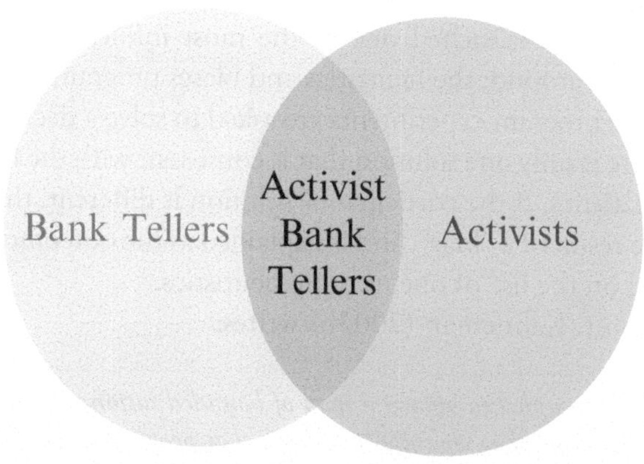

Fig. 3.4 The Linda Problem

information you have stored, based on your experience, tells you that 9 out of 10 pitches you receive are not worth listening to.

Another important heuristic is the availability heuristic, by which probability assessment is based on familiarity and ease of recall (media play an important role there). Due to the dramatic events of September 11, 2001, in the following months many Americans thought that traveling by car was bound to be safer than taking a plane. In fact, air travel had never been safer than in that period, thanks to the increased security measures. And the net result of choosing to travel by car was that there were many more fatal road accidents in the last quarter of 2001 than in the same period of prior years.

Last but not least, anchoring. You found the paint brush with which Leonardo da Vinci painted *La Gioconda*. At what price would you sell it? The question is a difficult one, as you have no reference/starting level to use. So in many cases in which you have to assess, for example, the correctness of a price, you need an anchor. But anchoring may produce mistakes. Imagine that you have just seen a pair of nice jeans selling at $100 in your local shop. Checking online, you later discover that a website sells the same jeans at $70. Chances are that you click and buy, glad to save $30. And you will never know that the correct price for those jeans was $50!

In Kahneman's view, all these heuristics can be useful in decision-making, but are prone to the generation of biases, that is, cognitive distortions, that in turn may lead to "irrational" decisions (we will examine biases in more detail in Chap. 4). This is the reason why a few decades ago Kahneman, Tversky, and others launched one of the most influential psychological research projects around: the heuristics and biases program. Typically, participants in the program experiments are asked to solve a decision problem for which there is only one solution that is consistent with the laws of probability and statistics. If the participants' solution is different, then it is considered as the result of a "bias", and is explained as the outcome of a mental process based on the use of one or more heuristics.

On this point, Kahneman (2003b) writes:

Our research attempted to obtain a map of bounded rationality, by exploring the systematic biases that separate the beliefs that people have and the choices they make from the optimal beliefs and choices assumed in rational-agent models. The rational-agent model was our starting point and the main source of our null hypotheses.

So, the whole program relies on the conceptual premise that the only possible rationality is the one advocated in conventional economics, that is, the one working in accordance with the rules of probability and statistics. This is quite at odds both with Simon's view by which rationality rests on realistic assumptions about human behavior and with the ecological rationality described by Gigerenzer (we'll introduce it later on).

In the second phase of their research, which led to the awarding of the Nobel Prize in 2002, Kahneman (and Tversky) highlighted the fact that, different from what conventional economics predict, decision-making under uncertainty is inconsistent with the maximization of expected utility, and developed "prospect theory", a more plausible alternative conceptual framework. Unlike expected utility, which is a normative theory (describes human behavior as it should be), prospect theory is a positive theory (describes human behavior as it is).

For the purposes of this chapter, the question we are interested in is: how much and what kind of "irrationality" is present in the decision-making process represented in prospect theory? In order to answer this question, let's quickly go through the main features of the theory itself.

First, in the prospect theory, utility doesn't derive from levels of wealth, but from gains and losses evaluated with respect to a reference level (typically current wealth). If John and Mary both reach a wealth of $100,000, their utility will be different if Mary's initial wealth was twice that of John.

Second, it is assumed that people perceive outcomes in terms of a "value function" defined over gains and losses relative to some reference point. Both the gain and loss functions display diminishing sensitivity, but the gain function is concave while the loss function is convex. This feature reflects the basic psychophysical principle (the Weber-Fechner law) that the difference between $10 and $20 seems bigger than the difference between $100 and $110, irrespective of the sign. The concavity over gains also highlights the fact that people tend to be risk-averse over most probability gains (I prefer a sure gain of $50 to a 50% chance

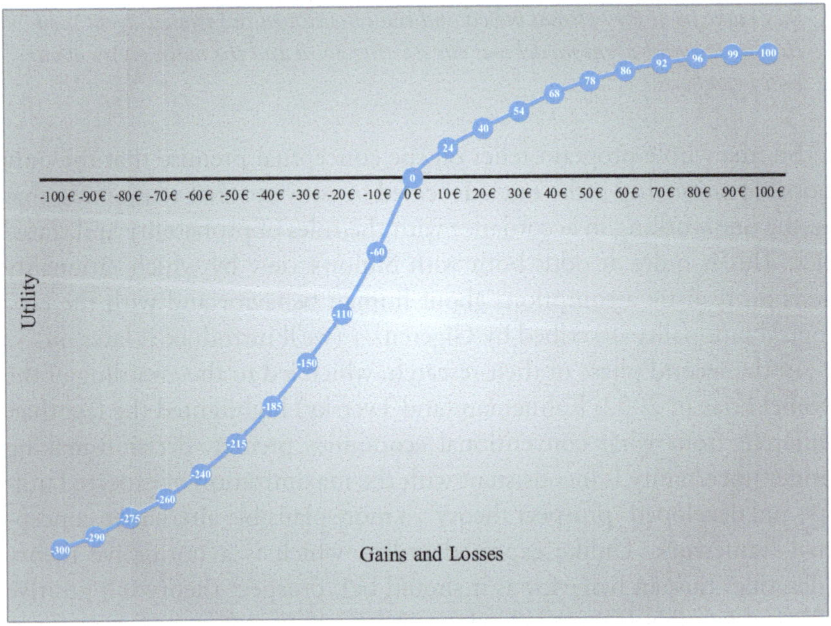

Fig. 3.5 Value Function

of $100). However, people also tend to be risk-seeking when it comes to losses (I prefer a 50% chance of losing $100 to losing $50 for sure). This explains convexity over losses. Then there is loss aversion. Losing $50 hurts more than gaining $50 yields pleasure. Loss aversion is generated as the value function is steeper in the region of losses than in the region of gains. Using the illustrative values of Fig. 3.5, losing $50 provokes a "dis-utility" of 215, almost three times the "utility" of gaining $50.

The fourth and final component of prospect theory is probability weighting, based on the π function which transforms stated probabilities.

Consider this gamble (see Table 3.2).

In this case people would choose option B, which is characterized by a higher expected value. And they should go for the same choice for any linear transformation of the probability structure (i.e. if you multiply all values in the probability line by the same number). But is it so? Let's try and multiply probabilities by 4 (see Table 3.3).

Table 3.2 A Simple Gamble

	A	B
Probability	0.25	0.2
Payoff	30	45
Expected value	**7.5**	**9**

Table 3.3 A Simple Gamble Transformed

	A*	B*
Probability	1	0.8
Payoff	30	45
Expected value	**30**	**36**

In contrast with what should be the neutrality of linear transformation, most people would now choose A*. Why? Because of the so-called *certainty effect*: the certainty of getting $30 is overweighted. People are most sensitive to changes in probability near the natural boundaries of 0 (impossible) and 1 (certain).

Thus, a 0.1 increase in probability has a greater effect on decisions when it changes probability from 0 to 0.1 (turning an impossibility into a possibility) or from 0.9 to 1 (turning a possibility into a certainty) than when it changes the probability from, say, 0.3 to 0.4. This explains why the same people may buy lottery tickets and insurance. In particular, Kunreuther et al. (2001) present strong evidence that people in risk areas accept to pay excessive premia to buy insurance against low probability natural hazards, for example, earthquakes, floods, and hurricane. Of course, whether probability theory is suitable for projecting future events with uncertainty ex ante is another matter, which we'll explore later. But a typical prospect theory probability weighting function $\pi(p)$ is concave for low probabilities (subjective probability weighted higher than actual probability) and convex for medium to high probabilities (subjective probability weighted lower than actual probability) (see Fig. 3.6).

Is all this irrational? Good question. Kahneman and Tversky give an articulate, if not ambiguous, answer when they say that

> *consistency is only one aspect of the lay notion of rational behavior……the common conception of rationality also requires that preferences or utilities for particular outcomes should be predictive of the experiences of satisfaction or*

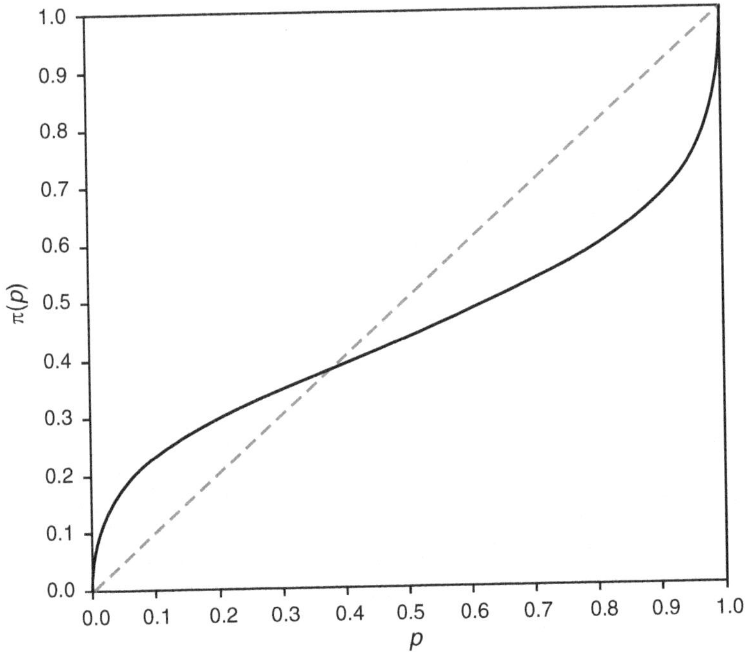

Fig. 3.6 The Probability Weighting Function

> *displeasure associated with their occurrence. ….. The predictive criterion of rationality can be applied to resolve inconsistent preferences and to improve the quality of decisions. A predictive orientation encourages the decision-maker to focus on future experience and to ask "What will I feel then?" rather than "What do 1 want now?* (Tversky and Kahneman 1981)

In the third phase of his career, Kahneman (2011) has explored the "physical" functioning of decision-making processes in the human mind and the concept of happiness.

In particular, the mind would respond alternatively to two coexisting systems: System 1 and System 2.

System 1 is quick as a hare, largely based on intuition, and is the first to be called into action in decision-making. System 2, which is slower, analytical (and more powerful) is, however, tiring and more "costly" in terms of elaboration, and so is activated only when needed (you can't fill

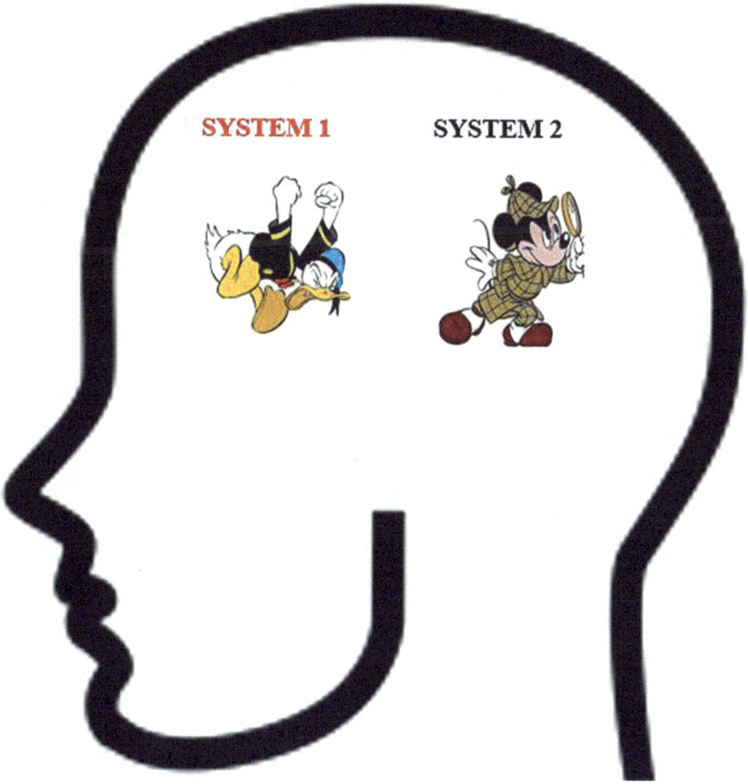

Fig. 3.7 The Two Mind System in Partition

correctly a tax form with just System 1). There is obviously a bias in favor of System 1. So whenever a problem looks easy on the surface, we switch it on (see Fig. 3.7).

A famous example is that of the ball and the baseball bat. Someone asks you what appears to be a very easy question: “If a ball and a baseball bat together cost $1.10, and the bat costs one dollar more than the ball, how much does the ball cost?” System 1 steps in: the ball costs 10 cents. Wrong, of course. It costs 5 cents.

So, System 1 is high risk in terms of probability of making mistakes. Accordingly, if we are rational, shouldn’t we just switch it off and rely exclusively on System 2?

Yes and no, says Kahneman. On the one hand, it is true that if we were rational in the "conventional" sense we would do it. But—here is the pessimistic angle in Kahneman's view—there is no escape from SYSTEMATIC mistakes. Interviewed on the matter by *Der Spiegel* on May 21, 2012, he plainly stated that

> "*we're all prone to make some very simple errors when we try to work out what to do. And we continue to make those mistakes even when they are pointed out to us*". For this there is no remedy: "*I don't have a recipe for avoiding the errors that we're all prone to, and I don't think there is one. It's the way we are*".

But why? Is it lack of willpower, or laziness, or what? Perhaps part of the answer lies with the "hedonic psychology", which is the area that Kahneman focused on in the last years. And in particular with the concept of happiness, which is the ultimate goal of every man, rational or irrational as he may be. Chances are that we LIKE System 1, irrespective of the mistakes it can deliver, because in many cases it has served us well, saving effort and time that we could devote to more pleasant activities. And this is especially true if such activities have produced what Kahneman calls "experienced" well-being (a matter of perception), which is wider than the "remembered" well-being (memory may fail). Could that be the reason why while French mothers spend less time with their children than American mothers, they enjoy it more.

* * *

Do you know the guy playing the accordion at the extreme right of this picture, taken some years ago during a dinner at Villa Giersch in Munich? Well, if you don't, you should.

He is no less than Gerd Gigerenzer, currently director of the Center for Adaptive Behavior and Cognition (ABC) at the Max Planck Institute for Human Development in Berlin, Germany.

Very much like Simon and Kahneman, he is a psychologist. And very angry with the "American" strand of behavioral economics (Kahneman and associates). Here is what he writes in his introduction to *The Behavioral Economics Guide 2016*", edited by Alan Samson (www.behavioraleconomics.com):

Source: Ernst Struengmann Forum c/o Frankfurt Institute for Advanced Studies

Fig. 3.8 Gerd on the Accordion

> In some corners of behavioral economics, researchers collect lists of people's biases, 175 of which are featured on Wikipedia. According to the Economist, human beings are fallible thinkers, being lazy, stupid, greedy, and weak. According to Newsweek, we are woefully muddled information processors who often stumble along ill-chosen shortcuts to reach bad conclusions. In their book Nudge, Thaler and Sunstein jokingly compare us with Homer Simpson, a character prone to bumbling stupidity, in order to justify governmental paternalism that protects us from ourselves. As you may know, this is not my view of humans. We already have plenty of paternalism, including an excess of surveillance, and certainly do not need more of it in the 21st century.

What especially makes Gigerenzer angry is the negative and partial view that "the Americans" have of heuristics, as that view can be considered an unacceptable distortion of Simon's discoveries. Again from the introduction to *The Behavioral Economics Guide 2016*:

> Herbert Simon, one of the founders of behavioral economics, held that heuristics were rational tools in situations of uncertainty. In AI, heuristics are used to make computers smart, yet in some corners of behavioral economics, heuristics are still seen as the reason why people aren't smart. The catch phrase is that heuristics are sometimes useful but often lead to serious errors. That is so true that it cannot be wrong. But the same truism applies to all complex models, from Pareto/NBD to multiple regression to Bayes. The fact that complex, fine-tuned algorithms tend to fail in situations of uncertainty should be a take-home message from the last financial crisis, where ratings, risk-weighted measures, and value-at-risk computations failed. Fine-tuning can make a system fragile and at the same time create illusions of certainty.

For Gigerenzer, the "American" view of heuristics suffers from at least two major problems. On the one hand, the excessively stylized description of reality implies behavior rules that are so "simple" that any deviation from them is labeled as "irrational". But, in fact, there are many circumstances (e.g. Brexit) in which it is unreasonable to expect the subject to construct an even approximate frequency distribution. Also, time limits can play a role in inducing "irrational" behavior. A nice illustration of why heuristics, and not optimizing rational procedures, are in fact the norm for most people around is given by Bookstaber (2017): "I wake up, fall out of bed, run downstairs to drink a cup of coffee, and grab some breakfast. Then I head back up to figure out what to wear. And then it is off to work.

If I were rational, at least the economic version of rational, this routine would not be as easy as it sounds. My mind would be running optimizations from the moment I opened my eyes. All possible breakfasts, all possible sets of clothes, and all paths to work: I would evaluate each one in turn given my current set of preferences, ranking each one against the others.... If I ran these optimizations every day I might never get out of bed".

On the other hand, the "Americans" obviously fail to accept the potential of heuristics in practical decision-making.

But what are heuristics? What is their correct definition? According to Gigerenzer and Gaissmaier (2011), "A heuristic is a strategy that ignores part of the information, with the goal of making decisions more quickly, frugally, and/or accurately than more complex methods".

To tell the truth, this definition doesn't seem the most satisfactory possible (a "strategy"? "quickly OR accurately"?), but let's have a look at the way in which Gigerenzer models heuristics. He does that using three "building blocks":

1. *Search*: it takes place in the environment and/or in memory. The more the available knowledge the more it is possible to select heuristics on the basis, among other things, of their past usefulness and/or cultural heritage
2. *Stopping*: of course, searching for information about available alternatives cannot go on indefinitely. One stopping rule can be the "one-reason" (or "take the best" rule): stop after you find the first discriminating cue. An example: I have to understand if during the weekend I will find more traffic going to seaside resort A or to seaside resort B. To infer that, the most valid cue is whether the specific resort is famous. Given that A is more popular, my conclusion will be that I will find less traffic if I choose B.
3. *Decision*: In the example just made, my decision will be to go to B.

Of course, in addition to the "one-reason", there are many other heuristics that could be considered, as the "recognition heuristic" (or fluency) or the "elimination heuristic" (using one cue after another in a specified order to narrow down the set of remaining possible categories until only a single one remains).

What is particularly interesting is Gigerenzer's view of "dynamic heuristics", that is, heuristics suitable for use in a sequential search.

As an illustration, he often uses the so-called "dowry problem".

In order to find a new adviser, Sultan Saladin summons a suitable candidate and tells him that he can marry the woman with the largest dowry in his sultanate, but he has first to select her out of a group of 100 beautiful women. If he fails, he will be executed. The women will enter the room one by one, declare their wealth, and the candidate can make his choice whenever he wants, but can't return to a woman he already let pass. At what point would it be optimal to stop the search?

Gigerenzer suggests the "37 percent rule". After the first 37 women pass, pick the first woman with a dowry higher than the highest of the first 36. In this way the chances of winning arrive at about one in three, so it can be considered "satisficing", as Simon would put it.

Of course, the "dowry problem" is an extreme case. In real life, we can go back to a shop we already visited, or divorce and get married again. But sometimes, although in a semi-strong version, the "dowry problem" applies: going back to a shop out of town can be costly in terms of time; also, if we declined to buy a house one month ago as we thought there could be better deals, and that was not the case, maybe that that specific house in the meantime has been bought by someone else.

This is why Simon's concept of satisficing by means of aspiration levels provides a tool for choice. An aspiration level is set, and search for alternatives is stopped as soon as the aspiration is met. Indeed, the concept of "aspiration level" is used by Simon broadly and vaguely, and in contexts dangerously near to expected utility maximization. But it is safe to equate the "aspiration level" to the "reservation price" of a seller. If you are selling your house and receive sequential offers, you simply sell whenever the price offered is the one you consider "about right".

So heuristics are not just as good as other decision-making instruments, but in specific circumstances, especially when uncertainty prevails and time is short, they are actually better!

This is why in order to catch a flying Frisbee, a dog doesn't just sit down and solve a system of differential equations, but moves and keeps its optical angle constant (see Fig. 3.9)!

And keeping your optical angle constant is what Gigerenzer calls a fast and frugal reasoning, which invokes an ecological, rather than procedural, definition of rationality. This decision-making process is ecologically rational if it is the best one for the specific environment/situation the decision-maker finds himself. And in many occasions—holds Gigerenzer—it is the best because of the "less is more" effect, by which too much information can actually do harm, whereas limited information can enable new cognitive and/or unconscious functions that would otherwise be absent. Seems a bit extreme? Think of the flying Frisbee!

Fig. 3.9 The Dog and the Frisbee

So, is Gigerenzer telling us that we should always go for uninformed decisions, and that this is the most (ecologically) rational approach we may have?

Not quite. Because he recalls the historical distinction—which in his view was neglected by Neoclassical Economics—between "risk" and "uncertainty".

Risk exists in situations in which alternatives, consequences, and probabilities are known for certain. If you are considering buying a lottery ticket, by looking at historical data, you can estimate probabilities of winning. In that circumstance, argues Gigerenzer, traditional statistical models can be effectively used and are a richer alternative than heuristics.

But in the majority of cases, the environment in which we operate is not stable, and in such cases statistical model would be of little use as they fit the past, but give no guidance for the future. Think of the situation in which Mark Zuckerberg decided to launch Facebook. How could he have known how people's preferences would evolve in the future? Were there historical samples to analyze in order to take an informed decision? The answer is no. Thus it is very likely that he relied on his personal heuristics! And chances are that that specific heuristics were to a significant extent unconscious, that is, with underlying reasons not immediately clear but strong enough to act upon.

And the additional complication is that many times it is not easy to distinguish between risky and uncertain situations. For example, the turkey featuring in a story by Nassim Taleb thought that it was in a risky situation when a man came. Initially, the turkey thought that the man was a killer, but instead he brought food, and continued to do so for weeks. So the turkey concluded that that was a situation of risk, in which probabilities could be calculated, and in order to estimate survival chances, it made recourse to Pierre Simon-Laplace's "rule of succession", by which the probability that something occurs again is equal to $(n + 1)/(n + 2)$, where n is the number of previous occurrences. So, after 32 days of the man bringing food, the turkey thought that the chances of being fed again were higher than 99%. It was only a pity that the following day was Thanksgiving: one important information was missing.

According to Gigerenzer, it is precisely to adequately face this kind of circumstance that we should be (or become) "risk savvy". In his view, people are not stupid, nor do they need the nudging guidance of governments (why should governments be less stupid than us, by the way?). The problem lies with the absence of any risk education. In order to be "savvy", we should be encouraged to understand that our life is full of risks and uncertainties, and that the only choice we have is to learn how to best handle them, rather than escaping from them. Sure, this means that we can make errors. But if these errors contribute to the development of our cognitive capabilities, they must be considered "good errors": "learn by failing, or you fail to learn". After all, Christopher Columbus wanted to open a sea route to India, and discovered America instead.

And he kept it simple, as predicated by the "less is more" rule. In this way he understood the nature of his mistake, and that gave him guidance for the future. Why? because of a very simple statistical property. The overall error we make when predicting is the sum of biases (unavoidable in situations of uncertainty) and a second component, as each variable has a given dispersion around the mean, which is called variance, and the more variables we use to make a prediction, the greater the total variance (the error) of the prediction itself.

So this is why the illusion of exactly measuring risk has to give way to a different approach, which recognizes the superiority of what seems a simpler approach, but it is not, resembling those cocktails whose ingredients (and the quantity of each ingredient) are only known by the barman who prepares them.

In Gigerenzer's view, the *homo heuristicus*' cocktail is prepared mixing up in subjective percentages: common sense, intuition and …courage. Because we should dare to know.

3.4 Human, All Too Human: The Global Crisis Case

In the previous chapter we used the global financial crisis as a test bed for evaluating the (in)adequacy of CE. Let us now use the same test bed to retrieve an interpretation of the crisis based on the kind of decision-making factors that are described by behavioral economics. A caveat first. In what follows we deal with behaviors which are not consistent with rationality as portrayed in CE, but we refrain from classifying them as satisficing (Simon's approach), irrational (as Kahneman would have them), or ecologically rational (à la Gigerenzer). For the purposes of this section, all that counts is that such behaviors would be inconceivable in a CE framework.

The main characters in the global financial crisis saga were the following three:

- Investors
- Borrowers
- Financial institutions (banks, regulators, and rating agencies)

Of course, the final catastrophe was generated by the interaction of the choices made by all three. But let us proceed in an orderly fashion and investigate the specific contribution of each leading character in turn.

3.4.1 Investors

Speaking of investors, what comes immediately to mind is their role in the creation (and in the burst) of the real estate bubble. Can we identify any behavioral factors among possible explanatory variables?

Creating the Environment for the Bubble

According to a popular theory, bubbles appear because investors extrapolate past events for predicting future outcomes (Barberis et al. 1988). In other words, people use the representative heuristic and extrapolate the past when making predictions about the future. In fact, representativeness is not just about the past. It has to do with the vividness of a story. And the recent positive performance of assets linked to the real estate market in the US was extremely vivid, through positive popular storytelling igniting an enthusiasm which was further amplified by the media, books, and magazines.

And given that historical records since the Great Depression (1929) showed that there was no single year in which house prices fell, it was not difficult to believe that investing in real-estate-linked assets was the right thing to do. As a matter of fact, between 1997 and 2003, house prices went up by 60%. And once you invested, the market was so good that it was difficult to get out.

Of course, history would tell that often prolonged and record-beating market rallies eventually succumb to the law of economic gravity. But as we know by now, many simply decided to neglect this empirical regularity. Why? Some would point to the so-called ostrich effect, generated by the confirmation bias (Karlsson et al. 2009). The confirmation bias makes us select the information that is (or can be interpreted as) supportive of our a priori convictions. The "ostrich effect" is the flip side of the coin, as it leads us to ignore information that conflicts with such convictions. So certain warning signals that could have eroded investors' faith in a never-ending bull market were simply ignored.

So the attitude of the market participants at the time was basically that despite past market records, "this time is different". There is also a different (not necessarily alternative) way of explaining such investor behavior that can be traced to Kahneman and Tversky's prospect theory. As visualized in the graph in III.III, in their subjective estimation, people tend to overweigh low probability events and, symmetrically, to under-weigh the probability of events when their statistical probability falls in a medium-high range (say between 0.5 and 0.8).

Herding

Under such circumstances, it was almost unavoidable that the effects of the confirmation bias were further reinforced by the creation of a "safety by numbers" environment. Especially when you "want" to believe in a story, doing what the others do (herding) can work as insurance policy, as it reduces potential regret and makes sure that you did not do worse than all the others (Muradoglu 2010). This may be important, as highlighted in III.II, as many behavioral studies have shown that relational factors (my income relative to my neighbor's) play a significant role in determining individual utility. Herding is often considered a typical illustration of irrational behavior leading people in the wrong direction. However, it should be noted that there may be circumstances, characterized by limited private information and a risky environment, in which the adoption of choices made by others can be considered fully rational. With scarce quantity and quality of information available to individuals, private signals are likely to be neglected, and there is an incentive to copy the behaviors of others. In this case, herding is the result of so-called information cascades, though collective choices may on occasion produce outcomes that are superior than those produced by individual judgments made in an ex ante environment (Surowiecki 2004).

Life Before and After the Bubble Burst

After many herds have heavily invested in the underlying assets, a moment arrives in which the bubble assumes a big enough size. At that moment, the question for investors is no longer whether the bubble will burst, but rather when this is going to happen and what to do about it.

Betting on the existence of a residual time cushion, some continued to buy, confident that a profit could still be made by selling to "a bigger fool" who would invariably appear before the crash. In behavioral terms, this approach would be an illustration of the so-called self-serving bias (the conviction that one's own ability is definitely way above that of other market participants). It worked. For a while.

Then, the end arrived. In normal circumstances (i.e. in a non-bubble environment), the "disposition effect" studied by Kahneman and Tversky would have prevailed: faced with moderate capital losses, investors would wait and stick to their depreciated assets in the hope that the market would bounce back to more normal levels. But circumstances in 2008 were not normal at all: observing changes in the "teaser rate" with borrower defaults on "liar's loans" and pondering what could happen next, investors realized there could be huge uncertainty ahead disfavoring them. When prices began to fall, the expectation was that they would fall further and further before reaching an unknown bottom level. In that context, was the rush to sell immediately irrational?

Let's make an example. Investor X bought a CDO bond at $60 in 2006. At the peak of the market in early 2007, the bond price reached $100, but in late 2007, after the news of an increasing number of subprime defaults, it is already down at $90.

What is the right strategy? By selling before all the others, investor X would bring home $90.

If he waited a while (say a month) and others would also decide to sell in the meantime, the resulting excess supply would drive the price downward at $80. If everyone (including investor X) panics and sells immediately, the price would drop to $60. But the worst outcome (a price of $40) materializes if all the others sell immediately, while investor X decides to keep her cold blood and wait. So the dominant strategy (i.e. the best whatever the others do) is to sell straight away (see Table 3.4).

Pity that all the others reasoned in exactly the same way. So, although she managed to avoid the worst scenario, in our example, investor X sold at $60 with a loss in the order of about 33%.

Table 3.4 Wait or Sell? Payoffs

	All other investors	
Investor X	Wait	Sell immediately
Wait	80	40
Sell immediately	90	60

3.4.2 Banks, Borrowers, and Regulators

Since the beginning of the century, US borrowers took full advantage of surplus cheap liquidity via subprime mortgages and lived in a seemingly unbreakable dream scenario, with house prices always going up and ridiculously low interest rates, which was deemed to last forever. Crucial factors that pushed this behavior may have been many, including the following:

- the "present bias" typically associated with hyperbolic discounting ("buy now, pay later") first explored by Laibson (1997)
- relational factors, for example, the need for "keeping up with the Joneses" (Haldane 2009)
- the tendency in a skyrocketing market to believe in "new era" stories (Akerlof and Shiller 2009)
- ignorance—Berthoud and Kempson (1992) show, for example, that a significant percentage of borrowing decisions are made without sufficient information about the exact costs of credit; so it is likely that many, even if they did not really realize the contents of mortgage contracts, signed them anyway only because they thought that house prices could only grow.

These are the main factors that unnaturally boosted demand for credit by people who in many cases did not have a stable job, savings, or other assets. But then one needs to explain the reasons why the supply of credit came to match demand. In other words, why did banks accept to extend loans to people with no financial coverage at all? Fact is that with markets so good, sensitivity to risk decreases and overconfidence steps in. And once you enter the overconfidence dimension, crises are seen as something belonging to other places (emerging countries) or other times, and you are a prisoner of the this-time-is-different syndrome (Reinhart and Rogoff 2010). So banks became overconfident not only in the ability of subprime clients to service their mortgages, and overconfidence was reinforced by the observation that institutional authorities—including government and rating agencies—were giving a benign eye to what was happening in the market. The case of rating agencies is particularly interesting. There was an original sin at work there, as agencies' fees were (are) paid by bond issuers. This means that all agencies have an intrinsic interest in letting new asset classes develop to make the overall size of the market grow continuously. And for the single rating agency, it is hard to maintain objectivity, as the bond issuer may just choose to turn to the competition. Furthermore, when these new asset classes are as complicated as CDOs (and "squared" CDOs!) representing baskets of financial flows originating from hundreds of different sources, chances are that agencies do not really have enough information (or will to collect information) about the exact contents of the "packages".

Last but not least, the financial viability of the system was undermined by the slippage (or in certain cases the collapse) of the ethical standards that kept the market working for decades. Bank officers were now paid on the basis of the number of mortgage contracts signed, irrespective of their credit quality, so in some cases they falsified documents or even lied to prospective borrowers; the bonus of top executives skyrocketed, as they were also merely a function of business volumes and short-term profitability. It was the triumph of greed. In the words of Gordon Gekko, the leading character in the movie *Wall Street*:

> *Greed, for lack of a better word, is good. Greed clarifies, cuts through, and captures the essence of the evolutionary spirit.*

As exciting as it could be, however, the party came to the end we know suddenly, leaving on the ground millions of victims around the world. Once again, the ignorance, greed, and cognitive distortions led man to build something that could not possibly stand for long.

Even though many thought that this creation would have been protected by the solidity of mathematical models, efficient markets, and the ultimate rationality of the *homo economicus*. In his book *Human, All Too Human*, Friedrich Nietzsche wrote:

> *When we see a waterfall, we think we see freedom of will and choice in the innumerable turnings, windings, breakings of the waves; but everything is necessary; each movement can be calculated mathematically. Thus it is with human*

Fig. 3.10 Source: http://mike-servethepeople.blogspot.it/2007/12/sub-prime-crisis-house-of-cards-waiting.html

actions; if one were omniscient, one would be able to calculate each individual action in advance, each step in the progress of knowledge, each error, each act of malice. To be sure the acting man is caught in his illusion of volition; if the wheel of the world were to stand still for a moment and an omniscient, calculating mind were there to take advantage of this interruption, he would be able to tell into the farthest future of each being and describe every rut that wheel will roll upon.

Unfortunately, *the homo economicus* does not exist. This is why this time it was NOT different.

Notes

1. https://www.socialsciencespace.com/2012/08/robert-shiller-on-behavioral-economics/
2. Bounded rationality was first introduced by Simon (1947). For an illustration of the satisficing concept, cf. in particular Simon (1956).

References

Akerlof, G., and R.J. Shiller. 2009. *Animal Spirits: How Human Psychology Drives the Economy and Why It Matters for Global Capitalism*. Princeton University Press.

Allais, M. 1953. Le Comportement de l'Homme Rationnel devant le Risque: Critique des Postulats et Axiomes de l'Ecole Americaine. *Econometrica* 94: 47–73.

Andreoni, J. 1990. Impure Altruism and Donations to Public Goods: A Theory of Warm Glow Giving. *Economic Journal* 100 (401): 464–477.

Barberis, N., A. Shleifer, and R. Vishny. 1988. A Model of Investor Sentiment. *Journal of Financial Economics* 49 (3): 307–343.

Bentham, J. 1789. *An Introduction to the Principles of Morals and Legislation*.

Berthoud, R., and E. Kempson. 1992. *Credit and Debt: The PSI Report*. Policy Studies Institute.

Blume, L.E., and D. Easley. 1984. Rational Expectations Equilibrium: An Alternative Approach. *Journal of Economic Theory* 34 (1): 116–129.

Bookstaber, R. 2017. *The End of Theory*. Princeton University Press.

Camerer, C. 1999. Behavioral Economics: Reunifying Psychology and Economics. *Proceedings of the National Academy of Sciences of USA* 96 (19): 10575–10577.

Easterlin, R. 1974. Does Economic Growth Improve the Human Lot? Some Empirical Evidence. In *Nations and Households in Economic Growth: Essays in Honor of Moses Abramovitz*, ed. Paul A. David and Melvin W. Reder. New York: Academic Press.

Eckel, Catherine C., and Philip J. Grossman. 1996. Altruism in Anonymous Dictator Games. *Games and Economic Behavior* 16 (2): 181–191.

Frank, R. 1999. *Luxury Fever: Money and Happiness in an Era of Excess*. New York: Free Press.

Gigerenzer, G., and W. Gaissmaier. 2011. Heuristic Decision Making. *Annual Review of Psychology*. 62: 451–482.

Gigerenzer, G., P. Todd, and ABC Research Group. 2000. *Simple Heuristics that Make Us Smart*. New York: Oxford University Press.

Gilboa, I. 2014. Rationality and the Bayesian Paradigm: An Integrative Note. *Bank of England Research Papers*.

Haldane, A. 2009. Rethinking the Financial Network. *Speech delivered at the Financial Student Association (FSA)*, Amsterdam.

Kahneman, D. 2003a. A Perspective on Judgment and Choice. *American Psychologist* 58 (9): 697.
———. 2003b. Maps of Bounded Rationality: Psychology for Behavioral Economics. *The American Economic Review* 93 (5): 1449–1475.
———. 2011. *Thinking Fast and Slow*. New York: Macmillan.
Kahneman, D., and A. Tversky. 1974. Judgment under Uncertainty: Heuristics and Biases. *Science* 185 (4157): 1124–1131.
Karlsson, N., G. Loewenstein, and D. Seppi. 2009. The Ostrich Effect: Selective Attention to Information. *Journal of Risk and Uncertainty* 38 (2): 95–115.
Kunreuther, H., N. Novemsky, and D. Kahneman. 2001. Making Low Probabilities Useful. *Journal of Risk and Uncertainty* 23 (2): 103–120.
Laibson, D. 1997. Golden Eggs and Hyperbolic Discounting. *Quarterly Journal of Economics* 112 (2): 443–478.
Lucas, R.E. 1981. Tobin and Monetarism: A Review Article. *Journal of Economic Literature* 19 (2): 558–567.
Moen, P., D. Dempster-McCain, and R.M. Williams. 1993. Successful Aging. *American Journal of Sociology* 97: 1612–1632.
Mullainathan, S., and R. Thaler. 2001. Behavioural Economics. *International Encyclopedia of the Social and Behavioral Sciences*.
Muradoglu, Y. 2010. The Banking and Financial Crisis in the UK: What is Real and What is Behavioural? *Qualitative Research in Financial Markets* 2 (1): 6–15.
Reinhart, C., and K. Rogoff. 2010. Growth in a Time of Debt. *American Economic Review* 100 (2): 573–578.
Schwartz, B. 2015. What Does it Mean to be a Rational Decision Maker? *Journal of Marketing Behavior* 1 (2): 113–145.
Schwartz, B., A. Ward, J. Monterosso, S. Lyubomirsky, K. White, and D.R. Lehman. 2002. Maximizing versus Satisficing: Happiness is a Matter of Choice. *Journal of Personality and Social Psychology* 83 (5): 1178.
Scitovsky, T. 1976. The Joyless Economy. An Inquiry into Human Satisfaction and Consumer Dissatisfaction. *Oxford University Press*.
Simon, H. 1947. *Administrative Behavior: A Study of Decision-making Processes in Administrative Organization*. New York: Macmillan Company.
———. 1955. A Behavioral Model of Rational Choice. *The Quarterly Journal of Economics* 69 (1): 99–118.
———. 1956. Rational Choice and the Structure of the Environment. *Psychological Review* 63 (2): 129.

———. 1959. Theories of Decision-Making in Economics and Behavioral Science. *The American Economic Review* 49 (3): 253–283.
———. 1990. Invariants of Human Behavior. *Annual Review of Psychology* 41 (1): 1–20.
Smith, A. 1792. *The Theory of Moral Sentiments*. London.
Sunstein, C., and R. Thaler. 2008. *Nudge: Improving Decisions about Health, Wealth, and Happiness*. New Haven, CT: Princeton University Press.
Surowiecki, J. 2004. *The Wisdom of Crowds*. New York: Doubleday.
Tversky, A., and D. Kahneman. 1981. The Framing of Decisions and the Psychology of Choice. *Science* 211 (4481): 453–458.
Werner, G., and H. Kliemt. 1998. The Indirect Evolutionary Approach: Bridging the Gap between Rationality and Adaptation. *Rationality and Society* 10 (3): 377–399.

Part II

Moving Forward: Seven Businesses to Finish

4

Introduction to Part II

The evidence presented in Chap. 2 clearly shows that conventional economics, epitomized by the principles of rational choice and discounted utility, is disconnected with the real world of finance and economics and reveals its weaknesses at the fullest as contemporary markets develop with ever more complexities, contingencies, and interdependencies.

As researches and new discoveries in behavioral economics are making their inroads to candidate themselves to mainstream practices in the field, there is perhaps a need to reflect on where behavioral economics stands, where it is moving toward, and how it meets challenges ahead in a world with loads of impossibilities.

Is behavioral economics an unfinished business? Yes. While unfinished business in behavioral economics may include somewhat limited explanatory power of cumulative prospect theory, we argue that the "unfinishedness" of behavioral economics is more conceptual than technical. We now present seven specific "businesses" that in our view should be urgently finished. For each issue we explain what the problem is and then propose hints for future research. All such hints meet specific conceptual requirements. Inter alia, they are general and "satisficing", in the sense that they fit plau-

F. Ghisellini, B. Y. Chang, *Behavioral Economics*,
https://doi.org/10.1007/978-3-319-75205-1_4

sible real-world decision-making, as advocated by Ho et al. (2006). The subsections in which we present the seven "unfinished businesses" of behavioral economics are the following:

4.1 How Many Real Biases Are There?

Behavioral economics badly needs an unequivocal definition to what really represents a bias, that is, a cognitive distortion susceptible to producing "wrong" decisions, as the ever-growing list (https://en.wikipedia.org/wiki/List_of_cognitive_biases) of alleged biases compiled over the years by behavioral scholars and practitioners resembles a never-ending stockpiling process. But many of them could in fact be more "design features" than distortions. For a selection of the most popular "biases", a simple and objective "screening" methodology is used to determine whether specific "biases" can be considered distortions in specific time/information and other situational contexts or even disappear when behavioral assumptions change.

4.2 How Do Real-World People Form Expectations?

The introduction of rational expectations has made the fortune of New Classical Economics. In contrast, behavioral literature is prolific on biases and beliefs, but is often silent on which expectation formation scheme fits better in a behavioral economics context. In fact, many behavioral researchers, on the one hand, seem to criticize rational expectations but, on the other hand, implicitly use them as a benchmark against which "irrationality" is measured. After discussing the functions of "biases" and beliefs in expectation formation, also taking account of findings in neural sciences, we stress the need for models that incorporate behavioral factors and at the same time remain empirically testable. In this respect, the theory of imperfect knowledge economics (IKE) and models based on a combination of rational expectations (in their weak/semi-strong form in terms of the role of information) and real-world intuitive factors represent promising avenues for research.

4.3 Time Discounting and Preferences

Some 20 years ago, behavioral economics introduced the concept of hyperbolic time discounting, by which people, when called to choose a sequence of positive events, are more impatient today than they will be in the future in seeking reward such as consumption. But are we really irrational if we change our preferences over time? Or do our apparently inconsistent choices depend also on different drivers? Some influential behavioral economists would say that the consistency of preferences is easily bypassed when emotional and/or visceral factors come to center stage. Others would point to the existence of conflicting multiple selves, for example, a myopic "doer" and a strategic "planner". An interesting alternative to be pursued further in research could be the one envisaging the interaction of multiple "specialized" selves, with diverse preferences, who are activated by the materialization of specific different circumstances.

4.4 Rationality: An Inferiority Complex?

The popular perception about behavioral economics is that of a discipline fiercely antagonistic of the standard Neoclassical Economics. So it is just paradoxical that people like Amos Tversky and Daniel Kahneman, considered by many the founders of behavioral economics, take consistency and coherency, the pillars of conventional rational choice, as benchmarks to measure people's irrationality, even though studies show there is no evidence that violations of consistency have any material consequences, such as lesser health, wealth, or happiness.

As a matter of fact, in the majority of behavioral research works, many decisions of real-world people are labeled "irrational", while there is only a minority striving to show that such decisions can be on occasion rationality-compliant. In both cases, however, reference is made to rationality as defined by conventional economics. But what if my "utility function" is in fact subjective and incorporates variables such as "feeling good socially" (in the family, with colleagues, etc.)? How could someone in that case claim the right to judge whether I am rational or not?

Future research could usefully focus on the setup of "satisficing" utility functions, for example, emotional well-being. So the utility function in this case lies in a band limited on one side by a conventional economic maximum and on the other by a minimum level of emotional acceptance.

4.5 The Problem with Behavioral Finance

In the past few years, behavioral finance has enjoyed noticeable success in the financial industry and a significant level of media coverage. The focus, however, has been again mainly on how biases of all sorts distort financial decisions and the best ways to "de-bias" such decisions. Much less importance has been given to the identification of genuine behavioral indicators for asset allocation.

In fact, there have been cases of research produced by influential behavioral scholars in which the framework used has been yet again the one (mean-variance approach) typical of conventional finance. Such framework, however, is only correct if the assumption is that investors are risk-averse, while in behavioral finance investors are assumed to be loss-averse.

Instead of mimicking conventional models, behavioral finance could, for example, propose "satisficing" asset allocation models, in which the investor who evaluates the prospects of a specific asset will be especially interested in estimating, together with expected returns, how much she can lose each time when a loss occurs and how frequently losses can be recorded.

4.6 Should Biased Nudgers Nudge Us?

Following the resounding success of the book *Nudge* (Thaler-Sunstein 2008), a number of governments (and private firms) have adopted active policies in many important areas (tax compliance, healthcare, etc.) to "gently push" people to take decisions which are deemed to be the best in terms of people's self-interest.

Many have criticized this "libertarian paternalism" on various grounds, arguing inter alia that authorities cannot really know people's true preferences or that, being made of people, governments are bound to be biased as well.

In light of such criticism, we propose that the focus of active policies should shift from the steering of few choices which actually leverage on biases to one—more democratic—which boosts people's autonomous decision-making capabilities.

4.7 What We Talk About When We Talk About Behavioral Economics

In this book we did not intend to present the usual wrap-up of concepts, which is a typical feature of conclusions in most economics books. We preferred to close with the seventh "unfinished business", which could in many ways be considered the most important: the achievement of clarity on how research is conducted and on the very nature of behavioral economics.

Reference

Ho, T., N. Lim, and C. Camerer. 2006. Modelling the Psychology of Consumer and Firm Behavior with Behavioral Economics. *Journal of Marketing Research* 43 (3): 307–331.

5

How Many Real Biases Are There?

Fig. 5.1 Confirmation Bias at Work

F. Ghisellini, B. Y. Chang, *Behavioral Economics*,
https://doi.org/10.1007/978-3-319-75205-1_5

5.1 200 and Counting?

In their seminal paper, Kahneman and Tversky (1974) (K & T) did not give an explicit definition of "bias", but highlighted the concept via a specific example: "For example, the apparent distance of an object is determined in part by its clarity. The more sharply the object is seen, the closer it appears to be. This rule has some validity, because in any given scene the more distant objects are seen less sharply than nearer objects. However, the reliance on this rule leads to systematic errors in the estimation of distance. Specifically, distances are often overestimated when visibility is poor because the contours of the objects are blurred. On the other hand, distances are often underestimated when visibility is good because the objects are seen sharply. Thus, the reliance on clarity as an indication of distance leads to common biases".

In their example, the usage of a mental "shortcut" like clarity (a heuristic rule) generates a bias (i.e. a distortion of the cognitive process that can lead to systematic errors).

K & T then proceed to present the biases associated with the main heuristic rules:

1. *Representativeness*. If event A is highly representative of B, it is likely that A originates from B. Example: Pierre is a former hippie living in Paris, in the Latin quarter (A). Is Pierre a movie director (B) or a civil servant (C)? Most people would say that Pierre is a movie director, as his profile fits better with that profession.

   But the representativeness heuristic leads mainly to insensitivity to prior probability of outcomes (there are many more civil servants than movie directors!)
2. *Availability*. The probability of an event is a function of the ease with which occurrences of that event come to mind. Example: Jane is old and has social relations mainly with people of her age. When asked whether doing crosswords is on average more popular than going to the movies, she thus chooses the former answer, as she knows many people who do crosswords.

The availability heuristic leads to biases due to the retrievability of instances (the number of people going to the movies is, of course, greater).

3. *Anchoring*. In many cases, estimates of a value require an initial input, especially when people are not in a position to develop autonomous estimates. Example: the "anchor" for the value of a stock X can be taken to be its current market price, for example, 100.

   But anchoring leads mainly to insufficient adjustment (if the initial estimate is 100 and the stock rallies to 110, it is sold on the conviction of making a juicy 10% profit not to be missed, whereas the "true" equilibrium value of X was, for example, 120).

Are biases then solely generated by heuristics? Of course not. To start with, the word "bias" may mean different things to different people. And not always negative things (in the Oxford Dictionary, one definition is "A concentration on or interest in one particular area or subject"). It is true, however, that a bias has been defined by many as a preparedness for acting, thinking, or judging in a specific manner.

Of course, the actual impact of biases will also depend on their strength (I could have a negative prejudice against women who drive, but it can be very light).

And for many researchers, biases fall into two distinct categories: cognitive and emotional, with the latter influencing the cognitive system from outside. Emotional biases would materialize when people are inclined to give more weight to information/decision options associated with the perception of pleasant consequences (conversely, less weight if associated with painful consequences). The distinction, however, appears artificial, as the interaction between cognition and emotions is in most cases inseparable.

In behavioral research, there is much confusion as to what a bias really is. In theory, a bias is a (cognitive, emotional) distortion in decision-making. Yet, as Gerd Gigerenzer has pointed out, in situations of uncertainty (as opposed to risk), there is a second source of error besides "bias," known as "variance," which is the source of overfitting. So for a rational mind, it is a question of striking a balance between these sources of errors. While heuristics simplify, and therefore reduce error from variance, how this works is part of the study of ecological rationality. The net result, however, is that we still lack a consensus view on how many biases there are, what they are, and how important they really are. If you Google "bias list", you come up with results like "the 12 cognitive biases that prevent you from being rational", "20 cognitive biases which screw up your decisions", and even (from Wikipedia) "Over 250 Cognitive biases, fallacies, errors, and more"! There are many duplicates with different names, scattered casually.

The feeling is that in the absence of any conceptual "filter", the number of could-be biases in the last few years has grown geometrically. And in a lot of cases, the actual real-world significance of specific biases has not been proved, so one wonders whether some are just describing what could be, not what actually exists.

So there is first of all a quantitative issue. Are we bound to be concerned with 250 (and growing) biases?

A wiser choice could be to focus on the main ones (i.e. the ones recurring more often in leading economic research), reported in this taxonomy, inspired by the one presented in John Mauldin's (2005) book *Just One Thing* (see Table 5.1).

Then comes the hardest part: the identification of a conceptual filter that can tell us whether any of these is indeed a bias, and if so whether such a bias is something that should be eliminated.

But what can be the much-needed filter?

Table 5.1

Some Important Biases

Cognitive	Heuristic driven	Emotional	Social
Overoptimism, illusion of control, illusion of knowledge	Framing mental accounting	Self-control hyperbolic discounting	Herding
Overconfidence	Anchoring	Ambiguity aversion	Cascades
Self-attribution bias	Gambler's fallacy	Regret	
Confirmation bias	Conjunction fallacy	Sunk cost fallacy	
Hindsight bias	Salience	Affect	
Cognitive dissonance	Home bias		
Disposition effect	Loss aversion		

Let's begin from the most common definition of bias: a distortion, that is, something which alters the normal functioning of the mind. So it is a negative thing. But what is the "normal" functioning of the mind, if not the way in which the mind works for the absolute majority of people from the Ice Age?

Kenrick and Griskevicius argue that people's decisions are driven by a "deep rationality"—a set of evolved biases that would have helped our ancestors and their genes to survive, and that continues to influence our choices in the modern world. Honed by lessons our ancestors learned, our decisions today (even our seemingly silly ones) reflect therefore a deep-seated evolutionary wisdom: "When we look at the deeper logic of decisions across the entire animal kingdom, it becomes clear that decision making in all critters, including us, is geared to promote deep-seated evolutionary goals. This is important because it suggests that many of our decision biases, errors, and misjudgments might not be design flaws; instead, they may be design features".

If this is true, then everything which is an ineliminable feature of human condition cannot be considered a "distortion", and thus a NEGATIVE bias. It will be just a "design feature".

On the basis of this first screener, we analyze and filter alleged "biases".

Some of them are clearly mind superstructures. Overconfidence is certainly not innate in the human being, and actually only some among us are overconfident. But can we say the same about loss aversion? Or hyperbolic discounting?

There is an interesting paper by Ashraf et al. (2005) that traces the first analysis of these "biases" to approximately 200 years before Kahneman and Tversky, when Adam Smith wrote *The Theory of Moral Sentiments*. In that book, Smith described some important ineliminable traits of the human nature, and, for example, wrote that

> *pain… is, in almost all cases, a more pungent sensation than the opposite and correspondent pleasure. The one almost always depresses us much more below the ordinary, or what may be called the natural state of our happiness, than the other ever raises us above it.*

A few pages later, dealing with time preferences, he wrote that

> *"the pleasure which we are to enjoy ten years hence, interests us so little in comparison with that which we may enjoy to-day, the passion which the first excites, is naturally so weak in comparison with that violent emotion which the second is apt to give occasion to, that the one could never be any balance to the other, unless it was supported by the sense of propriety"*. "*The spectator*", in contrast, "*does not feel the solicitations of our present appetites. To him the pleasure which we are to enjoy a week hence, or a year hence, is just as interesting as that which we are to enjoy this moment*".

It is therefore safe to assume that loss aversion and hyperbolic discounting can be considered innate feature designs, rather than distortions. A first screener could then be one by which an alleged bias is examined to find whether it is part and parcel of human nature. If that is the case, then it is not a bias.

So this screening should leave us with fewer main "biases" to be scrutinized. They are not necessary components of the human nature like loss aversion. But are all of them harmful? Couldn't it be that in specific circumstances they in fact serve a positive purpose?

Think, for example, of a situation (e.g., an investment decision) in which you have got little time to decide and/or the amount/quality of relevant information available is very small.

What can you do? You try to remember the important bits, you quickly check whether your prior beliefs can be supported by facts, you fill the gaps with best guesses or inputs from trusted sources (including friends, colleagues, etc.). In other words, you are not a victim of biases. You make recourse to them!

So many biases can be considered as a sort of heuristic rules, quick fixes that can help in many circumstances, especially those that are unforeseeable. Of course, they can also create problems, for example, in the context of financial decisions such as the choice of assets to invest in.

This is why making recourse to biases can be only justifiable in the presence of specific states of the world. In particular, when time is short and information is scarce.

There are trade-offs, of course, as an investment decision to be taken immediately elicits a different recourse to biases, depending on whether you are financially literate or not.

A second sequential screener could then be based on the following operating rules:

- Whenever both time and information are scarce, we would not be in the presence of a bias.
- In cases in which either time or information is insufficient, we could think of a new category, which we could label as that incorporating "justifiable" biases.

For any specific bias, Table 5.2 exemplifies the concept.

If the alleged bias under trial is not "acquitted" after these two screening tests, we can safely conclude that it is a true bias.

Shall we then apply our screening process to all the 250 biases listed by Wikipedia? That would require devoting an entire book just to that. So we go for a sample, choosing the biases which are most frequently analyzed in behavioral economics research. For the ease of reading, notes and references for each bias analysis are grouped together.

Table 5.2 When a Bias is a Bias

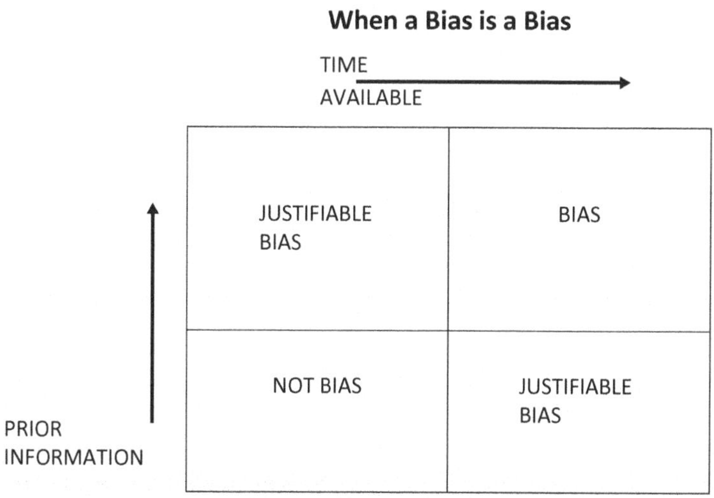

5.2 Screening Biases

5.2.1 Affect

Affect utilizes "gut feelings". It is driven by current emotion, which is shorter than a mood, such as fear, surprise, or pleasure in response to particular stimuli. Affect involves a subconscious and involuntary process without having to go through extensive periods of information search and calculations in decision-making, typically in situations of evaluating risks and benefits of some outcome.

Affect takes a leading role when one has strong feelings about the goodness or badness of a particular person, an object, or some other phenomenon. In the world of finance and economics, the theory goes that investors who take higher risks expect higher returns. However, findings by Ganzach (2001) showed that with familiar stocks, analysts judge risk-return relation as the same as what is in the theory, but with unfamiliar stocks, analysts tend to see them either generally good or generally bad with negative relations—low risk and high returns, or high risk and low returns.

Research findings show that if we have positive feelings about something, we tend to see low risk and high benefit and vice versa. So affect is considered as the first responder in a particular judgment. Here is an example of how affect works:

In a study conducted by Denes-Raj and Epstein (1994), subjects were offered an opportunity to win $1 each time they randomly drew a red jelly bean from a bowl, often preferred to draw from a bowl with more red beans than a smaller proportion of red beans, e.g., 7 in 100 was preferred to 1 in 10. According to Denes-Raj and Epstein, these subjects reported afterward that even though they knew the probabilities were against them, they felt they had a better chance when there were more red beans. A 7% probability versus 10% probability may be bad news, but it's more than made up for by the increased number of red beans. It's a worse probability, yes, but you're still more likely to win (Yudkowsky 2007a).

In this case, people trust their gut feelings more than the probability theory. After all, one may still not get a single red bean in the second pool after drawing ten times or more.

These gut feelings resonate with Antonio Damasio's (1994) somatic marker hypothesis, which says that: "thought is made largely from images such as perceptual and symbolic representations. These images then become 'marked' by positive or negative feelings linked directly or indirectly to somatic states". His findings also indicate that somatic markers increase the accuracy of the decision process, and the absence of these markers, mostly seen in people with certain types of brain damage, decreases the ability to make good decisions.

Screener 1: Is It Innate?

Affect is an intuitive and mostly automatic and subconscious process that relies on images, metaphors, and narratives. To judge whether affect is biased or not depends on the context as well particular beliefs or standards. For an ordinary investor in a developed market, such as in the US, who had never traveled abroad, it is only reasonable that he invests in US stocks as an affect heuristic. However, for a professional financier, this decision might be considered a bias in terms of his portfolio diversification. Given these differences, we refrain from the judgment of whether affect heuristics is biased or not for screener 1.

Screener 2: Used When Time/Information Scarce?

Studies show that affect is more salient when people have no time or resources to reflect. Under these circumstances, Finucane et al. (2000) found that time pressure greatly increased the inverse relationship between perceived risk and perceived benefit, consistent with the general finding that time pressure, poor information, or distraction all increase the dominance of perceptual heuristics over analytic deliberation. In addition, they predicted that individuals under time pressure would rely more heavily on their affect in order to be more efficient in the decision-making.

These researches, however, also state that feelings are not free from thoughts and thoughts are not free from feelings. The experiential system also takes past experiences into account—if a person has already experienced a certain issue, he or she is more likely to take more precautions toward the issue (Finucane et al. 2000). Given this argument, we classify affection as a justifiable bias under circumstances of scarce information/time, and as a bias in all other circumstances (Damasio et al. 1996; Denes-Raj and Epstein 1994; Finucane et al. 2000; Ganzach 2001; Hsee and Kunreuther 2000; Slovic et al. 2002; Yamagishi 1997; Yudkowsky 2007a).[1]

5.2.2 Disposition Effect

The disposition effect (DE) describes the behavior of investors or financial professionals when they sell winning position too soon or hold losing position too long. It is said that market participants tend to sell shares when price increases and keep assets that have decreased in value. Conventional methods in finance or economics consider this behavior irrational. It is "irrational" because investors should instead sell "losers" for tax reductions, or decisions on shorting or longing should depend on the expected future value of security and not the purchase price, which determines whether the seller is in a winning or a losing position. In other words, traditional theories imply that those who did not sell winning position too soon or hold on losing position too long are unbiased. But in a market where future prices are unknown, how do we determine who is biased or not?

According to Muermann et al., what is behind the DE are the expected feelings of regret and pride. There is the feeling of pride about having made the right decision when selling at a gain and the feeling of regret about having made a wrong decision when selling at a loss. Conventional theories, however, regard the DE as a bias and assume that more information should help to correct this bias. However, a study shows that both more-informed or less-informed investors can exhibit the DE in an incomplete information market environment, depending on the degree of information asymmetry between these two types of investors that changes over time (Dorn). On a related topic, Heimer (2015) conducted a study attempting to establish relations between heightened exposure to information via social media and increases in disposition effect, and looked into behaviors under uncertainty in terms of the impact of social networks on increase in the DE.

The study establishes causal peer-effects by comparing trader activities before and after exposure to new social conditions. It assumes further that the increase in the disposition effect reflects an asymmetry in the expected benefits from social interaction arising from competition and strategic consideration. The research suggests that trading under the social influence may asymmetrically favor winning positions or contribute to the increase of DE (peer influence and reputational concerns). Preliminary evidence from the study shows that social interaction contributes to the DE—when the fraction of gains sold exceeds the fraction of executed loss through a survival function.

Screener 1: Is It Innate?

DE occurs because the agent tries to avoid a negative feeling, which is associated with disutility or regret. At the same time, she seeks to receive a positive feeling (utility or pride). Selling winners works almost like an insurance against falling stock prices when investor still makes a profit, whereas holding losers works like a gamble to get lucky and earn a gain. The main argument is that investors try to ensure utility by selling winners and shift disutility by keeping losers. Since this perception of utility or disutility associated with negative or positive feelings among some investors is not universal and therefore cannot be considered as pure human nature, we do not acquit screener 1 criteria for innate causes. Meanwhile, research shows that social networks may help traders/investors to avoid regret and to seek/maintain pride that are explained in the DE.

Screener 2: Used When Time/Information Scarce?

In search of how time-varying information asymmetry influences the investors' behavior, Dorn and Strobl (2009) show that inexperienced investors rationally exhibit the disposition effect when information asymmetry between investors increases. To explain: if information disparity increases over time, uninformed investors learn very little about new information obtained by informed investors from the observed price. They rely more heavily on information revealed by past prices and are reluctant to revise their optimal stock holdings in response to the current price change. To put it differently, the demand for a stock from uninformed investors is less sensitive to news about changes in the asset value than that of informed investors. When new information suggests higher-than-expected payoffs, market clearing implies that the price will increase until the amount of shares that uninformed investors are willing to sell equals the amount that informed investors want to buy. The reverse is true when new information indicates lower-than-expected payoffs. In this case, the price will drop until uninformed investors are willing to buy shares from informed investors. In equilibrium, uninformed investors will therefore find it optimal to follow a contrarian strategy: they tend to decrease their stock holdings when good news drives prices up ("sell their winners") and to increase their stock holdings when bad news forces prices down ("hold on to their losers").

But when the degree of information asymmetry decreases over time as the spread of knowledge discrepancy narrows (as there are still some who are better-informed than others in relative terms), less-informed investors exhibit a reverse disposition effect: they keep their winners and sell their losers (if the majority keeps the stock, the position will continue to be in the winning). In this case, it is the better-informed investors who exhibit a disposition effect; they make a profit from selling shares that are still in the winning position before price goes down reflecting the news.

Similarly, and when the spread of knowledge or information among investors is narrow, new information about the asset value has a stronger impact on the beliefs of uninformed investors. Not knowing the signals received by informed investors in previous periods, uninformed investors learn more from this new signal and, hence, respond more aggressively to new information, forcing informed investors or traders to pursue a contrarian investment strategy. In other words, uninformed investors "overreact" to new information from the perspective of informed investors, who may be able to continue sustaining the winning position, if the majority holds. So the risk-averse investors can rationally exhibit the disposition effect even though past winners continue to outperform past losers in subsequent periods.

Another study shows that social networks (assuming they discuss about their trades implicitly or explicitly) decrease information asymmetry (Lin et al. 2009). Social and economic networks may have generated more better-informed traders/investors who are susceptible to DE. In this case, while some traders are better-informed than others in the network, the latter are better-informed than those outside. These changes in information structure would subsequently make many of the better-informed traders/investors susceptible to the DE, as illustrated in Dorn's study. Under information scarcity, we acquit the DE as a bias because both reduction in information asymmetry and peers effect, due to continued lack of certainty, contribute to the DE (Dorn and Strobl 2009; Fenton-O'Creevy et al. 2003; Frydman 2011; Jiao 2017; Lin et al. 2009; Mayraz 2011; Muermann and Volkman 2006; Bandura 1989; Knee and Zuckerman 1998; Langer 1975; Matute 2013; Sanger 2011).

5.2.3 Illusion of Control

Illusion of control (IOC) is a belief that we are able to control or have influence over some events, while the actual outcomes of these events are beyond our control or understanding. These misconceptions prevail and affect decision-making in economics and finance, education, and other important areas such as health. As Matute et al. (2015) put it: "This illusion rests at the heart of pseudoscientific practices and superstitious thinking". Subsequently, people's decisions are based on cognitive illusions rather than introspective insights possibly from differed or even contrasted knowledge.

Why does IOC occur? Traditional theories believe that humans have strong motives to have control over life events and their environment. Studies show that controllability dimension is considered an achievement and the failure of this measure may be attributed to personal causes. Thus, IOC is a defense mechanism associated with self-esteem for either an individual or, in some cases, for a nation. As one anecdote introduced earlier, when Mervyn King, the former governor of Bank of England, answered with "I don't know" during one of his financial hearings, the audience responded with disbelief, and it was regarded as a national disgrace.

The most noticeable instance of IOC in real life occurred in the risk management in the banking sector which significantly contributed to the 2008 financial crisis, when IOC indeed encouraged more risk-taking that ultimately became uncontrollable. And below are two additional examples of IOC in experiments:

1. Participants in a lottery experiment believed they had more control over the outcome if they chose their numbers rather than having them randomly assigned. Gamblers tend to throw the dice harder when they need higher numbers, evidencing an implicit belief that with "skill" they can somehow control their fortune.
2. The traders' ratings of their success measured their susceptibility to the IOC. This score was then compared with each trader's performance. Those who were more prone to the illusion scored significantly lower on analysis, risk management, and contribution to profits. They also earned significantly less.

While IOC may affect the quality of decision-making, others argue that it can foster mental health as people receive satisfaction by exerting some level of control in their life. IOC also motivates people to be persistent at some tasks when otherwise they would give up. Bandura (1989) argued that there is the adaptive effect of optimistic beliefs about control and performance in circumstances where control is possible, rather than perceived control in circumstances where outcomes do not depend on an individual's behavior.

Screener 1: Is It Innate?

Fenton-O'Creevy et al. (2003) argue that IOC may cause insensitivity to feedback, impede learning, and predispose toward greater risk-taking. Moreover, Knee and Zuckerman found that lack of IOC is associated with a non-defensive personality which is more prone to growth and learning with low ego involvement in outcomes.

More recent researches suggest that IOC is a cognitive effect rather than a motivational defense mechanism, and it is a corollary of how our cognitive system works when connecting effect with its causes. According to Matute, research results show that IOC is determined by the observed cause-effect coincidences rather than by a need to protect self-esteem. These findings were in line with the results of earlier experiments on unrealistic perceived control by Ellen Langer, which showed that there is a prevalence of IOC. More specifically, IOC is more common in situations of familiarity where subjects believe that there is some kind of pattern for cause-effect relations without taking into account other factors that may contribute to uncontrollability. Hence, there is no firm basis for us to acquit IOC as a bias.

Screener 2: Used When Time/Information Scarce?

IOC would strengthen under stressful competitive environment such as on the trading floors in financial markets. While time and information scarcity could be a related factor, it may not apply to all individuals. So IOC should not be acquitted under the circumstance and be considered a full bias.

5.2.4 Loss Aversion

Loss aversion is one of the most important concepts in behavioral economics and finance, and finds its most complete formal treatment in prospect theory (Kahneman and Tversky 1979). It is associated with the fact that the pain of losing is psychologically much bigger (typically, at least twice) than the pleasure derived from an equivalent gain. The existence of loss aversion explains why people are more willing to take or elude risks to avoid potential losses than they would be to achieve a gain. In some instances, loss aversion has also been used to explain the endowment effect (if you own something, you would not sell it at a price which is not higher than the one you paid) and the sunk costs fallacy (If we've spent resources on something, we're inclined to stay the course so as not to waste what we've already spent. In other words, we want to avoid feeling the loss of what's been spent, so we stick with our plan, hoping for a gain, even when sometimes it just leads to a bigger loss in the long run).

The classical example is a gamble in which the end result is to receive a fixed sum X. One option is being given the straight X. The other option is gaining twice the X and then losing X. The utility is exactly the same in both options. However, individuals are most likely to choose just receiving X because a single gain is generally preferred to having initially more and then suffering a loss. Loss aversion also explains why despite deciding you'll hate a concert ten minutes in, you'll stick it out for the whole two hours in misery. You've already paid for the ticket, so you don't want to "record" a loss by not attending.

Adam Smith wrote that "*pain, is, in almost all cases, a more pungent sensation than the opposite and correspondent pleasure. The one almost always depresses us much more below the ordinary, or what may be called the natural state of our happiness, than the other ever raises us above it*". For his part, Bentham does not question the rationality of the phenomenon, but simply accepts its reality to the extent of building it into the legislator's basic tool-kit of psychological presumptions. According to standard models of economic rationality, however, loss aversion is irrational. Behavioral economists disagree on whether loss aversion is a cognitive error, which might be corrected with better education and reflection, or is a perfectly rational reaction to perceived threats to well-being.

Screener 1: Is It Innate?

If people experience losses relative to a status quo as quite unpleasant, then loss-averse behavior is rational, because people are correctly anticipating and avoiding unpleasant sensations. As Kenrick-Griskevicius wrote in *The Rational Animal* (2013): "When considered in terms of evolutionary success, loss aversion makes perfect sense. Most animals, including our ancestors, lived very close to the margin of survival. Paleontologists who study early human civilizations have uncovered evidence that our ancestors faced frequent periods of drought and freezing. When you are living on the verge of starvation, a slight downturn in your food reserves makes a lot more difference than a slight upturn. Although we may not be living under the same conditions as our progenitors, we did inherit our brains from them".

Given that loss aversion can be considered part and parcel of human nature, according to S1 it cannot therefore be considered a bias (Smith 1759; Kahneman and Tversky 1979).

5.2.5 The Hindsight Bias

Hindsight bias (HB) is a tendency to overstate one's ability to have predicted an outcome or the belief that one actually predicted it correctly, either expected or unexpected, after the outcome is known. In reality, however, this belief is considered a bias because the claim to have predicted the outcome, which occurs after one learns the actual outcome, is an exaggeration of what one actually knew before the event that could not have been possibly predicted with certainty prior to the event. In essence, HB is one's claim to have known more than what one actually did, thereby distorting his previous judgment given the presence of new information. Since HB makes past events seem more predictable than they actually are, it can lead to substantial errors due to oversimplification or misjudgment in cause and effect relationships.

The HB was first introduced in research by Baruch Fischhoff in 1975 when he did an investigation presenting a historical scenario of the nineteenth-century British–Gurkha war to his participants. After giving the event outcome information to participants designated in the hindsight group who were asked to restore foresight judgments for probable outcomes, the hindsight participants judged the reported outcome to be more likely in advance than the foresight participants who were not informed about the outcome. The HB, which is also known as the knew-it-all-along effect or creeping determinism, has been shown to be a robust phenomenon in a variety of experimental as well as applied domains.

The HB, or the creeping determinism, is revealed through multifactor deficiencies and traits of limitations in humans. More specifically, physiological phenomena, for example selective memory retrieval, and cognitive symptoms, such as anchoring, are representations of self-fulfilling prophecy, illusion of foreseeability, and other personal motivations manifested in the HB. In addition to memory distortions, other traits of human biases could serve as activators for the occurrence of the HB. These traits, which are labeled under conventional human biases in the BEF are in line with the components such as the impressions of foreseeability and impressions of necessity studied by Hartmut et al. In the following, we provide examples of these biases such as false memory, anchoring, overconfidence, negativity bias in the context of the HB.

The study of false memory was initiated by psychologists Pierre Janet and Sigmund Freud. In severe cases, the person who has false memory recalls "a memory" that did not actually occur. In less severe cases, people recall or distort their foresight predictions which they did not actually do before the events occur. False memory is also associated with overconfidence, which could not be justified if false memory did not happen.

Here is an example of false memory in the context of the HB: Econometrics is your least favorite subject, and while you are nervous about the upcoming exam, you resented spending more time studying for it until the last minute. After the exam, you did not feel good about what you did and were unsure whether you would pass. But when you got your grade back with a B+, you were so excited and told your mother: "I knew I could pass that exam!" and eventually convinced yourself that you knew it in foresight.

Cognitive inputs such as illusions of foreseeability can lead to the HB. In the following, we introduce cases in anchoring and overconfidence.

Anchoring refers to decision-makers' tendency to focus on or paying too much attention to a salient or the first piece of information they receive, which may be an uninformative starting or random point in some process. Anchoring is considered an explanation for the HB in some cases when knowledge of the outcome of some event acted as an anchor in influencing one's judgment of his ability to predict the outcome (Hawkins and Hastie 1990). Anchoring is ubiquitous in financial investments. After reading an analyst report on gold performance, suggesting that the price would double or even triple in the coming months given the current economic situation. This was one of the very few good news that stood out in the investment world after continued recession. After purchasing the gold stock, the price surely went up. The investor tells his wife: "I knew I have predicted it right that it would go up!"

Overconfidence is when one's perception of or judgment on his/her ability to perform some task exceeds the actual objective outcome. Overconfidence is considered as a miscalibration of subjective probabilities, and it has been defined in three ways: (1) overestimation of one's actual performance, (2) overplacement of one's performance relative to others', and (3) overprecision in expressing unwarranted certainty in the accuracy of one's beliefs (Moore and Healy 2008). Overconfidence in the HB occurs when one sees the outcome of an event as more predictable than they really are. This view leads to the illusion of foreseeability of events and determinism in foresight. In the aforementioned example on the prediction of gold performance, the price of gold did not actually go up in linear terms. It went down quite a bit in between the months in that year. So the investor's assumption that the gold price will double or triple is bound to occur is an example of overconfidence.

Another factor that is associated with the HB is personal motivation; for example, there are needs to defend one's position for reasons of responsibility or ego. In general, people have a need to see the world as in good order and predictable while trying to avoid being blamed for some responsibilities. In malpractice suits, the more severe the negative outcome, the more dramatic the jurors' HBs are. In a perfectly objective case, the verdict would be based on the physician's standard of care instead of the outcome of the treatment. However, studies show that cases that ended in severe negative outcomes such as death were results of higher levels of hindsight bias.

Screener 1: Is It Innate?

Though an analysis by Heuer (1999) attributes the HB to the nature of human mental processes and deems it to be exceedingly difficult to overcome, perhaps we should trace the development of the human mental processes from the last hundreds, if not thousands, of years, to the human consciousness, the willpower to conquer our surroundings, and the insatiable desires to know. These unique characteristics had made human the king and the queen of all living species, yet we have forgotten that there are limits in human capacity to know with certainty in foresight at both the individual and institutional levels even with the most advanced methodology and technology we have developed. While it may be true that the drive to know is inherent in the human nature, it is a misunderstanding that events that have already occurred were predictable before they took place. In other words, while it is a dilemma between the belief in the power of knowing and the reality that we cannot know with certainty in foresight, the HBs, which are exaggerations and distortions of what we really know, are mismanagement of this conflict. While previous research defines two causal motives of the HB, for predictability and a self-presentation (Campbell and Tesser 2003), as a need, we think it is rather a human desire, which is not necessarily a part and parcel of human nature at all times, that contributes to the distortions of foresights in hindsight and hence deny acquitting for this screener.

Screener 2: Used When Time/Information Scarce?

In terms of the time factor, studies show that there is a relationship between the amount of time participants are given to respond and their level of bias when recalling their foresight judgments. The results support the idea that the HB bias index is greater among participants who are asked to respond rapidly than among participants who are allowed more time to respond. However, the HB is not about bias as a corollary of shortage of time in the decision-making but a discrepancy in the interpretations of judgments before and after the event or the attitudes in working toward the unknowns, albeit there are differences in the degrees of the discrepancy.

One aspect of behavior in the HB relating to time is worth noticing. The HB implies two levels of judgment, in foresight and in hindsight, that involve time. Timing, which embraces change in the course of an event and incomplete information ex ante, is a pivotal factor in the HB that creates uncertainty. While research results show that the subjects are aware of the uncertainty factor, it is another matter whether they realize what it means: uncertainty could derive from obsolete learned cognitive skills and knowledge in many cases. For the HB, if the outcome is a surprise, subjects would feel the need to exaggerate or recreate facts as justification of the usefulness of learned knowledge, ego repairment, and for other motivational causes. In other words, the HB disregards or works against the implications of the timing and imperfect information factors ex post. While the HB exerts the power of human will to predict and the reinforcement of the usefulness of knowledge, it ignores the power of change in between times and the unknown consequences that uncertainty enforces and enlightens. As in the ancient Chinese saying: there are ten thousand things happening at the same time in the process of change that takes time. The implication: it is more a matter of luck than skill if one makes a precise prediction in foresight. Thus we are not acquitting the HB.

As the HB does not pass both screeners, we consider it a bias in human judgment. The HB can be a problem when it stops us from learning from our mistakes. It breeds myopic attention to simple causal understanding of the past while neglecting other possible and reasonable explanations, as well as encouraging overconfidence in the certainty of one's judgments (Blank and Nestler 2007; Campbell and Tesser 2003; Calvillo 2012; Fessela et al. 2009; Harley 2007; Hartmut et al. 2008; Hawkins and Hastie 1990; Hertwig et al. 2003; Heuer 1999; Sanna 2007; Werth et al. 2002; Moore and Healy 2008; Nestler et al. 2008; Roese and Vohs 2012).

5.2.6 The Conjunction Effect/Fallacy

The conjunction fallacy (CF) was proposed by Daniel Kahneman and Amos Tversky in the 1980s as a result of the "Linda's problem" we introduced earlier. So the questions is,

Which is more probable?

1. Linda is a bank teller.
2. Linda is a bank teller and is active in the feminist movement.

As you may recall from previous discussions, according to Kahneman and Tversky, the answer with conjoint probability is a fallacy or an error, given that two probabilities together, hence in conjunction, are always less than, if not equal to, the probability of either of the probability in mathematical terms. Or to put it differently, the probability of a conjunction can never be greater than the probability of its respective conjunct according to the rule of probability, so formally: Prob (A) => Prob (A Λ B) <= Prob (B). And to give an illustration of the probabilities in simple mathematical terms, say that the Prob(Linda is a bank teller) = 0.10 and the Prob(Linda is a feminist) = 0.90, assuming independence, the Prob(Linda is a bank teller and a feminist) = 0.10 × 0.90 = 0.09, which is lower than the Prob(Linda is a bank teller). Using formal logic as a norm, Kahneman and Tversky had determined in their initial experiment that conjunction is a fallacy since the probability of two things being true can never be greater than the probability of either one of them being true, as illustrated earlier, while each must be true in order for both to be true. From the experiment, Kahneman and Tversky generalized that judging the conjunction being more likely than one of its conjuncts is a corollary of a scenario more likely imagined in the process of an inference, hence an erroneous belief that works at odds with the probability rule.

In 1982, Kahneman and Tversky conducted an experiment simulating an earlier version in the 1970s for the probability of some propositions:

Bill is 34 years old. He is intelligent, but unimaginative, compulsive, and generally lifeless. In school, he was strong in mathematics but weak in social studies and humanities.

Which may or may not be true, and are not mutually exclusive or exhaustive, starting with the most probable propositions and ending with the least probable propositions:

A: Bill is an accountant.
B: Bill is a physician who plays poker for a hobby.
C: Bill plays jazz for a hobby.
D: Bill is an architect.
E: Bill is an accountant who plays jazz for a hobby.
F: Bill climbs mountains for a hobby.

The result showed that 92% of 94 undergraduates at the University of British Columbia gave an ordering with A > E > C. Or the vast majority of subjects indicated that Bill was more likely to be an accountant than an accountant who played jazz for a hobby, and more likely to be an accountant who played jazz for a hobby than simply a jazz player for a hobby. Subsequently, the ranking E > C was displayed by 83% of 32 graduate students in the decision science program of Stanford Business School and all of whom had taken advanced courses in probability and statistics (Yudkowsky).

Similarly, according to the rule of probability, for all X and Y, Prob(X Λ Y) <= Prob(Y), there is a conflict in logic or the paradox according to this rule of probability if we say that Bill is more likely to be an accountant who also plays jazz for a hobby than just a jazz player. Conjunction was labeled as a fallacy because the probability that X and Y are valued to be more likely than that of Y violated the rule of probability.

Hertwig and Gigerenzer's research (1999) concluded that it is an error to impose the rules of probability as the norm for making rational inference under uncertainty, and researchers have mistaken intelligent inferences as reasoning errors. This conclusion refers to the idea that norms should be content-blind with the assumption that sound reasoning follows the conjunction rule of probability theory. They argue, however, that content-blind norms overlook the intelligent ways that humans deal with uncertainty, for example,, when drawing pragmatic inferences. In a series of studies, they show that people infer nonmathematical meanings of the term "probability" in the Linda conjunction problem and demonstrate that one can design contexts in which people infer mathematical meanings of the term and are therefore more likely to conform to the conjunction rule. They report evidence that the term "frequency" narrows the spectrum of possible interpretations of "probability" down to its mathematical meanings, and that this fact accounts for the low proportion of violations of the conjunction rule when people are asked for frequency judgments. Finally, they conclude that rational responses may be misclassified as fallacies when one fails to recognize the human capacity for semantic and pragmatic inference.

Likewise and after the classic "Linda's problem" initial experiment, Tversky and Kahneman (1983) tested the CF problem by using frequencies instead of probabilities and found that the effect of thinking diagrammatically sharply reduced or eliminated some forms of the CF (Mellers et al. 2001). One of the experimental questions from Hertwig and Gigerenzer in the Linda problem was reformulated as the following:

There are 100 persons who fit the aforementioned description (that is, Linda's). How many of them are:

- Bank tellers (out of 100)?
- Bank tellers and active in the feminist movement (out of 100)?

While 85% of the participants showed the "CF" in the previous experiment (bank teller and active in the feminist movement), the participants gave an answer as expected in the reformulated experiment (Gigerenzer 1991). In this case, participants were given some shared traits and specific numeric information and instructions that made the problem less abstract, more consistent, and clearer.

Screener 1: Is It Innate?

It is a human innate characteristic to utilize our intuitive heuristics or intelligent ways, as Gigerenzer put it, in composing a judgment under uncertain situations that are not bound by the conjunction rule. Hence, we acquit conjunction as a fallacy for all circumstances. As Tversky and Kahneman admitted, a conjunction can be more representative and easier to imagine or to retrieve than instances of a more inclusive category, so the representativeness and availability heuristics can make a conjunction appear more probable than one of its constituents. And systematic violations of the conjunction rule are observed in judgments of lay people as well as of experts in a variety of contexts, including estimation of word frequency, personality judgment, medical prognosis, decision under risk, suspicion of criminal acts, and political forecasting (Tversky and Kahneman 1982, 1983; Bonini et al. 2004; Gigerenzer 1991, 1996; Hertwig and Gigerenzer 1999; Mellers et al. 2001; Tentori et al. 2004; Wedell and Moro 2008; Yudkowsky 2007b).

That's all, folks! For obvious reasons of space, we cannot screen all the alleged biases listed in the literature. However, the small sample we focused on turned out to be a mixed bag. Out of six, two were found not to be biases at all, and two were justifiable when information and/or time were scarce. If we extrapolated this result (but of course that would be a gross approximation), we would have real biases around 70–80 or fewer, rather than the almost 200 listed by popular science sources like Wikipedia. And the vision of researchers would be noticeably less blurred, which could imply less time devoted to the discovery of yet another "bias", and more time allocated to solve some of the important problems still hampering the development of behavioral economics.

Notes

1. "Affect Heuristic: How our Emotions Speed Up Decision-Making Being Human". April, 1, 2013. http://www.beinghuman.org/article/affect-heuristic

References

Ashraf, N., C. Camerer, and G. Loewenstein. 2005. Adam Smith, Behavioral Economist. *Journal of Economic Perspectives 19* (3): 131–145.

Bandura, A. 1989. Human Agency in Social Cognitive Theory. *American Psychologist 44* (9): 1175.

Blank, H., and S. Nestler. 2007. Cognitive Process Models of Hindsight Bias. *Social Cognition 25* (1): 132–146.

Bonini, N., K. Tentori, and D. Osherson. 2004. A Different Conjunction Fallacy. *Mind and Language 19* (2): 199–210.

Calvillo, D.P. 2012. Rapid Recollection of Foresight Judgments Increases Hindsight Bias in a Memory Design. *Journal of Experimental Psychology: Learning, Memory, and Cognition 39* (3): 959.

Campbell, J.D., and A. Tesser. 2003. Motivational Interpretations of Hindsight Bias: An Individual Difference Analysis. *Journal of Personality 51* (4): 605–620.

Damasio, A.R. 1994. *Descarte' Error: Emotion, Reason, and the Human Brain.* Avon.

Damasio, A., B.J. Everitt, and D. Bishop. 1996. The Somatic Marker Hypothesis and the Possible Functions of the Prefrontal Cortex. *Philosophical Transactions: Biological Sciences* 351 (1346): 413–1420.

Denes-Raj, V., and S. Epstein. 1994. Conflict Between Intuitive and Rational Processing: When People Behave Against Their Better Judgment. *Journal of Personality and Social Psychology 66* (5): 819.

Dorn, D. and Strobl, G. 2009. Rational Disposition Effects: Theory and Evidence.

Fenton-O'Creevy, M., N. Nicholson, E. Soane, and P. Willman. 2003. Trading On Illusions: Unrealistic Perceptions of Control And Trading Performance. *Journal of Occupational and Organizational Psychology 76* (1): 53–68.

Fessela, F., K. Epstudeb, and N.J. Roese. 2009. Hindsight Bias Redefined: It's About Time. *Organizational Behavior and Human Decision Processes 110* (1): 56–64.

Finucane, M.L., A. Alhakami, P. Slovic, and S.M. Johnson. 2000. The Affect Heuristic in Judgments of Risks and Benefits. *Journal of Behavioral Decision Making 13* (1): 1.

Frydman, R. 2011. *Beyond Mechanical Markets: Asset Price Swings, Risk, and the Role of the State*. Princeton University Press.

Ganzach, Y. 2001. Judging Risk and Return of Financial Assets. *Organizational Behavior and Human Decision Processes* 83 (2): 353–370.

Gigerenzer, G. 1991. How to Make Cognitive Illusions Disappear: Beyond Heuristics and Biases. *European Review of Social Psychology 2* (1): 83–115.

———. 1996. On Narrow Norms and Vague Heuristics: A Reply to Kahneman and Tversky. *Psychological Review 103* (3): 592–596.

Harley, E.M. 2007. Hindsight Bias in Legal Decision Making. *Social Cognition 25* (1): 48–63.

Hartmut, B., S. Nestlerb, S. von Collanib, and V. Fische. 2008. How Many Hindsight Biases are There? *Cognition 106* (3): 1408–1440.

Hawkins, S.A., and R. Hastie. 1990. Hindsight: Biased Judgments of Past Events After The Outcomes are Known. *Psychological Bulletin 107* (3): 311.

Heimer, R. 2015. *Peer Pressure: Does Social Interaction Explain the Disposition Effect?* Federal Reserve Bank of Cleveland.

Hertwig, R., C. Fenselow, and U. Hoffrage. 2003. Hindsight Bias: Knowledge and Heuristics Affect Our Reconstruction of the Past. *Memory 11* (4–5): 357–377.

Hertwig, R., and G. Gigerenzer. 1999. The 'Conjunction Fallacy' Revisited: How Intelligent Inferences Look Like Reasoning Errors. *Journal of Behavioral Decision Making 12* (4): 275.

Heuer, R.J., Jr. 1999. *Psychology of Intelligence Analysis*. Washington, DC: Center for the Study of Intelligence, Central Intelligence Agency.

Hsee, C.K., and H. Kunreuther. 2000. The Affection Effect in Insurance Decisions. *Journal of Risk and Uncertainty 20* (2): 141–159.

Jiao, P. 2017. Belief in Mean Reversion and the Disposition Effect: An Experimental Test. *Journal of Behavioral Finance 18* (1): 29–44.

Kahneman, D., and A. Tversky. 1974. Judgment under Uncertainty: Heuristics and Biases. *Science 185* (4157): 1124–1131.

———. 1979. Prospect Theory: An Analysis of Decision under Risk. *Econometrica 47*: 278.

Kenrick, D.T., and V. Griskevicius. 2013. *The Rational Animal: How Evolution Made Us Smarter Than We Think*. New York: Basic Books.

Knee, C.R., and M. Zuckerman. 1998. A Nondefensive Personality: Autonomy and Control as Moderators of Defensive Coping and Self-Handicapping. *Journal of Research in Personality 32* (2): 115–130.

Langer, E.J. 1975. The Illusion of Control. *Journal of Personality and Social Psychology 32* (2): 311.

Lin, M., N.R. Prabhala, and S. Viswanathan. 2009. Can Social Networks Help Mitigate Information Asymmetry in Online Markets? *ICIS 2009 Proceedings Paper*.

Matute, H. 2013. The Illusion of Control: Cognitive Bias or Self-Esteem Problem? http://mappingignorance.org/2013/10/22/the-illusion-of-control-cognitive-bias-or-self-esteem-problem/

Matute, H., et al. 2015. Illusions of Causality: How They Bias Our Everyday Thinking and How They Could Be Reduced. *Frontiers of Psychology 6*: 888.

Mauldin, J. 2005. *Just One Thing*. New York: John Wiley & Sons.

Mayraz, G. 2011. Wishful Thinking in Predictions of Asset Prices. *CEP Discussion Paper*.

Mellers, B., R. Hertwig, and D. Kahneman. 2001. Do Frequency Representations Eliminate Conjunction Effects? An Exercise in Adversarial Collaboration. *Psychological Science 12* (4): 269–275.

Moore, D.A., and P.J. Healy. 2008. The Trouble with Overconfidence. *Psychological Review 115* (2): 502.

Muermann, A., and J.M. Volkman. 2006. Regret, Pride, and the Disposition Effect. *PARC Working Paper Series*.

Nestler, S., H. Blank, and G. von Collani. 2008. A Causal Model Theory of Creeping Determinism. *Social Psychology 39* (3): 182–188.

Roese, N.J., and K.D. Vohs. 2012. Hindsight Bias. *Perspectives on Psychological Science 7* (5): 411–426.

Sanger, S. 2011. The Illusion of Control. http://psychcentral.com/blog/archvies/2011/10/03/the-illusion-of-control.

Sanna, L.J. 2007. Metacognitive Experiences and Hindsight Bias: It's Not Just the Thought Content That Counts! *Social Cognition 25* (1): 185–202.

Slovic, P., M. Finucane, E. Peters, and D. MacGregor. 2002. Rational Actors or Rational Fools: Implications of the Affect Heuristic for Behavioral Economics. *Journal of Socio-Economics 31* (4): 329–342.

Smith, A. 1759. *The Theory Of Moral Sentiments*. London: Regnery Publishing.
Tentori, K., N. Bonini, and D. Osherson. 2004. The Conjunction Fallacy: A Misunderstanding about Conjunction? *Cognitive Science 28* (3): 467–477.
Tversky, A., and D. Kahneman. 1982. Judgments of and by Representativeness. In *Judgment under Uncertainty: Heuristics and Biases*, ed. D. Kahneman, P. Slovic, and A. Tversky. New York: Cambridge University Press.
———. 1983. Extensional Versus Intuitive Reasoning: The Conjunction Fallacy in Probability Judgment. *Psychological Review 90* (4): 293.
Wedell, D., and R. Moro. 2008. Testing Boundary Conditions for the Conjunction Fallacy: Effects of Response Mode, Conceptual Focus, and Problem Type. *Cognition 107* (1): 105–136.
Werth, L., F. Strack, and J. Förster. 2002. Certainty and Uncertainty: The Two Faces of the Hindsight Bias. *Organizational Behavior and Human Decision Processes 87* (2): 323–341.
Yamagishi, K. 1997. When A 12.86% Mortality Is More Dangerous Than 24.14%: Implications For Risk Communication. *Applied Cognitive Psychology 11* (6): 495–506.
Yudkowsky, E. 2007a. Affect Heuristic. http://lesswrong.com/lw/lg/the_affect_heuristic/
———. 2007b. Conjunction Fallacy. LessWrong. http://lesswrong.com/lw/ji/conjunction_fallacy/

6

How Do People Form Expectations in the Real World?

6.1 Expectations Before Behavioral Economics

During the first part of the twentieth century, the theme of expectation formation was considered of secondary importance in economic theory. In most economic models, such as the input-output model, economic agents (producers, consumers, etc.) were assumed to react mechanically and passively to stimuli coming from endogenous economic shocks and/or government policies. One (notable) exception in the treatment of expectations in the first half of the century is delivered by Keynes (1936). He assumes that in order to optimize the level of output, entrepreneurs have to form long-term expectations on the return of investment. Defining expectation formation as a tool to establish grounds for belief leading to an action, Keynes had a different perspective on the use of probability associated with uncertainty. His view was that while quantified probability based on frequency distributions was a special case, the general case was uncertainty, where even nonquantifiable (ordinal) probability may not be identifiable. However, Keynes introduced the determinant of confidence on the outcomes of an event through the notion of

F. Ghisellini, B. Y. Chang, *Behavioral Economics*,
https://doi.org/10.1007/978-3-319-75205-1_6

weight of argument, where weight is generally higher, the higher the amount of relevant evidence brought to bear. But Dow (1995) noted that what is relevant is itself theoretically loaded, and theoretical understandings can change. Also, there is no direct correspondence between degree of confidence and degree of probability, so there may, for example, be high confidence that an outcome has low probability, and vice versa. What this leads to are two folds in the path: (1) entrepreneurs' optimistic expectations and a willingness to ignore the uncertainty surrounding these expectations, and this is the meaning of Keynes' animal spirits, and (2) public institutional conventions that promote public-spirited behavior, which would address the consequences of uncertainty in the economy and in society, albeit on the basis of uncertain knowledge (Davis 1994).

Acting in the context of uncertainty, that is, with scarce information, Keynes' entrepreneurs therefore first collect the data that the market is able to generate in a regular way and, taking account of the specific level of confidence associated with such data, use them to form subjective expectations which will determine the chosen level of investment. From a qualitative point of view, Keynes' approach was thus quite advanced for the times.

Other than that, unfortunately, the best expectation scheme that economics could produce in the first 60 years of last century was the adaptive one.

The Adaptive Expectations model as developed by Nerlove (1958) is based on the notion that economic agents develop forecasts of a variable based on past realizations of the variable adjusted for their own past expectations. For instance, in the case of inflation, expected inflation $\mathrm{E}[\pi_t]$ would be given by:

$$\mathrm{E}[\pi_t] = \mathrm{E}[\pi_{t-1}] + \theta\{\pi_{t-1} - \mathrm{E}[\pi_{t-1}]\}$$

where the term in curly brackets represents the forecast error made by the economic agent in attempts to determine the previous rate of inflation and θ is an "error adjustment" term.

Adaptive expectations do not therefore make any use of current information, and it was precisely for this reason that they were instrumental in supporting the Phillips curve theory developed by Milton Friedman (1968) and reviewed in Chap. 2, by which, given the stickiness of workers' expectations and ensuing wage requests, government were able to achieve the desired rate of unemployment just by changing the rate of inflation.

As it turned out only after few years, markets are much quicker to adjust to government interventions. This finding made even clearer that the treatment of the way in which people formed their forecasts in the first six decades of the last century was largely unsatisfactory. Then something changed. Almost simultaneously, two economists introduced innovative approaches in expectation modeling.

Consider, for example, the approach developed by G. L. S. Shackle in the mid-60s, which describes the complexity of the expectation formation process (Shackle 1966).

He argued that in true uncertainty, it is the possibility, not probability, that is ultimately relevant, and probability must be abandoned in favor of possibility and a means must be sought to define the degrees of that possibility. This is in line with our earlier discussions that people are more sensitive to the changes in the extremes of possibility or impossibility, which relates to the degree of "potential surprise" according to Shackle. Subsequently, he developed a function of subjective possibility in expectation formation or of potential surprise to market outcomes, $\varphi = \varphi\ (G, y)$, in a range of desirability to undesirability of hypothetical outcomes, G, and each expectation element y. Shackle defines further that the expectation element has a vector of two entries: one represents the decision-maker's valuation of a hypothesis regardless of its capacity to become actual, for example, whether it is a profit or loss, and the other represents a measure of the degree of possibility of this hypothesis. He believes, however, that the decision-maker can simplify or manipulate these elements or his thoughts, a natural psychic entity and the fusion of thoughts and feeling at the core of the act of decision. Shackle's views on expectations formation resonated with those of neuroeconomics in later discoveries.[1]

Shackle's work was, however, largely ignored by mainstream economists, mainly because of its complexity. Academics needed something which was at the same time more realistic than static/adaptive expectations and simple enough to be easily incorporated into tractable economic models.

This is why the Rational Expectations Hypothesis (REH), which is generally considered the most innovative theoretical innovation in economics of the second half of last century, really made the fortune of the New Classical school.

As reported in II.II, the hypothesis was first proposed by John F. Muth in his paper *Rational Expectations and the Theory of Price Movements* (1961). Muth's point was that agents know the true model governing the economy and make optimal use of all available information—including news—so that market outcomes are, on average, in line with expectations (forecasts "are essentially the same as the predictions of the relevant economic theory"). The hypothesis was then expanded by New Classical economists such as, among others, Nobel Laureate Robert Lucas, Thomas Sargent, and Robert J. Barro. As a matter of fact, the importance of the expectation revolution in economic theory is highlighted by the amount of research focused on expectations. According to Google scholar, the number of economic research papers with the word "expectations" in the title jumped from about 2000 in the 1950–1970 period to about 15,000 in the following two decades.

The dominance of the REH (and of its implications, such as the efficient markets hypothesis) began to come seriously into question with the burst of the dot.com bubble at the outset of this century, and came to a virtual end with the global financial crisis of 2007, which exposed the inadequacy of New Classical Economics to explain/forecast real-world phenomena (cf. Chap. 2). In the same period, behavioral economics was on the rise.

6.2 Expectations (or Their Absence) in Behavioral Research

In this context, it was therefore logical to assume that behavioral economics would also provide a new and more convincing model for the formation of expectations. Unfortunately, however, most behavioral research has so far underrated the importance of identifying a general scheme of expectation formation that can work as an alternative (or as a complement) to the one generated by rational expectations. In fact, the situation turned out to be quite paradoxical.

In the words of Frydman and Goldberg (2013), "behavioral economists, who have uncovered massive evidence of REH's empirical failure, generally subscribe to this belief, and have interpreted their findings as evidence that individuals fall short of 'full rationality'. Of course this statement is entirely correct only if it refers to the 'American school' (cf. Chap. 3), but given the dominance of this school, it can be considered representative of what goes on in most behavioral research. Consider, for example, financial problems such as asset allocation strategies. We know that according to behavioral economics, investors are loss-averse, rather than risk-averse. So, in evaluating the expected performance of a specific asset, they are bound to form a forecast of future losses. Hence, there is a need to specify how these forecasts are generated. For example, in most behavioral research, significant importance is given to cognitive biases such as overconfidence or disposition effects that can distort allocation choices, but we are told very little about the forecasting process in itself. Speaking of expectations, behavioral economics has been instrumental in helping us to reject what is unrealistic and surely does not work, like the REH in its strong form (people know the true model, use all the existing information, and have unlimited computing capacity). But what about weaker forms of the REH, like those postulating that, although endowed with limited information and computing capability, people still make the best possible use of all the information available to them? Seems reasonable, doesn't it? Still, as yet behavioral research does not seem ready to take a consensus position on this and we are left with a big conceptual hole. There is little doubt that that hole should be filled, though. Understanding expectation formation is critical for behavioral economics because it addresses key unsolved issues such as "biases" and "irrationality" as well as unanswered questions in order for the field to move forward and to make improvements in the market. As we introduced earlier, in an imperfect knowledge world, people form expectations utilizing two types of resources, the explicit or external knowledge and skills, where they attempt to find the most relevant information within a particular time frame and possibly build a quantitative model and conduct an analysis from the data, and the implicit or internal knowledge, where they learned and remembered from past experiences that sometimes called intuition, the critical use of which under uncertainty was even confirmed by conventional economics theorists as noted earlier.

In the case of asset price swings, "behavioral finance theorists have assumed that REH is the way to represent how rational participants understand the effect of fundamental factors on asset prices. This has led them to seek accounts of price swings that make 'less than full rationality' and/or irrelevant considerations primary factors driving market participants' expectations of payoff-relevant outcomes" (Frydman and Phelps). So "American" behavioral theorists have claimed market participants' behavior to be "irrational" or "biased" when there is high market volatility or absence of absolute market consensus. Are these labeling in describing individual behaviors used simply too loosely without realizing market participants' intrinsic needs in responding to market changes that are in dissonance with previous expectations or simply from observations that there is a wide range in individual judgments because of differences in experience, skills, knowledge, and innate abilities (Kahneman and Tversky 2002) in forming expectations? Or is it because of the conflict between probability theories and intuitive judgment—as in the Linda problem—that leads to "conjunction fallacy"[2]? It seems to be inevitable that one must choose between two types of models: consistent REH models representing conventional economics that rule out an active role for participants' expectations in driving outcomes and inconsistent behavioral models that allow for such a role (Frydman and Phelps). Clearly, this alleged duality is a problem—it is almost saying that we make decisions by choosing either System I or II of our brain functions but never both. But is this how we form expectations in reality? A prominent economist lit up during a seminar on what were purported to be "biases": "*Ah, I see,*" he said, "*behavior is either rational or it's psychological*" (Cosmides and Tooby 1994).

Do conventional economics theorists genuinely believe that the assumptions in the REH model represent reality or that REH should be the norm and represents how rational participants should forecast? Is this devout belief in "rationality" because of its scientific appeal or its pursuit for tractability and control and that the human elements such as emotions or heterogeneous individual precepts, which are considered less manageable, can be easily corrected or abandoned in correspondence with unknown events in a complex market?

While the mainstream component of the American school has implicitly accepted the REH, other behavioral researchers have explored different territories. In particular, they have focused on two fundamental and interrelated issues:

1. mechanisms governing the accumulation of knowledge/information and
2. the degree of subjectivity in making forecasts.

Expectation formation can be thought of as a process in which knowledge plays a crucial role. As a matter of fact, what comes first is the quality as well as the quantity of knowledge available to forecasters.

Some researchers working on approaches developed by the "American" behavioral school have been more innovative than others on the matter. In Chap. 3 we reported, for example, the important work done by Daniel Kahneman (2013) on the two systems governing our mind processes. Instead of the intuitive System I and the reasoning System II, physicist Ned Herrmann, while heading the management at the GE Corporation, compiled the four quadrants as the whole brain thinking process developed by other brain scientists in a way that can be approximated by a graph[3] (see Fig. 6.1).

While the right and left sides of the human brain in the graph are similar to the concept of Systems I and II, respectively, the upper and lower parts are divided as intellectual and instinctive with the interactions of both Systems I and II functions in them. Similarly, Camerer et al. (2005) had carved out the four quadrants by controlled or automatic, from left to right, and by cognitive or affective, from upper to lower, parts of our brain-processing functions. To put them in more comprehensive terms, the dimensions of the four quadrants in cognitive functions are controlled cognitive, controlled affective, automatic cognitive, and automatic affective.

Fig. 6.1 The Brain and Its Four Quadrants

Considering that knowledge is imperfect—and there are always unknown-unknowns—theories on the role of intuition have been developed to explain an expectations formation process which has both quantitative and qualitative characteristics. As Kahneman (2013) had defined, information or data stored in System I are slow learning but stickier than those in System II. From a certain perspective and given how our memory systems and cerebral mechanisms work, we could consider System I as some type of data bank we carry with us, as it is influenced by experience and memory, from where we could retrieve information when we are encountered with particular stimuli in the environment or when we associate with the workings of the System II, for example, in the midst of data analysis with new information. This is the instinctive or intuitive part of human brain that plays an important role, and at times a subjective part, in the expectations formation process with scarcity of observable data. Indeed, all the following factors are necessary in forming expectations (see Fig. 6.2).

Fig. 6.2 The Funnel of Expectations

This is confirmed by findings which show that automatic and deliberate processes can operate simultaneously and thus jointly shape thought and action, and thus the ideal case of pure intuition or pure deliberation does not exist in reality (Betsch 2016). In Betsch's (2016) words:

> *when distinguishing different strategies of thinking on the empirical level, one should seek to specify the relative contribution of the two processes. If automatic processes dominate, one should expect that the judgments or decisions are reached very quickly by virtue of parallel processing. At the same time, judgments and decisions should reflect a strong sensitivity for entire samples of prior experiences even if the sample is huge because parallel processes can handle a large amount of information. Moreover, intuitive judgments and decisions should be prone to undervalue the weight of new evidence because they strongly rely on consolidated knowledge.*

Behavioral research has thus done quite well in identifying the complex mechanisms governing the formation of the knowledge base which is necessary for generating expectations. What is still missing, however, is the incorporation of these mechanisms into tractable and empirically testable models.

And as if things were not already very complicated, consider the role of subjectivity.

In order to claim that the REH does contain elements of realism, some often quote Muth's statement that the REH "does not assert that expectations are all the same" (Muth 1961: 317). However, Frydman and Goldberg (2013) show that in a rational expectations model, the REH can only hold in the aggregate if any change in the expectations of a group of agents is symmetrically compensated by changes in expectations held by the rest of participating agents.

So what generally is absent in the RE models is the indispensable qualitative side that includes autonomy, true heterogeneity, and other characteristics such as heuristics or intuitions in decisions and behavioral changes given changes in situations and in the environment. To various levels, these qualities are implied or infiltrated even in the quantitative side of the adaptive agent-based model. For example, the proportion of the fixed parameters we input in a one-period forecasting error can be highly subjective. Other examples of subjectivity include the selection of information given restrictions of time frame, and the amount, sources, and quality of information available. For some, newspaper headlines may be sufficient in forming particular types of expectation while personal views influenced by individual temperament may apply in the process.

But one of the most extreme forms of subjectivity is intuition. The importance of human intuitive functions in an uncertain environment is also highlighted by Tversky and Kahneman in their earlier work on the psychology of intuitive judgment. They have asserted clearly that intuitive judgment is often the only practical method for assessing uncertainty because we normally do not have adequate formal models for computing the probabilities of future events.

To provide empirical evidence supporting these claims, a study by Harteis and Gruber found that in most cases intuitive predictions of stock market development are better than rationally justified ones and that experts predict more precisely than novices on a descriptive data level. Since there is the speculative nature in the expectation formation to some extent, as discussed earlier, because there is always some crucial information missing that is necessary to determine factors objectively given the nature of change in time, the study concludes that intuition is an important component of professional competence in the market because it allows individuals to act appropriately in situations when they lack information. Thus intuition promotes the quality of forecasts on the stock market. Moreover, the empirical findings confirm that intuitive forecasts were significantly closer to the effective values than were the rationally justified forecasts. In fact, the US dollar was intuitively predicted with almost perfect accuracy (Harteis and Gruber 2007).

As is illustrated vividly by George Soros (2013) from his years of practice in the financial markets, what generate expectations are both subjective and objective realities of participating agents that make up the so-called feedback loop and the reflexivity system of the market. For illustrative purposes, Fig. 6.3 visually approximates the process for the simple case of a market in which just two agents interact.

As the agent's expectation or subjective reality turns into action that feeds into objective reality, the latter becomes part of the information source of our expectation in the next time horizon; so subjective reality is based partly on observable information. This empirical finding is in line with the assertion that outside the domain of random sampling, probability theory does not determine the probabilities of uncertain events (Kahneman and Tversky 2002). As market realities comprise both past objective information and current subjective opinions, market outcomes at a particular point in time are realities of both the observable data and the less observable subjective opinions and expectations leading to manipulations and speculations as shown in Fig. 6.3.

So a subjective trait like intuition is important. But the subjectivity of expectations is also shaped by other drivers, such as emotions and personal beliefs. Among the attempts to build theoretical frameworks capturing the impact of various subjective drivers, mention should be made of the theory of possibility (TOP) introduced by Zadeh (1978), which has been set up to deal with decision-making situations in which information is incomplete.[4] TOP is based on viewpoints of both subjectivity (e.g., personal beliefs) and objectivity (e.g., belief generated from data observations in representing degree of uncertainty). By using a pair of dual set-functions (possibility and necessity measures), it makes the process easier to capture partial ignorance.

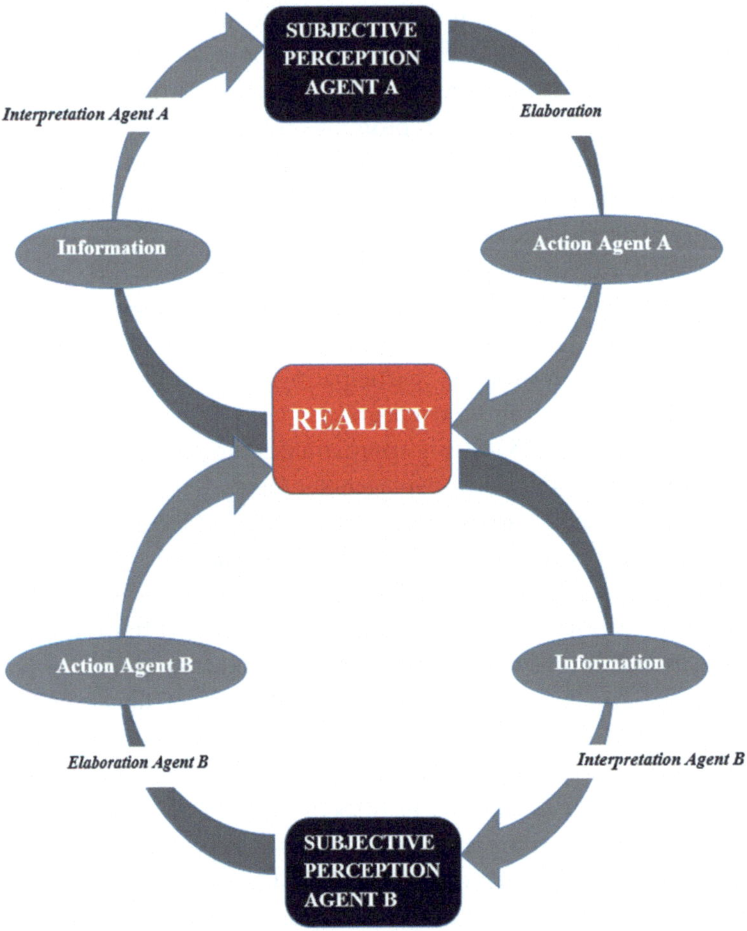

Fig. 6.3 Soros' Expectations

There are a few behavioral implications in TOP. First, we discussed earlier how the surprise factors are associated with market behaviors and in turn contribute to market volatility, for example, a bank run when there is a surprise market outcome; or when in defense, emotions take over. The explicit measure of surprise, which is the reverse of the possibility measure, can potentially tame market over- and under-reactions. Second,

TOP broadens the perspective of what could happen; it is a far cry from the attempt to characterize an individual's "attitude to risk" by a single ratio, and is a tool which should offer possibilities to advanced empirical psychology (Shackle). And expectation, after all, is imaginative creation within the free space conferred by uncertainty—a bounded space, however, confined to the "possible" according to the laws of nature and of human nature as the individual decision-maker conceives them (Shackle). This is when some of the human behavioral traits such as fear provide a means of understanding and anticipating what the human mind will go through when sizing up how imperfect a possibility of a particular outcome is (Earl 2012). Lastly, but hardly the least, unlike a probability measure which is singleton in nature, possibility measures have a plural approach in exploring likelihood outcomes, reflecting exactly what the essence of uncertainty is—a plurality of outcomes of a future event. So it can have any number of distinct and mutually exclusive outcomes without limit.

More specifically, possibility measures may rectify behavioral tendencies discovered from the prospect theory such as people tending to overweigh low probability events. In this context, mention should be made of how the TOP approach has further embraced the theory of evidence originated by the Dempster-Shafer theory.[5] There are two, dual, nonadditive measures—the possibility measure π and the necessity measure η, which consist of the belief measure (*Bel*) and the plausibility measure (*Pl*). These measures follow the max/min rules such that: $\pi(A \cup B) = \max(\pi(A), \pi(B))$ and $\eta(A \cap B) = \min(\eta(A), \eta(B))$. And in most cases, $\pi(A \cap B) < \min(\pi(A), \pi(B))$ and $\eta(A \cup B) > \max(\eta(A), \eta(B))$. Shackle's possibility and surprise theories in dealing with uncertainty using barriers were more conceptual and qualitative, albeit with some measurements involved. Similarly, Zadeh had attempted to differentiate degree of possibility from that of probability: "A basic assumption which underlies our approach to approximate reasoning is that the imprecision which is intrinsic in natural languages is, in the main possibilistic rather than probabilistic in nature.... possibility relates to our perception of the degree of feasibility or ease of attainment, whereas probability is associated with the degree of belief, likelihood, frequency, or proportion". So

Zadeh's treatment in the degrees of possibility is about how easy or feasible an action leading to a particular outcome is, which differs from the measure of how plausible a proposition is true in the fuzzy logic. However, with the possibility-necessity dual function approximation since Zadeh, the latter or the necessity function, which comprises both a belief and a plausible function, is more quantitative, and possibility measures are therefore, in some cases, supported by more quantitative measures of the plausible function.[6]

So, while keeping Shackle's conceptual notion of possibility or the ease and feasibility of the occurrence of an event in mind, the general usage in quantitative terms is that the degree of possibility is the upper probability and the degree of necessity is the lower probability. The lower probability is interpreted as the "degree of potential surprise" or "degree of provability" if A failed to occur. Here is an example of the possibility and necessity measures applying these rules: in the subprime mortgage lending case, suppose x = the low-income group, A = event of default, and S = possibility of financial crisis, the question is what is the possibility that the subprime group could default and cause a finance crisis or $x \in A \subset S$?

First, you may want to maximize your imagination for the possibilities that event A can happen that results in market behaviors such as sell-offs, leading to a market meltdown. So the possibility function is $\Pi(A) = \max_{s \in A} \pi(s)$. Then develop degrees of possibilities that $x \in A$ and that A causes S under various possible scenarios. For the necessity function $N(A) = 1 - \Pi(A^c) = \min_{s \notin A} 1 - \pi(s)$, where A^c is the complement of A which can be the increase in interest or unemployment rate. Here, you look for the degree of certainty or necessity, from sources such as supporting data or intuitive inductions and deductions, to which π implies A and that $x \in A$.

As we can see, the functions in beliefs and plausibility consist of both subjective and objectivity factors in the judgment of an agent, distinguishing what is believable or plausible from what is less believable or plausible, based on the agent's knowledge and available data in assigning possibility values. Such functions may explain the phenomena of overweighting low probability, the degree of necessity, and, underweighting high probability, the degree of possibility.

6.3 Is There a Tractable Way to Model Expectations in a Behavioral Model?

As interesting as it can be, however, the TOP is hardly usable in the context of a parsimonious economic model. Some would say that this may be disappointing, but it is a somewhat foregone conclusion when you deal with expectations. Inputs are so numerous and diverse, and subjectivity so pronounced that modeling expectations often based on "animal spirits" in an accessible way is practically impossible. In the words of Phelps (2008), "*animal spirits can't be modeled.*"

In spite of this, recently Frydman and Goldberg have engaged in a courageous effort to come up with a theory that could on the one hand take into account most of the subjective and objective factors driving expectations and on the other hand remain tractable enough. The name is imperfect knowledge economics (IKE).

In their research, they first tried to produce a weighted ranking of fundamental factors influencing expectations (Frydman and Goldberg 2011). In the case of daily stock prices, they found such factors to include (1) the economy (gross domestic product, productivity, consumer income, employment, job creation, etc.), (2) fed funds level, discount rate, treasury yield, (3) inflation (producer price index, consumer price index, wages), (4) earnings, and (5) company variables (bankruptcy, CEO/CFO leaves, malpractice, dividends, etc.). Let us see an example of the weights in quantitative measures in terms of the influences of factors on the formation of expectations of the top 10 factor frequencies over the entire sample from the same study (% overlap for some factors):

- Fundamentals: 99% (in dynamic)
- Earnings: 65%
- Psychological considerations: 55%
- Psychology with fundamental: 54%
- Economy: 47%
- Interest rates: 38%
- Sales: 23%
- Company variables: 23%

- Inflation: 20%
- Oil prices: 19%

The sample corollary from this particular study by Frydman and Goldberg shows that while the fundamentals in dynamic form alone had almost all the influences on the expectation for stock prices, the weight on the combination of psychology and fundamental takes more than half of the influence on the expectation formation for future prices. The 55% psychological considerations, which may carry a wide range of traits, for example, from bearish to bullish and other shades in between, could easily move away from the more observable but historical fundamental trends, or swing in either direction depending on subjective viewpoints, which may be regarded as "biased" at times. However, personal or subjective views are intrinsic and part and parcel of the inputs in determining stock price because of the unpredictable or uncertain market conditions and movements in a free or quasi-free capitalist environment given limits in fundamentals serving as historical information.

Looking at the overlapping realities in the weights between the observable and the less observable or the conscious and subconscious characteristics influencing the expectation formation, the real challenge lies in the delineation of the two in exact or quantitative terms. The former may dominate in a more stable environment, while the latter takes charge during uncertain times such as before a major financial crisis or under a particular political upheaval.

The overall IKE project is thoroughly explained in Frydman and Goldberg (2013).[7] Basically, IKE uses nonstandard probabilistic distributions to overcome what is deemed to be the main weakness of REH models, that is, the inability of accounting for revision of forecasting strategies in the presence of nonroutine changes in the structure of the economy (in REH models changes in expectations are supposed to materialize only as a result of the arrival of "news"). In applying IKE to financial assets price dynamics, Frydman and Goldberg specified inter alia that:

- aggregate price expectation is a weighted sum of heterogeneous forecasts (as those typically associated with "bulls" and "bears").

- as causal variables are not fully specified, expectation strategies can be revised to account nonroutine changes in market structure.
- as in Keynes (1936):
  - the awareness of imperfect knowledge leads market participants to revise in "guardedly moderate ways" their view of how the market works.
  - although psychological factors play a role in a decision-making process that, given imperfect knowledge, remains however rational, fundamentals continue in any case to be the main driver in expectation formation.

Although they consider the contingent and qualitative nature of IKE to be very important for incorporating heterogeneity and psychology into empirically testable models, Frydman and Goldberg acknowledge that outside the realm of finance (e.g., in macroeconomic policy modeling), IKE can as yet turn out to be of limited utility.

To be sure, there are also other problems with IKE. For example, their paper does not explain in any detail the way in which psychological factors concur to expectation formation. But one of the (many) great merits of IKE remains that of stressing that subjective psychological factors (including those called "biases" by most "conventional" behavioral research) do NOT lead to irrationality.

Since most of the alleged "biases" typically emerge given limits in information, while norms, for example, a particular dominating market force, are computed after the event rather than in advance, according to Kahneman and Miller (1986), they do not necessarily represent underlying market "truth" or capabilities. So we may not be "biased", as some of the norm and subjective opinions (e.g. from Rajan[8]) turn out to be an accurate objective reality. In that respect, it was the more intuitive approach for the sources in forming expectations (e.g., the way we interpret data or factors we use) that play a key role in putting the market on a certain path. As the behavioral economist Bob Shiller succinctly put it, we need more expectations theories and less EMH (Ritholtz 2011)!

Overall, the treatment of the expectation issue in behavioral economics is therefore unsatisfactory. Most of behavioral research has mainly to do with criticism of the simplistic and unrealistic features of the rational expectations hypothesis, but as yet no consensus alternative expectation theory has been produced. The situation is made worse by the presence of some conceptual confusion on the definition of what a "behavioral expectation" is.

On the one hand, there have been cases in which expectation models have been unduly labeled as "behavioral". For example, Levine (2012) writes: "*Undoubtedly, real people are not unboundedly rational. They can scarcely be expected to rationally forecast 'equilibrium' prices. Let us instead consider a 'behavioral' model: let us suppose that firms forecast prices next period to be whatever prices were last period. This is exactly the behavioral model of adaptive expectations formation that was widely used before the rational expectations revolution of which behavioral economists are so critical*". This text contains at least two puzzling elements. First, the expectation scheme described by Levine is static, rather than adaptive (as reported earlier, adaptive expectations are slightly more sophisticated as they incorporate an "error correction" mechanism). Most importantly, it is not clear at all on what grounds the scheme should be defined as "*exactly the behavioral model*". To our knowledge, although some could hold that extrapolative/regressive/adaptive expectations are more likely to prevail in the real world, there is no official (or unofficial) consensus behavioral model of expectations. In this context, it is also to be noted that some rationality-related concepts have on occasion been presented as conflicting, while this is not necessarily the case. For instance, Mallard (2016) writes that "*the economics profession has favoured the rational expectations view and has, at various times and in various forms, sought to sideline Simon's alternative of bounded rationality*". But this statement would be correct only if the sole possible version of the REH or its representative EMH were the "strong" one (by which people know exactly the "true" model, and have all the information and advanced computing capabilities). If the EMH form considered is the "weak" or semi-strong (by which people just make good use of whatever information is available), then a conceptual difference with bounded rationality remains (in the weak or semi-strong EMH, people still optimize and make quantitative forecasts) but it becomes much less pronounced.

On the other hand, in behavioral research, the very meaning of the word "expectation" has been sometimes distorted and confused with other concepts. For example, there are cases in which the difference in meaning between an expectation and a belief turns out to be significantly blurred. Being a conviction, a strong opinion about someone/something, a belief is a "structural" concept. In contrast, an expectation is a guess about the punctual realization of a variable, though not without influences of past experience. To illustrate the difference, consider the case of the future price performance of a specific asset, for example, the share of company X. I may have the belief that X shares are structurally overvalued, but at the same time have the expectation that, due to current momentum trends, X shares will appreciate further in the short term.

While all these complexities and subjectivities are no doubt there and their inclusion in the analysis contributes to making the description of expectation formation more complete, at the same time they represent an obstacle to the generation of a tractable and simple theoretical scheme. The crucial challenge would then be: how can we model the aforementioned in a way that is general, somewhat tractable, and allows for a consensus formal rendering? With the realistic factors involving both human traits and the environment delineated earlier, we could phrase the question differently: how do we introduce in our models of expectation schemes which lead to decisions and market behaviors that are more in line with reality for both market participants and policymakers?

A further attempt to make progress on these issues is presented in a recent research paper on "natural expectations" by Fuster et al. (2010) (FLM for short). "Natural expectations" are defined as a weighted average of rational and (naive) intuitive expectations. The weighting parameter, λ, assumes values comprised between 0 and 1. It is important to note that natural expectations work on an "as if" basis. In other words, agents do not calculate intuitive and rational components separately, but go through a deliberative process in which the two components are unconsciously mixed.

But what are intuitive expectations? In their paper, FLM equate them to extrapolative expectations, on the grounds that in a number of studies, forecasts are found to be based on the extrapolation of recent market trends.[9] So, intuitive expectations of the change in a variable x are generated by an autoregressive process ($\Delta x_{t+1} = \varphi \Delta x_t + \varepsilon_t$), with parameter φ estimated from historical data. In contrast, rational expectations are formed on the basis of a regression on standard causal variables.

FLM's model is parsimonious, as λ is the only free parameter. When $\lambda = 1$, forecasts are only based on intuition. When $\lambda = 0$, expectations are entirely rational. The higher the value of λ, the higher the possibility that, with the arrival of news, momentum trends are translated into large price swings, while expectations fail to fully incorporate mean reversion.

While extremely interesting, FLM's model has its problems. For example, asset price volatility generates consumption patterns which are unrealistically volatile. So the model is only an initial step in what could, however, be considered the right direction. What is still missing is a formulation of heterogeneous expectations consistent with a parsimonious and empirically testable model.

In more recent years after the financial crisis, the personal or subjective factor in the expectation formation has gained more attention. For example, in a study on expectations formation about future inflation by scholars from NBER (Malmendiery and Nagelz 2013), personal experiences were found to have played an important role. Findings in the investigation show that

> *individuals adapt their forecasts to new data but overweight inflation realized during their life-times. Young individuals update their expectations more strongly in the direction of recent surprises than older individuals since recent experiences make up a larger part of their lives so far.*

What a normal person with behavioral rationality but no privileged skills or information would do to forecast an asset price in a foreseeable future? Most likely, his/her expectation would be a weighted average of three factors, and the third of them would be highly subjective:

1. Index performance (recent and relevant, where relevant simulates/tracks current trends)
2. Forecasts available (recent and relevant) via media/web and other social means (Note: the amount and quality of information selected are subject to personal judgment, as:

   (a) Some people may be content with news headlines
   (b) Information selected can be "filtered" by "confirmation biases"

(c) Shiller/Cape expectational index or expert expectational index (latter for policymakers)

3. Personal views (if any) to the extent and the direction of markets/ economy changes (and what we call "confirmation bias" can have a role here too). To put it in equation:

$$E_t\left(S_{t+i}\right)=S_t+\beta F_t+p\left[\gamma F_{t+i}^{*}+\left(1-\gamma\right)F_{t+i}^{p}\right]+e_t$$

where

$E_t(S_{t+i})$ is the expectation of next year price,
βF_t is the sensitivity of stock price to the performance of the Index at time t
$0 < \gamma < 1$ is the weight assigned to F_{t+i}^{*} as personal prior beliefs (which may incorporate biases) for time $t + i$
F_{t+i}^{p} is the price expectation held by media, colleagues, friends, and so forth.

Typically, a person who is not confident in her capacity to forecast will rely on F_{t+i}^{p} (implying $\gamma \to 0$), whereas one who feels confident will assign great importance to her prior F_{t+i}^{*} (implying $\gamma \to 1$). The e_i term tracks what we missed in the projection, which may be taken into account in the next round of attempt.

Weight assignments to each of the three factors change from person to person and also depend on the situation and the nature of the matter. What does the equation imply in terms of "proposing avenues for research"? In practice, what we just described is a "behavioral rational expectations" mechanism, in the sense that:

Factor 1 is a classic input for both adaptive and rational expectations; factor 2 belongs to classical REH, but is filtered with BEF features; factor 3 resembles the Bayesian prior mechanism, but also tainted with BEF features. In addition, people, different from what REH predicts, do NOT know (even partially) the "true" model, as the model used is a mix (with subjective weights) of media and personal views (if factor 3 weighs about zero, for

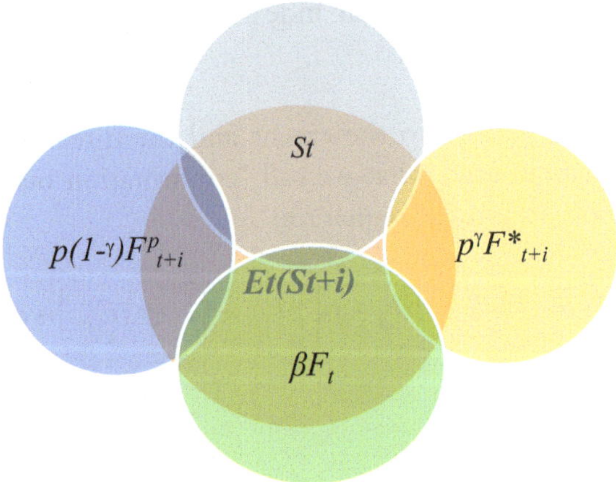

Fig. 6.4 Expectations as Overlapping Sets

example, there would be—though filtered by confirmation bias—"herd" behaviors). To translate this equation to relations in sets, we have Fig. 6.4.

At the center is the dependent variable of the expectations for the stock price in the next period of time. While the four variables that shape the expectation are supposed to be independent in the equation, they overlap in some form of relations in reality. These overlapping relations among important factors in the expectation formation are in line with other findings (Frydman and Goldberg) discussed earlier, and human psychology, whatever the forms are in the effect, bullish or bearish, had played more than half in the factors. The weight therefore plays a critical role in decisions as the decision-maker needs a single solution in the situation given.

Another example model: at the end of 2015, the task is to forecast US housing prices in 2016.

The general formula could be

$$E_t\left(P_{t+1}\right)=P_t+\alpha\left(P_t-P_{t-1}\right)+\beta\left[\gamma\, P_t^*+\left(1-\gamma\right)I_t^p\right]$$

where

$E_t\,(P_{t+1})$ is the expectation of 2016 prices

$(P_t - P_{t-1})$ is the 2015/2014 change in prices

$0 < \gamma < 1$ is the weight assigned to P_t^*, personal prior beliefs (which may incorporate biases)

I_t^p is the price expectation held by media, colleagues, friends, and so forth.

We consider three different investors: not confident (low weight to prior), confident (high weight to prior), and neutral (equal weights to all parameters and static prior) (see Table 6.1).

Using actual data as inputs and with an actual 2016 housing price index of 105.6, the most accurate forecast would have been that of non-confident people, that is, people who would assign the greatest importance to I_t^p, the price expectation held by media, colleagues, friends, and so forth. The worst forecast would have been that of confident people (i.e. people who believe in their prior forecast) (see Table 6.2).

Of course the crucial challenge remains: how can you model contents similar to the above in a way that is general, tractable and allows for an empirical testing? On the surface, it seems like mission impossible. As Shackle (1966) noted, historical data or the most recent "news" has been so shaped by an interplay so complex and subtle as to defy explicit analysis. However, expectation formation is also shaped by market designs under a particular choice architecture that could form "bounded uncertainty" to an extent. In this vein, we could say, for example, that the 2008 crisis was the failure of market design in the choice architecture, which was expected by some, as shown below (see Table 6.3).

Table 6.1 A Matrix of Heterogeneous Investors

	Not confident	Confident	Neutral
α	0.6	0.6	0.5
β	0.4	0.4	0.5
γ	0	1	0.5

Table 6.2

Not Confident	Confident	Neutral
105.0	103.9	104.4

Table 6.3 Choice Architecture and the Global Crisis

Traditional Morgage Lending	
Loan on Book	Bank as Originator
Mortgage Lending Before Crisis	
Investors as Lenders	Brokerage Firms Create MBSs
Choice Among Agents	
Investors are free to flee	Mortgagees free to abandon homes

Among the causes of the 2008 market failure, one could therefore have to do with poor market design and the choice architecture with misaligned incentives, obligations, issues of transparencies, and ultimately ignorance in the impact of fundamental uncertainties when interest rates change while the ratio of home mortgage debt to disposable personal income ration in the US increased sharply, exceeding 100%, and personal savings rate reached zero between 1978 and 2007, an indication of strenuous personal financial conditions. However, mortgage lending continued to expand until 2008, when the crash occurred.

Because expectation formation has a key function in driving and shaping the market, and in turn the overall economy, whether it weighs more on observable data or subjective opinions based on some of the data, future research on behavioral expectations might be improved by expanding and deepening the IKE and the TOP models with the inclusion of behavioral and subjective traits we have discussed and discovered so far and the factors highlighted in the example just presented for model generality, empiricality, and tractability. Of course it could be that even such enrichment may not capture all elements in changing forms to fit entirely a reality which, to an extent, remains to be unforeseen, as Keynes and some post-Keynesian economists would stress, non-ergodic (i.e. subject to nonroutine change), and transmutable by the decision of economic agents. This is why Keynes stressed that the

> *"state of long term expectations" involving non routine matters that are "very uncertain" form the basis for important economic decisions involving investment, the accumulation of wealth, and finance. In these areas, agents "know" they are dealing with an uncertain, nonprobabilistic creative economic external reality.*

What we know, though, is that we have got to move forward, as we cannot continue to pretend that elegant but extraneous RE models can be a satisfactory answer to our problem. Expectation formation is about seeking all possibilities surrounding an event with or without boundaries of uncertainty and given the subjective and objective realities driving human behavior. For policymakers, the outstanding issues in an economy may be analogous to those in human biology, where even the most advanced medical technology may not conquer in normative or positive terms. However, if effective control methods, given understandings of the fundamental problems in humans, could prevent the malignancies from spreading for the most part, it should still be considered a form of cure. As Lars Syll (2012) put it:

> *The future is not about known probability distributions. It is not about picking the right ball from an urn. It is about new possibilities. It is about inventing new balls and new urns to put them in.*

Notes

1. Neuroeconomists argue that the function of the brain is not likely to contain a single "reasoning" module, such as in the expectation formation process, and suggest that there are two, not one, mechanisms in the process of judging the likelihood of an event—some explicit, driven by controlled processes, others implicit driven by automatic processes (CLP, 45). This view is further supported by other experts in the field of neural/psychology. In his paper on neural mechanisms for economics, Craver (Craver Carl F. (2008), No Revolution Necessary: Neural Mechanisms for Economics, Economics and Philosophy, 24, 381–406, Cambridge University Press) wrote:

Many decision-making tasks, such as evaluation of utility, judgments of probability, choice, etc., *straddle these quadrants. Moreover, automatic and affective dimensions, scientists are finding, influence judgment and behavior much more than one would expect given the standard economic theory's emphasis on controlled and cognitive processes. For example, judgments about whether or not one agrees with a given editorial, how probable an event is, whether a given stimulus is positive or negative, whether consumption should be delayed or not, and many others, all take place at the intersection of several of the four quadrants (CLP). Yet only one of these processes, the controlled cognitive one, is captured by the expected utility theory.*

2. The "conjunction fallacy" in Linda's problem defies the probability axiom which says in mathematical terms that the probability of combined events occurring together is always less than that of a single event.
3. Herrmann, N. <http://www. Herrmannsolutions.com/what-is-whole-brain-thinking-2/>.
4. "The name 'theory of possibility' was coined by Zadeh in 1978, in Fuzzy Sets and Possibility Theory". *Journal of Artificial Intelligence.*
5. Cf. Shafer (1976).
6. The starting point is a unique representation of π by a possibility distribution function π: X → [0,1] via the formula $\pi(A) = \max_{x \in A} \pi(x)$, where the possibility of a state or an outcome A is the maximization of the possibility of x which is an element of A. If the possibility of a state $\pi(s) = 0$, it means that state s is rejected as impossible; if $\pi(s) = 1$, it means that state s is totally possible (= plausible). If, for example, the degree of plausibility $x = s$ and denoted $\pi_x(s)$, and $\pi_x(s) = 0$ iff $x = s$ is impossible, then it is a total surprise as the surprise measure $1 - \pi_x(s) = 1$. But if $\pi_x(s) = 1$ if $x = s$ is normal and fully plausible, then it is unsurprising, though there is no certainty (Dubois).

   For a simple example "does event A occur?", where A is a subset of state $S = [0,1]$, the possibility and necessity functions are: $\Pi(A) = \sup_{\mu \in A}\pi(\mu)$ and $N(A) = \inf_{s \notin A} 1 - \pi(\mu)$, where $\Pi(A)$ evaluates to what extent A is consistent with supremum value of π, while $N(A)$ evaluates to what extent A is certainly implied by infimum value of π. The possibility-necessity duality is expressed by $N(A) = 1 - \Pi(A^c)$, where A^c is the complement of A.
7. Cf. Frydman and Goldberg (2013).
8. Rajan, Raghuram, an IMF economist at the time, who correctly warned about the financial market before its crash in 2008.
9. Cf. for example Ernan et al. (2007).

References

Betsch, T. 2016. The Nature of Intuition and Its Neglect in Research on Judgment and Decision Making. https://www.researchgate.net/profile/Tilmann_Betsch/publication/267701225_The_Nature_of_Intuition_and_Its_Neglect_in_Research_on_Judgment_and_Decision_Making/links/54d09c750cf29ca81101ed68.pdf

Camerer, C., G. Loewenstein, and D. Prelec. 2005. Neuroeconomics: How Neuroscience Can Inform Economics. *Journal of Economic Literature 43* (1): 9–64.

Cosmides, L., and J. Tooby. 1994. Better than Rational: Evolutionary Psychology and the Invisible Hand. *The American Economic Review 84* (2): 327–332.

Davis, J.B. 1994. *Keynes's Philosophical Development*. Cambridge: Cambridge University Press.

Dow, S. 1995. Uncertainty about Uncertainty. In *Keynes, Knowledge and Uncertainty*, ed. S. Dow and J. Hillard. Aldershot: Edward Elgar.

Earl, P. 2012. Kahneman's Thinking, Fast and Slow from the Standpoint of Old Behavioral Economics. https://shredecon.files.wordpress.com/2012/06/hetsa-2012-earl.pdf.

Ernan, H., Y. Lahav, and C.N. Noussair. 2007. Traders' Expectations in Asset Markets: Experimental Evidence. *American Economic Review 97* (5): 1901–1920.

Friedman, M. 1968. The Role of Monetary Policy. *American Economic Review* 58 (1): 1–17.

Frydman, R., and M. Goldberg. 2011. *Beyond Mechanical Markets: Asset Price Swings, Risk, and the Role of the State*. Princeton, NJ: Princeton University Press.

———. 2013. The Imperfect Knowledge Imperative in Modern Macroeconomics and Finance Theory. In *Rethinking Expectations: The Way Forward for Macroeconomics*, ed. R. Frydman and E. Phelps. Princeton University Press.

Fuster, A., D. Laibson, and B. Mendel. 2010. Natural Expectations and Macroeconomic Fluctuations. *Journal of Economic Perspectives 24* (4): 67–84.

Harteis, C., and H. Gruber. 2007. Intuition and Professional Competence: Intuitive versus Rational Forecasting of the Stock Market. *Vocations and Learning 1* (1): 71–85.

Kahneman, Daniel. 2013. *Thinking, Fast and Slow*. New York: Farrar, Straus and Giroux.

Kahneman, D., and D. Miller. 1986. Norm Theory: Comparing Reality to Its Alternatives. *Psychological Review 93* (2): 136.

Kahneman, D., and A. Tversky. 2002. Extensional Vs. Intuitive Reasoning: The Conjunction Fallacy in Probability Judgment. In *Heuristics and Biases: The Psychology of Intuitive Judgment*, ed. T. Gilovich, D. Griffin, and D. Kahneman. Cambridge University Press.

Keynes, J.M. 1936. *The General Theory of Employment, Interest and Money*. London: Macmillan.

Levine, D., ed. 2012. *Is Behavioral Economics Doomed?* Cambridge: Open Book Publishers.

Mallard, G. 2016. *Bounded Rationality and Behavioral Economics*. Routledge.

Malmendiery, U., and S. Nagelz. 2013. Learning from Inflation Experiences. *NBER and CEPR*.

Muth, John F. 1961. Rational Expectations and the Theory of Price Movements. *Econometrica* 29 (3): 315–335.

Nerlove, M. 1958. Adaptive Expectations and Cobweb Phenomena. *Quarterly Journal of Economics 72* (2): 227–240.

Phelps, E. 2008. Our Uncertain Economy. *Wall Street Journal*.

Ritholtz, B. 2011. Shiller: More Expectations Theory, Less Efficient Market Hypothesis. http://ritholtz.com/2011/06/shiller-more-expectations-theory-less-efficient-market-hypothesis/

Shackle, G. 1966. *The Nature of Economic Thought*. Cambridge University Press.

Shafer, G. 1976. *A Mathematical Theory of Evidence*. Princeton: Princeton University Press.

Soros, G. 2013. Fallibility, Reflexivity, and the Human Uncertainty Principle. *Journal of Economic Methodology 20* (4): 309–329.

Syll, L.P. 2012. David K. Levine is Totally Wrong on the Rational Expectations Hypothesis. *Real-World Economics Review Blog*. https://rwer.wordpress.com/2012/02/16/david-k-levine-is-totally-wrong-on-the-rational-expectations-hypothesis

Zadeh, L.A. 1978. Fuzzy Sets as a Basis for a Theory of Possibility. *Fuzzy Sets and Systems* 1 (1): 3–28.

7

Time and Preferences

Do I contradict myself?
Very well then I contradict myself
(I am large, I contain multitudes.)
—Walt Whitman, Song of Myself, section 51

OK, today I have just received as a gift, something I always dreamed about, but given its cost, I never resolved to buy: a white truffle. I like it a lot, especially grated over Piedmont tagliolini (sort of egg-rich fresh pasta thinner than fettuccine). And I know that I have to eat it within a week. So, when will I eat my truffle? Tonight? Or shall I delay my consumption, so that each day I will know that there is a white truffle waiting for me in the fridge? Which option gives me more pleasure?

This intertemporal choice is not trivial at all.

According to conventional economics, preferences are stable. (Un)fortunately, as shown below, real-world experiences tell us a different story, with preferences changing over time and not always in an orderly way. Could that be the result of the way in which we discount utility? Or are there different factors at work? One of the most important challenges

F. Ghisellini, B. Y. Chang, *Behavioral Economics*,
https://doi.org/10.1007/978-3-319-75205-1_7

highlighted by behavioral research relates to the fact that, in some contexts, people make choices that seem to conflict with earlier intentions. Is it possible to set up models that reconcile time-inconsistent preferences with "rational" decision-making?

Strange as it may seem, the matter of intertemporal choice has begun to be properly investigated less than 200 years ago. In 1834, the Scottish economist John Rae wrote *The Sociological Theory of Capital*, in which he stated that someone's time preferences are explained by his "effective desire of accumulation". This desire is in turn determined by four factors:

1. The bequest motive
2. Self-restraint
3. Uncertainty of human life
4. Excitement of immediate consumption

In particular, 1 and 2 favor accumulation, whereas 3 and 4 push in the opposite direction. But all four interact. If you live in a well-ordered system and have a reliable job, then 1 and 2 prevail, whereas volatile living conditions and prospects drive you toward immediate and often superfluous consumption.

In the decades after Rae's seminal work, intertemporal choice became very technical and was treated as a matter of efficiency. Jevons (1888) stated that if you keep constant over periods, the value given by the multiplication of each period's marginal utility of consumption and the probability of x% of the good remaining consumable will give you the optimal length of the period within which the good should be consumed.

Then came Paul Samuelson, who wrote a very influential paper entitled *A Note on the Measurement of Utility* (Samuelson 1936). His main finding was the discovery of the constant discount rate, that is, the rate that period after period reduces the utility of consuming a good X. So each period we have a different value for discounted utility. And the exercise in which the economic agent engages is that of maximizing the value given by the sum of all discounted utilities.

So there exists a discount function that assigns a weight to utility at every time period, because when an individual sacrifices consumption of money in the present in order to save it for the future, it is natural to assume that he takes into account the fact that money will yield an interest during this time.

Assume that my yearly income *Y* is partly spent for basic needs *N* and that leaves a residual *X* (no residuals are likely in the future). I have to decide whether to consume immediately *X* or postpone its consumption for two years, which is when I retire from work.

If at time 0 there is a two-year interest rate *R* and *I* invest *X* instead of consuming it, at time 2, I will have

$$X_2 = X_0 (1+r)^2$$

Which when inverted gives

$$X_0 = \frac{1}{(1+r)^2} X_2$$

Or more generally for period t

$$X_0 = D_t X_t$$

where $D_t = \dfrac{1}{(1+r)^t}$ is an exponential function.

Although Samuelson himself was skeptical of the real-world relevance of what he considered mainly a mathematical exercise,[1] the scientific community rapidly endorsed the model, mainly for a couple of very practical reasons:

- the discounted utility (DU) model is simple, tractable, and elegant in its formulation, and
- exponential discounting is the only discount function that guarantees dynamic consistency, that is, whatever the specific period he is in, an

individual sticks to his time preferences. Without exponential discounting, the fact that I prefer to receive $100 on Monday rather than $110 on Tuesday would NOT necessarily imply that I prefer to receive $100 on Wednesday rather than $110 on Thursday. So exponential discounting became the only model capable of ensuring rationality as defined by conventional economics.

As it is the case with many conventional economics tenets, however, exponential discounted utility (EDU) has proved handy, elegant, highly usable, BUT scarcely capable of explaining many instances of real-world decision-making.

To start with, there is no such thing as a stable discount factor. Frederick et al. (2002) show that D_t varies noticeably, across individuals and time, implying a discount rate ranging from −6% to infinity! Among possible reasons mentioned by the authors, the fact that uncertainty and the existence of utility functions are impacted by visceral factors. What is certain is that EDU has little empirical validity.

One of the most significant among the "anomalies" that EDU cannot explain has to do with the increased utility generated by the expectation of a pleasurable event and, speculatively, with the reduced utility generated by the immediate realization of a looming unpleasant event. In particular, Prelec and Lowenstein (1991) show that for given outcomes, people prefer to arrange them in such a way as to generate an improving sequence.

These outcomes are at odds with EDU. According to EDU, given that the present utility of future gains and losses is reduced via the discount rate and if one can choose temporal allocations, one will try to realize gains immediately and allocate losses in the most remote future possible.

Lowenstein and Thaler (1989) confirm these findings and introduce the concepts of "savoring" (utility of anticipating future pleasant events) and "dread" (get rid as soon as possible of certain unpleasant events).

The classical example has to do with kisses and electric shocks. Assume that you are absolutely certain within a week to receive:

- a kiss from your favorite movie star
- a moderate electric shock

The only choice you have is to allocate the two events in specific days within the week. Given that in EDU the future is discounted (i.e. future events—positive or negative impact less on utility), for an EDU person it would be natural to place the kiss in the first day and the shock in the last.

Unfortunately, empirical tests tend to give the opposite result. People prefer to receive the shock immediately and then live a few days enjoying the expectation of a wonderful kiss.

Generally speaking, the kiss-shock sequence issue challenges one of the very basic tenets of EDU: utility independence, by which the only factor that affects the distribution of utility across periods is discounting. So, net of discounting going from worst to best or the other way around should make no difference. But can it be true? Even if overall utility is the same, would you really be indifferent between an increasing and a decreasing wage dynamics?

Not only that.

First, if utility independence rules, then the past doesn't count when deciding on the future. So, if you prefer Italian food to Chinese food, you should always go for an Italian restaurant, irrespective of the fact that you just had pasta all'amatriciana, Parma ham, and parmigiana di melanzane the previous night. Is this realistic?

Second, utility independence implies the absence of any desire to spread consumption over time.

But assume you are a respondent to the following two questions:

(a) I am given the option to have dinner at an Italian restaurant once in the coming week. When shall I have it?
(b) I am given the option to have dinner at an Italian restaurant twice in the coming week. When shall I have them?

For question (a), it is likely that you choose to have your dinner in 4 or 5 days.

For question (b), you probably end up having your first dinner the following day and your second dinner at the end of the week, so that your consumption is spread as smoothly as possible over time.

It should be noted that recently the phenomenon of preference for improving sequences has been found to be less robust empirically than it

Table 7.1 Preferences and Sequences

Factors Favoring Deteriorating Sequences	Factors Favoring Flat Sequences	Factors Favoring Improving Sequences
Uncertainty on better outcomes actually occurring	Diminishing marginal utility of consumption	*Anticipatory utility*: Delaying the good extends the period of savoring and accelerating the bad reduces the period of dread
Desire to avoid an opportunity cost (so that excess outcomes can be reinvested)	Fairness in allocation among future "selves"	*Contrast effect*: Deferring the good minimizes the adaptation-level effect (by which a higher level of well-being becomes quickly the "normal")
Pure time preference (present-biased preferences)	Simple 1/*n* heuristic (if you have *n* alternatives, you just weigh them equally)	*Extrapolation*: Although the sequence is truncated, people may believe that the improvement scenario becomes permanent

was thought before. Frederick and Lowenstein (2008) first present a useful matrix of nine factors theoretically explaining the preference for sequences with different profiles (see Table 7.1).

Then they proceed to explain why the alleged empirical superiority of improving sequences claimed, among others, by Prelec and Lowenstein (1993), was mainly the result of restricting measurement practices to pre-set sequences differing in trend. In contrast, they find that when people are given the option of freely allocating outcomes among multiple periods, there is no prevalence of improving sequences. As an example, they mention the case in which people are told that they would suffer 30 intense headaches over the next 8 years and to indicate how they would allocate them over the years. In all, 27% of respondents preferred a declining sequence (fewer headaches in later years), 34% opted for the improving sequence, and 39%, the relative majority, chose a flat sequence, with headaches distributed evenly across years. Apparently, the main factor behind the preference for flat sequences is the simplest: the 1/*n* heuristic, by which you, given uncertainty, are reluctant to assume responsibility, and just go for equal allocations.

What is the truth then? Flat is preferred to improving, or the other way around? Apparently, there is no clear directional evidence. One thing is certain, however. The dispersion of preferred sequences is in any case a violation of the EDU model, as the constant (and positive) discount rate, which is a conceptual pillar of EDU, would command a systematic prevalence of deteriorating sequences (in an EDU model, you go for the good things first, as the present is discounted less than the future).

Can we say that all these deviations from EDU predictions represent "anomalies"? Of course not, as they are termed "anomalies" only by reference to a model that was accepted as a benchmark just because its main implication, that is, dynamic consistency, made things easily tractable, without regard to its descriptive validity.

But can we at least rescue dynamic consistency as a normative principle? In other words, would it be legitimate to argue that people should conform to their previous decisions? If this were the case, it would mean that we consider our previous "self" to be better and worthier of respect than our current self. On what grounds should we come to this conclusion? The answer to this question simply does not exist.

But the best documented "anomaly" for EDU has to do with the way in which people discount the future in the real world. When the intertemporal choice to be made is in the near future, they discount delays more heavily. EDU would predict that if the delay between two options is the same, then discounting would be the same, irrespective of when the choice is to be made. Still, many people prefer $100 now to $110 in a day, but very few people prefer $100 in 30 days to $110 in 31 days. And when 29 days have passed, they would reverse their preferences back to their preference to receiving immediately $100. Such "preference reversals" have been observed both in humans and in pigeons (Green et al. 1994).

This behavior can be generated by hyperbolic time discounting. Formally, in the simple formulation ("quasi-hyperbolic discounting") introduced by David Laibson (1997), the discount factor DF can be described as:

$$1 \text{ for } D\left(\text{delay from today}\right) = 0\left(\text{no discount}\right);$$

$$\alpha\beta^{D}$$

where α, β are parameters with a value higher than 0 and lower than 1 for $D > 0$.

A very important difference of this model from the conventional economic model is the addition of a present bias parameter (α) that works together with the conventional discount factor (β). Time-inconsistent preferences (present bias) occurs as $\alpha < 1$.

The following graph (drawn with $\alpha = 0.6$, $\beta = 0.8$) highlights the difference between conventional exponential discounting and hyperbolic discounting (see Fig. 7.1).

With hyperbolic discounting, people are more impatient in the very short term but exhibit greater patience than with exponential discounting in the long term. Thus, the extent to which the choice between two future rewards is discounted depends BOTH on the length of the delay and WHEN the choice occurs.

In the same vein, consider the following example, inspired by Akerlof (1991).

Suppose that if I begin exercising this month I would have an immediate benefit of −6 (i.e. a cost), and a future benefit of 10 which materializes

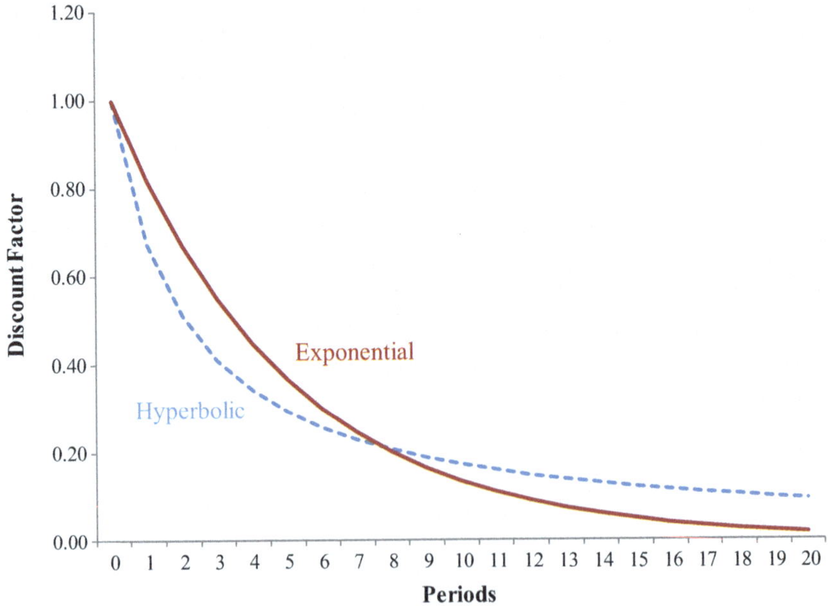

Fig. 7.1 Hyperbolic and Exponential Discounting

one month later, with a one-month delay discount factor of 0.4 and a two-month discount factor of 0.3.

Shall I begin to exercise immediately? My payoff would be

$$-6+0.4\times 10=-6+4<0$$

So the answer is negative.

Choose today to begin exercise next month? Yes, as

$$0.4\times(-6)+0.3\times 10=-0.24+0.3>0$$

But when next month arrives, the payoff I face would again be

$$-6+0.4\times 10=-6+4<0$$

So I'll put exercising off again.

Some researchers argue that hyperbolic discounting is the opposite of delayed gratification ("savoring"), so they cannot coexist in real-world behavior. But that needs not to be the case. Hyperbolic discounting predicates that, given an equal delay, people are more impatient in the short term than they are in the long term. Savoring tells us that anticipation of pleasure boosts utility, so the actual consumption of pleasure is delayed to a later stage—quite different concepts.

What is more interesting is the criticism of EDU scholars that hyperbolic discounting is "time inconsistent" because an optimal decision made at time t may no longer be optimal when reevaluated at a later stage.

The classical illustration of the concept has to do with problems of addiction and self-control. For example, just after enjoying a succulent pasta all'amatriciana we often feel guilty, and vow to forego all short-term food temptations in exchange for the greater long-term rewards of improved health. But when shall we start our healthier diet? Right now? The problem with immediate action is that at time zero, when we have to bear the "cost" (disutility) of giving up all the good things to eat, there is no discounting, so it really hurts. It looks like we'd rather postpone the

Fig. 7.2 Preference Reversal

plan and include it in New Year' resolutions. But when January 1 arrives, the problem looks as if it were exactly the same. May be we can put it off again just for a few months, until summertime? And so on.

Figure 7.2 gives a visual illustration of the phenomenon. Choices A and B become available in period 8 and 10, respectively. The *x*-axis shows the moment in which the two alternative choices are evaluated, and the *y*-axis shows the present value of the two choices. Initially, choice B is preferred, but as period 8 approaches, choice A gains in appeal and becomes the preferred one in period 7, just before it turns out to be available.

But where does hyperbolic discounting come from? Some, including Walther (2010), suggest that it originates from a nonlinear way of weighting probabilities. So, the role of uncertainty seems central.

But is there a consensus view on hyperbolic discounting? Hardly.

From a theoretical point of view, a recurring criticism is that hyperbolic discounting is efficient from a descriptive point of view, but lacks a psychological basis. In other words, the reasons why people should use the hyperbolic discounting process remain largely unexplained. But is that the case? If you subscribe to hyperbolic discounting, you can search psychological foundations in an evolutionary approach. Our ancestors would prefer to kill and eat the passing scrawny antelope immediately, even if they knew that if they spared it more antelopes would be available tomorrow.

And how robust is the empirical evidence for hyperbolic discounting?

Some would say that empirical evidence is strong not so much for hyperbolic discounting per se, but rather for preference reversals. This distinction is important as hyperbolic discounting is not the only theory generating preference reversal. According to Rubinstein (2003), preference reversal may simply be caused by the fact that people use a heuristic which measures and discounts delays "in percentage". Receiving a reward in 11 years rather than in 10 years is not a large percentage delay, so I would give more weight to the amount of the reward; receiving the same reward in 2 years rather than in one year, on the contrary, would really put my patience to the test.

Others[2] hold that the evidence for hyperbolic discounting does not rely solely on the preference reversal component.

Be that as it may, the preference reversal component of the theory is, however, extremely robust from an empirical point of view.

In this context, the most interesting question has to do with causality: can dynamic inconsistency be considered, rather than an "anomaly", or the result of a conflict, the norm in decision-making? And what if what is termed "inconsistency" is instead a completely different concept, defined by the way in which our mind actually works?

According to conventional economics, if somebody asks you whether you prefer beer or red wine, your answer should bind you in a consistent way to always prefer beer to red wine, or the other way around.

Assume that your good faith answer to the question is that you, generally speaking, prefer beer.

But the following day, when you are invited to an exclusive dinner in a French restaurant, you would not drink beer with your beef bourguignon, and rather have a more appropriate vintage Bordeaux.

You would also opt for wine if the following week you manage to date a beautiful girl for dinner, as the choice of wine is more likely to give her a positive impression of you.

Is this dynamic inconsistency? Or is it rather a question of context, so that people in different situations can have or use different preferences from the ones held or used previously?

As yet, mainstream behavioral economics does not provide an answer to these questions, and this is indeed one of the "unfinished businesses" to be fixed. But how?

Some would argue that much of the preference inconsistency phenomenon is simply due to "optical" factors: when we evaluate events/choices which are distant in time we do that in an abstract fashion, and can only appreciate the true relevance of the event/choice when the time for it becomes near (Soman et al. 2005).

An expanding strand of research points to the interaction between multiple selves. Thaler and Sunstein (2008), for example, envisage an individual "containing two semiautonomous selves" with different levels of "impatience". Note that the concept of multiple selves can be extended to incorporate setups in which a single person can switch from one state to another.

The crucial point to be specified, however, relates to the way in which either self (or state) takes the lead as a result of different circumstances.

Bernheim and Rangel (2004) suggest an explanation that bears some resemblance to the "System I and II" setup developed by Kahneman. Although the analysis takes place in the addiction context typical of drug and alcohol usage, it could be easily generalized. The explanation is simply that there are two distinct modes governing people's choices. Normally we decide in a "cold" mode, which allows us to evaluate costs and benefits rationally. The "hot" mode is triggered whenever the addictive option is offered: in that case people would choose it, whatever the longer-term consequences. This model is similar to those in which the utility function incorporates "visceral" factors such as the craving for tasty food, sex, and so forth.[3]

When experiencing a visceral state, people focus primarily on goals associated with their current state and downplay the importance of other goals. And typically they suffer from a "hot-cold" empathy gap, a bias which leads them to underestimate the extent to which visceral factors determine actual decision-making. What is also very interesting in the visceral model is that, on the one hand, the extent to which visceral preferences operate may be endogenous (if I had copious amounts of food yesterday, I will be less hungry today) and, on the other hand, the fact that the visceral state may be activated as the "temptation" date approaches.

Both these features can be useful in explaining preference reversal processes.

In all these cases, the switch from "self 1" to "self 2" is almost automatic, as it depends on the nature of the choice and/or the passing of time.

Thaler and Shefrin (1981) introduce the concept of conflicting selves. There is an altruistic planning self who cares about the long-term utility of all future selves, who in contrast are myopic doers just caring about their own short-term utility. So the planner can try to commit the doer to optimal choices (e.g. the planner can pay in advance for gym sessions), but eventually it is the doer who decides what to do. The overall result resembles that of a never ending bargaining process.

But is conflict between selves unavoidable? And are there just two selves, the "good" and the "bad"?

Kenrick and Griskevicius (2013) present a particularly promising version of the "multiple selves theory", which, rather than on conflict between patient and impatient doers, is based on "specialization".

According to this theory, inside our mind there are many "subselves", each with different preferences. Depending on the features of a specific situation/context, a particular "specialized" subself is summoned to express its particular preferences, which may be at odds with the preferences expressed only an hour ago in a different situation by a different subself.

And all this, once again, would have an evolutionary origin, linked to the crucial basic needs of our ancestors. Broadly speaking, these needs could be assembled in distinct groups:

(a) Self-protection against physical harm
(b) Self-protection against diseases
(c) Conquer (of a mate, of friends, of social status)
(d) Maintenance (of sex, friends, status, family)

For each group, preferences do change. So, if I am in a risky situation for my very existence, I will go for choices that are inspired by absolute loss aversion. But if, having just escaped danger (group (a)), I am confronted with a passing beautiful representative of the opposite sex, I will do everything—including maybe a risky session of bungee jumping—to get myself noticed (group (c)).

More generally:

- The self-protection subself against physical harm can be activated by all sorts of danger and typically pushes people to blend with the others. In financial markets, the self-protection subself can thus be activated by "bubble" situations, and may result in herding-like behavior. The self-protection subself against disease leads people to avoid contact by becoming more introverted and less tolerant of novelties.
- The conquer subself is often willing to take risks to attain mating and status. Above all, the status subself wants to be respected and needs self-affirmation. In many cases, many behaviors that appear quite innocent (including volunteering in helping the elderly) are in fact attempts to show off and to demonstrate one's value.
- The retention subself is activated by cues that celebrate or threaten a long-term relationship. And notice that such relationship need not be a family one. If you are a historical investor in company X and company X is about to engage in a capital increase exercise, the mate retention subself is likely to push you to participate in the exercise. Conquer is typically associated with a lower degree of risk aversion. But conquer and retention are of course related, as in both cases social status is definitely a target.

Think about what motivates people to engage in charitable activities.

Is it because of an altruistic motivation? Or do people just want to show off, as being nice and helping the others enhance a person's status? Both explanations can be true, the former as a proximate cause and the latter as an ultimate cause.

The general lesson is, however, that the conventional wisdom of CE (by which people at any point in time seek to maximize the same target variable, e.g., wealth) is not empirically robust. In sum, it seems that an appropriate description of the interplay between intertemporal choices and preferences cannot be reduced to finding the appropriate discount rate, even if we were to allow discount rates which vary over time as it is the case with hyperbolic discounting.

There is much more, given that not only discount rates but also preferences themselves are far from being univocal, and they seem to be functions of specific context we find ourselves in.

Depending on the context and therefore on which goal they currently have in mind, consciously or subconsciously, people will have very different preferences and make very different choices.

The question is: how to make sense of all this and develop a "satisficing" model capable of explaining why and how preferences may change over time?

Let's proceed in order. We have seen that empirically the DU model is not significantly supported, mainly because of the frequent occurrence of preference reversal. Shall we therefore just embrace the hyperbolic discounting model and get over with it? Not so simple. For one thing, there are other models (among others, the visceral factors model) which can generate preference reversal outcomes.

What is even more important, however, is that it is not always the case that preferences are reversed. Of course, that may be the result of preferences that are so strong that the passing of time has little effect on planned choices. But there might be reason to believe that preference dynamics respond to a variety of factors.

As highlighted in Frederick et al. (2002),[4] combining insights from different models could be very important to explain real-world phenomena: "For instance, a preference for improvement may interact with hyperbolic discounting to produce preferences for U-shaped sequences—for example, for jobs that offer a signing bonus and a salary that increases gradually over time".

In fact, the management of a choice based on a seemingly more general decision-making rule can be as demanding as those of different preferences arising from different models. In conventional economics, the *homo economicus* is an unbounded decision-maker, endowed with complete information, high computing capabilities, and no time constraints. Given the highly unrealistic nature of these assumptions, part of conventional economics research has turned to decision-making models characterized by constrained optimization. In these models, the agent behaves as the unbounded decision-maker as long as the costs of collecting additional information are smaller than related benefits. When costs become greater than benefits, the agent stops searching and decides on the basis of currently available information. This could seem more realistic, but actually it is not, as in order to accurately estimate the implied cost-benefit balance, the agent should have the same kind of informational and computing endowments which are associated with unconstrained optimization!

That is why real-world people use heuristics, that is, mental "shortcuts" that allow for quick decisions on the basis of limited information. And it is interesting to note that, although heuristics are "ecologically rational" (i.e. your best choice given the circumstances), some decision scientists continue to consider them as something most likely leading to second-best outcomes (Kiker et al. 2005).

In fact, the "fast and frugal heuristics" research program (Gigerenzer et al. 1999) is based on the logical premise that ignoring some information is the only way to have robust, efficient, and transparent decision mechanisms. It is robust because simplicity is the key to adapt to ever changing external circumstances. It is efficient because heuristics are quicker to use, and in this way allow us to save the most valuable resource in a competitive environment: time. And it is transparent because, given their simplicity, heuristics can be communicated and shared with everybody else. But are heuristics too naive to work? Surprisingly they are not.

Czerlinski et al. (1999) contrasted the predictions of heuristics about, inter alia, house prices with those arising from multiple linear regression models, and repeatedly found heuristic-based forecasts to be more accurate than those generated by sophisticated algorithms.

In the preference-shaping exercise we conduct here, the assumption for the sequence setup could be something similar to that associated with the "Take the best" heuristic.

The "Take the best" heuristic is a mental tool used when making a decision based on inferences about a situation (Gigerenzer and Goldstein 1996). Inferences are based upon criteria ("cues"), each of which has a specific weight. A decision-maker will tend to work his way down from the most important cue, to cue of lesser importance, whenever the most important cue does not yield a clear result, and stop after you find the first discriminating cue.

An example can help to understand how the "Take the best" heuristic works.

Consider the problem that I could have in choosing between restaurant A and restaurant B. May be I shouldn't, but among possible choice criteria ("cues"), I assign the highest value (0.9) to a TripAdvisor rating of 4 dots minimum IF the rating is supported by at least 500 reviews. The second most important cue for me is friends' advice, and in case the first two cues don't help me to sort the question out, my last criterion would be the results of a visual checking of the two restaurants.

Restaurant A has fewer than 4 dots from TripAdvisor, while the TripAdvisor criterion for restaurant B generates a verdict that can be classified as "unknown" (Restaurant B has four dots but fewer than 500 reviews). So I turn to the "Friends advice" criterion, and my search stops there (no need to go on and check the place) as friends recommend restaurant A and are in contrast negative on restaurant B (see Table 7.2).

The second constraint may have to do with the contents, that is, the selection of a theory as general as possible. In order to do so, one could use the conceptual common denominator in the multiple selves/states research, that is, the concept that preferences can be context-dependent.

In a "Take the best" context, the assumption could therefore be that whenever certain stimuli/contexts (let's call them "emotions" for short) are present, they prevail on any other considerations in determining preferences. If that is not the case, then people would choose on the basis of the prescriptions of hyperbolic discounting.

Table 7.2 Two Restaurants

		Restaurants	
	Cue Validity	A	B
Trip Advisor: 4 Dots with at least 500 Reviews	0.9	Negative	Unknown: <500 reviews
Friends' Advice	0.7	Positive	Negative
Place Checking	0.5		

There can, however, be situations in which the presence of emotions is not certain. As we shall see in what follows, in that case subjective probabilities may have a crucial role.

Again, things are likely to be clearer if we use an example.

And when it comes to hyperbolic discounting and procrastination, one of the most used examples is the gym situation we introduced earlier.

One month ago I decided to begin exercise this month, as the payoff of procrastinating looked like

$$0.4\times(-6)+0.3\times 10=-2.4+3>0$$

In the absence of different considerations, I would now tend to put exercise off again as today's payoff is $-6 + 0.4 \times 10 = -6 + 4 < 0$.

But what kind of different consideration could make me decide differently? The ideal candidate would relate to an emotion that is a sort of common denominator for the models based on multiple selves/state and on visceral factors AND can be relevant in the decision to begin physical exercise.

In order to find that common denominator, let's first have a look at a correspondence table between visceral factors and the "specializations" of multiple selves as defined in Kendrick-Griskevicius (2013). We can identify three main blocks (in descending order of importance).[5] Notice that while for the first two blocks correspondence is immediate, the third block represents more a causal relationship, as the reported emotions are usually associated with threatening or preservation of objects of maintenance (see Table 7.3).

In the gym case, block 2 could be extremely relevant, especially in its sex component.

More specifically, assume that just before I take my decision on the gym, I am told by a friend of mine that the pretty girl I spotted a couple of days ago might be going to the same gym. If after investigation and that turned out to be the case, of course I would forget about hyperbolic discounting and join the gym immediately!

Say that in this case a simplified "Take the best" structure could look like this (see Table 7.4).

Table 7.3 Visceral Factors and Multiple Selves

	Visceral Factors	Multiple Selves
1	Somatic Factors (e.g. pain/avoidance of pain, disease/avoidance of disease) and Survival Drives (e.g. hunger/ avoidance of hunger)	Self-protection against harm and disease
2	Social Drives (e.g. sex)	Conquer (of sex, of a mate, of friends, of status)
3	Emotions (e.g. anger, fear, well-being)	Maintenance (of sex, of friends, of status, of family)

Table 7.4 The Gym and the Pretty Girl

	Cue Validity
Pretty Girl at the Gym	0.8
Hyperbolic Discounting	0.4

- *Scenario 1*: It is certain that the pretty girl is going to the gym. Search stops there. I am going as well, so there would not be any preference reversal with respect the decision I took last month on the basis of hyperbolic discounting.
- *Scenario 2*: Not sure that the pretty girl is going. In this case I can decide on the basis of λ $(0 < \lambda < 1)$, my prior probability that the pretty girl would be there, weighting it with the relative importance I assign to cues. So if $\lambda \times 0.8 > (1 - \lambda) \times 0.4$, I would still go.
- *Scenario 3*. The pretty girl is definitely not going. In this case, normal hyperbolic discounting would apply, and I will continue to procrastinate.

Overall, this example is thus representative of the combination of insights from different models advocated by Camerer et al. (2004) in order to investigate further preference dynamics and the non-systematic occurrence of preference reversal. In addition, as to avoid indeterminacy of results, the mechanism described is hierarchical and sequential (hyperbolic discounting operates as a "reserve" model, whenever the visceral/multiple selves model is not in a condition to determine preferences).

Are we bound for theories that, unlike exponential discounted utility, are so complex that they become intractable? This is a very important aspect, and precisely in order to minimize this risk in the example given, we have made recourse to the "Take the best" heuristic, one of the simplest real-world decision-making tool. Of course a higher level of generality may require the adoption of more sophisticated model frameworks. But the fact that solving one puzzle opens the door to even more complicated questions is precisely what makes research so important.

Notes

1. "The idea that such a [mathematical] investigation could have any influence upon ethical judgments of policy is one which deserves the impatience of modern economists" (Samuelson 1937).
2. Cf., for example, DellaVigna (2009).
3. Cf. in particular Loewenstein (2000).
4. Camerer et al. (2004).
5. In the table we do not consider "pathological" factors, such as drug addiction.

References

Akerlof, G. 1991. Procrastination and Obedience. *American Economic Review 81* (2): 1–19.

Bernheim, B., and A. Rangel. 2004. Addiction and Cue-Triggered Decision Processes. *American Economic Review 94* (5): 1558–1590.

Camerer, C., et al. 2004. Time Discounting and Time Preference: A Critical Review. In *Advances in Behavioral Economics*. Princeton University Press.

Czerlinski, J., G. Gigerenzer, and D. Goldstein. 1999. How Good are Simple Heuristics? In *Simple Heuristics that Make Us Smart*, ed. G. Gigerenzer and P.M. Todd. New York: Oxford University Press.

DellaVigna, S. 2009. Psychology and Economics: Evidence from the Field. *Journal of Economic Literature 47* (2): 315–372.

Frederick, S., and G. Lowenstein. 2008. Conflicting Motives in Evaluations of Sequences. *Journal of Risk 37* (2–3): 221–235.

Frederick, S., G. Loewenstein, and T. O'Donoghue. 2002. Time Discounting and Time Preference: A Critical Review. *Journal of Economic Literature 40* (2): 351–401.

Gigerenzer, G., and D.G. Goldstein. 1996. Reasoning the Fast and Frugal Way: Models of Bounded Rationality. *Psychological Review 103* (4): 650.

Gigerenzer, G., P. Todd, and the ABC Research Group. 1999. *Simple Heuristics That Make US Smart*. New York: Oxford University Press.

Green, L., N. Fristoe, and J. Myerson. 1994. Temporal Discounting and Preference Reversals in Choice between Delayed Outcomes. *Journal of Psychonomic Bulletin & Review 1* (3): 383–389.

Jevons, W.S. 1888. *The Theory of Political Economy*. London: Macmillan.

Kenrick, D.T., and V. Griskevicius. 2013. *The Rational Animal*. New York, NY: Basic Books.

Kiker, G.A., et al. 2005. Application of Multicriteria Decision Analysis in Environmental Decision Making. *Integrated Environmental Assessment and Management 1* (2): 95–108.

Laibson, D. 1997. Golden Eggs and Hyperbolic Discounting. *Quarterly Journal of Economics 112* (2): 443–478.

Loewenstein, G. 2000. Emotions in Economic Theory and Economic Behavior. *AEA Papers and Proceedings*.

Lowenstein, G., and R.H. Thaler. 1989. Anomalies in Intertemporal Choice. *Journal of Economic Perspectives 3* (4): 181–193.

Prelec, D., and G. Lowenstein. 1991. Decision Making over Time and under Uncertainty: A Common Approach. *Management Science 37* (7): 770–786.

———. 1993. Preference for Sequences of Outcomes. *Psychological Review 100* (1): 91.

Rubinstein, A. 2003. Economics and Psychology? The Case of Hyperbolic Discounting. *International Economic Review 44* (4): 1207–1216.

Samuelson, P. 1936. A Note on Measurement of Utility. *Review of Economic Studies* 4 (2): 155–161.

———. 1937. A Note on the Measurement of Utility. *Review of Economic Studies*.

Soman, D., et al. 2005. The Psychology of Intertemporal Discounting: Why are Distant Events Valued Differently from Proximal Ones? *Marketing Letters Springer 16* (3–4): 347–360.

Thaler, R.H., and C.R. Sunstein. 2008. *Nudge: Improving Decisions about Health, Wealth, and Happiness*. New Haven, CT: Yale University Press.

Thaler, R.H., and H.M. Shefrin. 1981. An Economic Theory of Self Control. *Journal of Political Economy*.

Walther, H. 2010. Anomalies in Intertemporal Choice, Time-Dependent Uncertainty and Expected Utility—A Common Approach. *Journal of Economic Psychology 31* (1): 114–130.

8

Rationality: An Inferiority Complex?

8.1 The (Almost) Unchallenged Dominance of Conventional Rationality in Behavioral Economics

In Chap. 3, we highlighted the apparently fierce debate between the "American" school and the "German" school on whether real-world decision-making can be considered rational. The "Americans", with their long list of biases, would have a fairly negative view on that: many—if not most—human decisions are to an extent irrational. In contrast, the "German" school would argue that what counts is "ecological" rationality; that is, apparently irrational choices (like those driven by heuristic rules) can turn out to be completely rational if appraised in the context of the particular environment in which those choices are made.

Different views, but with an important feature in common: the crucial importance of rationality as a yardstick against which decisions are to be evaluated. Then the questions to be answered are at least two:

- What does behavioral economists mean by rationality?
- Should rationality be the most important element in human decision-making?

F. Ghisellini, B. Y. Chang, *Behavioral Economics*,
https://doi.org/10.1007/978-3-319-75205-1_8

As in this section we focus on the first question, we would begin by searching the definition of rationality in Kahneman's influential books and papers.

Most of the times Kahneman doesn't really define rationality directly, though within each individual work, he usually defines what rational action would be for that case. For example, in a paper about how individuals are biased when making forecasts, he explains what a rational, unbiased forecast would look like by contrast. However, there is one instance in which rationality is defined directly. It is a famous paper written with Amos Tversky (Kahneman and Tversky 1981), opening by the following statement:

> The definition of rationality has been much debated, but there is general agreement that rational choices should satisfy some elementary requirements of consistency and coherence. In this article we describe decision problems in which people systematically violate the requirements of consistency and coherence, and we trace these violations to the psychological principles that govern the perception of decision problems and the evaluation of options.

Consistency? Coherence? Aren't those the requirements of rational choice theory, the cornerstone of conventional economics, by which if you prefer A to B, and B to C, then you are bound to prefer A to C? They are. So rationality for the "Americans" is very much the same as it was for the conventional economists. As noted in a recent paper (Buturovic and Tasic 2015):

> *By using rational choice as a normative standard against which errors and biases are identified, Kahneman et al. reinforce rather than undermine the rational choice framework. Keeping in mind that Kahneman's work is widely regarded as the greatest challenge to standard neoclassical economics today, it is paradoxical that his work is so deeply rooted in the same neoclassical version of rationality that he outwardly opposes.*

Ok then, but what about the "Germans"? One of the most complete treatments of the kind of rationality that should be relevant to decision-making is in a research produced in 2001 (Gigerenzer and Selten 2001):

Traditional definitions of rationality are concerned with the internal order of beliefs and inference, such as consistency. The notion of ecological rationality, by contrast, is not concerned with internal criteria. The question of ecological rationality concerns the match between a strategy and an environment. … Heuristics that are matched to particular environments allow agents to be ecologically rational, making adaptive decisions that combine accuracy with speed and frugality. The degree to which a match exists (e.g., the cues in the environment may only be approximately non-compensatory) determines how accurate a heuristic is. ….

Given that simple heuristics tend to be more robust when environments are noisy and information is scarce (see below), one-reason decision making can actually become more accurate than regression…….. To summarize, the reasonableness of models of bounded rationality derives from their ecological rationality, not from coherence or an internal consistency of choices. A strategy is ecologically rational to the degree that it is adapted to the information in an environment, whether the environment is physical or social.

Basically, this quote tells us that what counts in decision-making in an uncertain world is not the respect of some abstract logical criteria, but rather the final result in terms of "accuracy". But accuracy with respect to what target?

The target is the same of conventional economics, that is, utility maximization. The only difference is that when in uncertainty, rationality need not be obeyed.

But what if, instead of uncertainty, we have risk? Risk, according to Knight (1921), refers to a situation of perfect knowledge: the decision-maker knows the probabilities of all outcomes for all alternatives. This makes it possible to calculate the only correct, or optimal, response. Uncertainty, in contrast, refers to situations where probabilities are unknown or unknowable.

In his Introduction to the *Behavioral Economics Guide 2016* (http://www.Behavioraleconomics.com/BEGuide2016.pdf), Gigerenzer writes:

Under risk, it pays to fine-tune an algorithm to the past sample of available data because the world is known and stable, meaning that the future is like the past. Under uncertainty, where the future cannot be easily foretold, too much fine-tuning on the basis of past data can produce greatly distorted results because it entails "overfitting" the past. The Pareto/NBD model illustrates this danger.

> *The important point is that when dealing with risk one should rely on probability theory and optimize; with uncertainty one should rely on heuristics and simplify.*

So Gigerenzer says that, whenever we face (what we think is) risk, we should optimize. But how? Gigerenzer and Volz (2012) tell us that

> *claims that the rational brain always works by Bayesian calculations are founded on the assumption that what is rational in a world of risk is also rational in an uncertain world—the world our brain has to deal with most of the time. … Bayesian inference works in small worlds where there are reliable data for probabilities and only a few alternatives and cues.*

And what is more rational than Bayesian learning?

In Bayesian learning, you choose a prior probability distribution on the set of all possible worlds. Then, after observing some event, adopt a new probability distribution called posterior probability distribution. Henceforth, use the posterior probabilities for predictions and decision-making. Repeat ad infinitum. Any further observation leads to further conditioning. The posterior probabilities at one stage serve as prior probabilities at the next. As a matter of fact, Bayesian updating is generally considered to be the only rational approach to learning once one has a prior.

So the tool choice method predicated by Gigerenzer seems pretty clear: it is "conventional" optimization for quantifiable risk and heuristics for uncertainty.

One important question is the following, however: out of clearly "uncertain" environments in which statistical tools are of no help, can we always tell FOR SURE when "*the world is known and stable, meaning that the future is like the past*"? Or is it not often the case that, given our limited knowledge set, we easily mistake risk for uncertainty? In other words, it may well be that in certain situations there are empirical regularities that could be estimated ("risk") but we simply are not aware of them; hence we think that we are in an "uncertain" environment, and use heuristics instead of optimization techniques.

Maybe then further reflection on this point is needed?

8.2 Unconventional Rationality and Unconventional Utility Functions

We already hinted about the reasons why, in spite of an anticonventional image, Daniel Kahneman is fully aligned with the conventional definition of rationality. As aptly reported by Buturovic and Tasic,[1] an undisputable proof of this alignment is given in his bestseller *Thinking, Fast and Slow*:

> *Kahneman begins by informing us that while people are good intuitive grammarians, they are intuitively bad statisticians.*
>
> *Whereas even four-year-olds routinely follow the rules of grammar as they speak, educated adults fail at questions that involve what Kahneman and his colleagues assume are elementary statistical reasoning skills.*
>
> *Before examining the evidence for people's statistical incompetence, one must stop and wonder about the aptness of the comparison between grammar and statistics. … Stating that people are good or bad at statistical reasoning tells us something about their knowledge of and talent for this particular skill and not much else. A passionate physicist without much interest in the outside world could observe that people are very good at manipulating objects but embarrassingly inept at solving problems in theoretical mechanics. Few of us would treat such a statement as evidence that people should gain more knowledge of theoretical mechanics or that they are irrational.*

So, the conventional economics definition of rationality accepted by Kahneman is flawed, as it contains irrelevant elements (why would the knowledge of statistics be a prerequisite for being rational?).

Not only that.

The conventional definition of rationality fits perfectly with the famous Oscar Wilde's quote: "*A cynic is a man who knows the price of everything, and the value of nothing*".

As reported by Buturovic and Savic, the concept is illustrated beyond any reasonable doubt by the "revolutionary" Kahneman when he explains the so-called endowment effect" through the story of Professor R. The Professor buys a bottle of vintage wine at an auction for a price X, and would not sell it unless the bid was higher than X. In Kahneman's view, this means that Professor R is dominated by a bias, and Richard Thaler defines this behavior as "not rational". Neither considers for a second that Professor R is not a profit maximizer: he collects wine for pleasure, and his collection would not be complete without the bottle just bought.

But there is more.

To start with, conventional rationality is meant to be "objective" (i.e. based on consensus data and information), whereas the kind of rationality used in "private" decisions is highly "subjective".

To appreciate the difference, the following example, taken again from Gilboa (2015), may be useful.

> *Assume that I'm a juror on a murder case. The defendant, Mr. A, is accused of having murdered his girlfriend. There is something very troubling about the behavior of the guy in court. He seems to be sneering and the tone of his voice makes me believe that he's a psychopath. However, considering all evidence, including a psychologist's expert testimony, Mr. A's lawyer makes a very convincing case that guilt has not been established beyond a reasonable doubt. Together with the other jurors, I find myself voting for acquittal. As I come home, I see my 20-year-old girl dressing up.*
>
> *Asking her about her plans, she says she has a date with no other than Mr. A. No way, honey, I reply, nothing of the kind is going to happen.*
>
> *Assuming that my daughter and I are a single decision maker (and that she needs my advice), my decision about the date differs from my voting decision in court. In court, I try to be objective. I attempt to put aside all my hunches and the distrust I feel for the guy, and base my vote on what I believe can be said to be objectively established. However, when I make a decision for myself (or my daughter), I do wish to use all sources of information, including my intuition, even if it cannot be proved.*

Am I irrational?

Of course not. Because, given that my overriding goal is to protect the safety of my daughter (I also want her to have fun, but not when risk is excessive), I think that overall I took the best decision in order to reach my goal.

According to Herbert Simon (1945), "*Behavior is purposive in so far as it is guided by general goals or objectives; it is rational in so far as it selects alternatives which are conducive to the achievement of the previously selected goals*". And given that there cannot be any external authority charged with the task of assessing whether the alternative selected is "*conducive to the achievement of the previously selected goals*", to the extent that I am genuinely convinced that I have done the right thing, I am rational (no need for statistics!).

And what, in turn, does "doing the right thing" mean? Is there a universal definition for it?

Neoclassical economists (and the "American" behavioral school) thought that the answer was positive, and that the "right thing" was wealth maximization. But there is growing evidence that this approach fails to incorporate the complexity and the width of real-world "utility functions" (in Simon's words "previously selected goals").

And if my "utility function" is subjective and incorporates variables which, unlike wealth, may or may not be measured in an objective way, how can someone claim the right to judge whether I am rational or not?

In conventional economics, the individual has a utility function in which costs are to be minimized while benefits should be maximized. And costs and benefits are usually expressed with reference to income or financial wealth. But why should it be so?

Hirschauer et al. (2015) highlight the fact that "*an individual may enjoy—besides consumption—leisure, low stress levels, and a supportive, non-competitive work place environment*".

That is, he/she may have a multidimensional goal system that is very different from a narrow-minded *homo economicus* who exclusively maximizes income. Making the choices that would be rational for the so-defined *homo economicus* will not maximize the utility of the multiple-goal individual.

Contrasting the term "externality," the disregard of negative linkages between the individual's multiple utility components has been coined "internality" by Frank (1999).

To be more precise, acting like *homo economicus*, while in fact having a multidimensional goal system, is the result of two kinds of bounded rationality. The first error arises if the correlations between different utility sources are ignored. High incomes, for instance, are often correlated with high stress levels and little time for leisure and family. Consequently, the net increase of utility achieved by a higher income is either much less than what has been previously assumed, or—depending on the strength of the correlation—it may even be zero or become negative. In line with expected utility theory, increasing risks (e.g. job insecurity, environmental uncertainties) constitute an additional reason why an increase of income levels may do little to foster average happiness. The second error arises when people ignore the fact that their "tastes" will change over time. "Changing tastes" refers to the fact that, even if all correlations are considered correctly, people's relative evaluation of different outcomes, such as income and leisure, may change over time and/or as a consequence of their choices.

What if either costs or benefits (or both) are not financial, but rather associated with emotional well-being? Let's make an (admittedly extreme) example. Assume that I am an investor, and my utility function is such that:

- my benefits derive essentially from "feeling good socially" (in the family, with colleagues, etc.) at the very moment in which I take a specific decision, irrespective of future financial implications;
- conversely, in my costs, social exclusion weighs much more than financial losses.

The investment implications of such a utility function are likely to generate what is considered by "American" scholars a biased behavior: "herding". I will tend to replicate the investment choices of people in my community, with of course no need for statistical analysis and information search. Would that be irrational? Not if I subscribe to Simon's definition of rationality, that is, if I think that buying the same asset people have bought is actually "*conducive to the achievement of the previously selected goals*" (feeling good socially and minimize the risk of exclusion).

The fact—the kind of utility that may not be associated with a poor proxy like wealth, but rather with the "real thing", that is, well-being or happiness—is not new. Already in the nineteenth century, the English philosopher Jeremy Bentham (1789) stated that

> *Nature has placed mankind under the governance of two sovereign masters, pain and pleasure. It is for them alone to point out what we ought to do, as well*

as to determine what we shall do.... They govern us in all we do, in all we say, in all we think.

Bentham therefore equates utility with pleasure and disutility with pain—a utility function theory later referred to as hedonism or hedonic psychology (Kahneman et al. 1999). Conventional economics has often rejected the hypothesis that happiness (or well-being) can be equated with utility.

In particular, the utilitarian concept, as proposed by Bentham, has been replaced in consumer theory by a reductionist behaviorist concept which assumes that we can only observe what people do. Thus, utility is a reflection of people's choices; happiness is a reflection of people's feelings. As artificial as this distinction may be, recent research has, however, established a functional link between happiness and utility. In particular, Kimball and Willis (2006) distinguish lifetime utility and current affect ("happiness") as follows:

- Lifetime utility is the extent to which people get what they want, where they want is indicated by their choices (where choices include noneconomic goods like freedom, ecology, satisfying social and love relationships, etc.). The economic goods component of lifetime utility is the standard welfare measure in CEF, and represents the discounted sum over time of "flow utility".
- Current affect is how positive people's feelings are at a given time.

The functional form which links utility and happiness is identified in the following one:

Affect = *baseline mood* + *elation*

where elation is short-run happiness—which depends on recent news about lifetime utility; baseline mood is long-run happiness. So, utility and happiness are connected in two ways: on the one hand, long-run happiness (baseline mood) is an argument of the flow utility function; on the other hand, short-run happiness (elation) depends on news about lifetime utility.

Of course the direct or indirect inclusion of noneconomic components in the individual's utility function makes it even more difficult to conceptually justify objective tests of rationality.

In turn, such objective tests become even harder to justify given that, if subjective well-being is in or linked to utility functions, then this opens the door to a potentially devastating (for CE) second-order effect. The point here is that subjective well-being depends not only on actual facts, but also on the way in which facts are perceived, that is, by the emotions that facts are generated.

And this begs the question: how do we know that humans are motivated, consciously or otherwise, to be rational?

Before we even approach this million-dollar question, let's start from how emotions can be defined. Oatley and Jenkins (1996) suggest this three-part definition:

1. An emotion is usually caused by a person, consciously or unconsciously, evaluating an event as relevant to a concern (a goal) that is important; the emotion is felt as positive when a concern is advanced and negative when a concern is impeded.
2. The core of an emotion is readiness to act and the prompting of plans; an emotion gives priority for one or a few kinds of action to which it gives a sense of urgency—so it can interrupt, or compete with, alternative mental processes or actions. Different types of readiness create different perceived relationships and opportunities with others.
3. An emotion is usually experienced as a distinctive type of mental state, sometimes accompanied by or followed by bodily changes, expressions, and actions.

The role of emotions in decision-making is still to be completely explored.

However, they seem to be important in explaining what conventional (and "American" behavioral) economists would define "violations of rationality". Take loss aversion, as explored by prospect theory. One hypothesis is that a loss gives rise to emotions that have greater negative intensity, such as fear, embarrassment, dread, and threatened loss of control, relative to positive emotions. Likewise, one explanation for the endowment effect could be that ownership acquires a greater emotional significance in defining and displaying our claimed status and social identity to others. This is the reason why we would never sell our bottle of vintage wine at the same price we bought it.

And how about emotions related to interpersonal comparison? Mui (1995) tells the story of a Chinese villager who was very popular in the community until he became rich through a series of well-done businesses. Then envy stepped in, and his property was destroyed by neighbors.

The reason was that the businessman's resource endowment (or utility level) was an argument in fellow villagers' utility function, so envy was, formally, a type of negative externality.

The existence of interpersonal emotions in the utility function adds to the inadequacy of individualistic utility function specified in most economic models. As a matter of fact, the personal significance of events is bound to change if the context in which such events take place change. This is where, for example, fairness and equity play a role. There are many cases in which a person would be happier to receive a small bonus, if the bonus is bigger than that granted to colleagues, than to get the same bonus as others.

The fundamental question is then the following: is it possible to imagine a theoretical setup which incorporates all the complexities of real-world decision-making AND remains tractable from an analytical point of view?

There have been a series of attempts in that direction. An interesting one is the research by Parada Daza (2004), which postulates the existence of an emotional well-being utility function. Basically, a hypothesis develops from other families of functions, with the utility function being a borderline or extreme solution (mathematically, the outer envelope function, with another utility function serving as the inner envelope function). A new function, called emotional well-being, develops between these envelope functions. Emotional well-being describes a behavioral mix between the rational economic individual and the individual who does not follow this norm.

The newly developed function gives a framework in which to understand this behavior, from which, obviously, the functioning of purely economic rationality does not escape. Nevertheless, purely economic rationality is always implicit in the analysis, since the actions are carried out between a band of two economic utility functions. The function shows emotional well-being to lie between a maximum that coincides with the economic maximum and a minimum level of emotional acceptance defined as a satisfaction minimum.

Notes

1. Cf. Kahneman and Tversky (1981).

References

Bentham, J. 1789. An Introduction to the Principles of Morals and Legislation. Oxford Clarendon Press.

Buturovic, Z., and S. Tasic. 2015. Kahneman's Failed Revolution Against Economic Orthodoxy. *Critical Review* 27 (2): 127–145.

Daza, P.J.R. 2004. The Utility Function and the Emotional Well-Being Function. *Journal of Business Ethics and Organization Studies.*

Frank, R. 1999. *Luxury Fever: Money and Happiness in an Era of Excess*. New York: Free Press.

Gigerenzer, G., and R. Selten. 2001. *Bounded Rationality: The Adaptive Toolbox*. Dahleme Workshops.

Gigerenzer, G., and K.G. Volz. 2012. Cognitive Processes in Decisions under Risk are not the Same as in Decisions under Uncertainty. *Frontiers in Neuroscience* 6: 105.

Gilboa, I. 2015. Rationality and the Bayesian Paradigm. *Journal of Economic Methodology* 22 (3): 312–334.

Hirschauer, N., M. Lehberger, and O. Musshoff. 2015. Happiness and Utility in Economic Thought—Or: What Can We Learn From Happiness Research for Public Policy Analysis and Public Policy Making? *Social Indicators Research* 121 (3): 647–674.

Kahneman, D., E. Diener, and N. Schwarz, eds. 1999. *Well-Being: Foundations of Hedonic Psychology*, 3–25. New York: Russell Sage Foundation Press.

Kahneman, D., and A. Tversky. 1981. The Framing of Decisions and the Psychology of Choice. *Science* 211 (4481): 453–458.

Kimball, M., and R. Willis. 2006. *Utility and Happiness.* LSE Papers.

Knight, F.H. 1921. *Risk, Uncertainty, and Profit*. Hart and Schaffner.
Mui, V.L. 1995. The Economics of Envy. *Journal of Economic Behavior & Organization* 26 (3): 311–336.
Oatley, K., and J. Jenkins. 1996. *Understanding Emotions*. Oxford: Blackwell.
Simon, H.S. 1945. *Administrative Behavior: A Study of Decision-Making Processes in Administrative Organization*. New York: The Free Press.

9

The Problem with Behavioral Finance

9.1 The Easy Victory of Behavioral Over Conventional Finance

Perhaps it is not by chance that the fallacies of conventional economics/finance are especially apparent when it comes to money management. And for good reasons, as there are plenty of statistics and market data recording what real-world investors actually do, as opposed to what they are supposed to do.

Within the basic framework of conventional economics, built upon Bernouilli's decreasing marginal utility of money and hence risk aversion, people would never buy a lottery ticket. Why on earth would you spend a dollar just to have one probability over a million of winning 1000 dollars? That's not rational. But you would be even more irrational if, just after you bought your lottery ticket, you bought a home insurance against earthquakes (and you don't live in risky areas like California). Because you would make the opposite mistake, as each year you would be required to pay a non-negligible amount of money for protection against a very remote event.

But that is what many people actually do (Friedman and Savage 1948)!

F. Ghisellini, B. Y. Chang, *Behavioral Economics*,
https://doi.org/10.1007/978-3-319-75205-1_9

So, people don't really follow the conventional mean-variance approach first developed by Markowitz (1952). In the mean-variance world, investors:

- are always risk-averse, irrespective of whether they are evaluating gains or losses;
- care only about wealth levels, irrespective of whether the achievement of a specific wealth level implies a big or a small change;
- use objective probabilities and statistics. This is why in maximizing return, they mainly care about expected values (mean) subject to risk containment at a given level (variance). Risk is equated to volatility, irrespective of whether deviations from the mean generate gains or losses.

A basic precondition for mean-variance optimization is thus portfolio diversification (i.e. selection of uncorrelated assets).

All these three basic tenets were severely questioned by Kahneman and Tversky's prospect theory (1979), by which investors:

- are willing to take risks when this implies avoiding a sure loss, while they remain risk-averse when considering alternative gain prospects
- evaluate gains and losses with respect to a specific initial reference point
- overweigh low probabilities, both for gains (lotteries) and for losses (insurance). Rather than risk-averse, they are loss-averse (i.e. volatility in itself is not a problem)

In general, portfolio diversification is thus not a prerequisite for asset selection. It is more so because of investment rules generated by mental accounting. In behavioral finance, mental accounting—which is typically considered a bias, that is, a distortion of the decision-making process—refers to the fact that, contrary to what is posited by conventional finance, people do not consider money to be fungible. Sometimes it is the origin of money that determines its allocation: it is more likely that I buy 100 dollars of champagne with the 100 dollars just won with the lottery rather than with the 100 dollars I usually manage to save each month out of my wage. In investing, different mental accounts form the layers of a pyramid. The base layer is targeted to finance the most basic needs (food, housing, etc.). But if the base layer is labeled "security", how many other layers are there? It depends on how articulated mental accounting is. For illustrative purposes, the case is often made for three levels (from bottom to top), which, as interpreted by Lopes (1987), can be identified as targeted to:

1. *security*, that is, the satisfaction of most elemental needs. Given this, no loss can be accepted, so money allocated to this layer has to be invested in liquid and risk-free assets (e.g. savings)
2. *potential*, that is, the hope to increase current wealth by accepting a limited level of risk. In practice, money is allocated to market instruments such as CDs, government or high-grade corporate bonds. It is important to underline, however, that in Lopes' view, survival and potential could also be considered as a single composite layer, where allocations vary depending on individual loss aversion.
3. *aspiration*, that is, pure risk-taking targeted to a radical change in wealth. Apart from lottery tickets, money is invested in highly speculative instruments (e.g. high yields or derivatives).

Behavioral portfolio theory, as fully described by Shefrin-Statman (2000), is really the product of a combination of mental accounting (which provides the basis for a layered pyramid-like asset allocation) and prospect theory (which determines the way in which the pyramid is built and investors behave). In particular, crucial importance attached to the following features of prospect theory, which explains why typically investors hold on to "losers" while quickly selling "winners":

- overweighting of low probabilities (it determines the simultaneous presence of "insurance" in the base layer and "lottery" in the aspiration layer of the pyramid)
- reference point (most of the times, it is the initial purchasing price of an asset, against which to measure loss prospects)

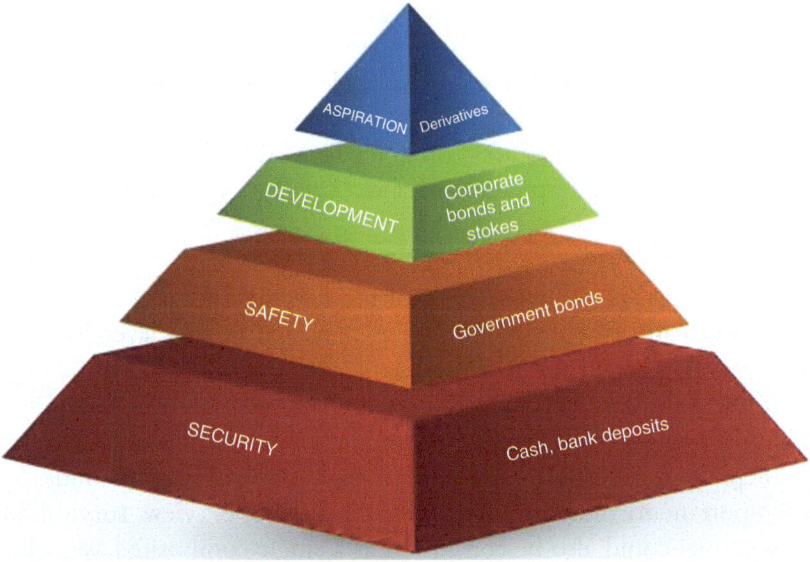

Fig. 9.1 Behavioral Investment Theory: A Four-Layer Pyramid

Behavioral finance has shown that real-world investors use different mental accounts, similar to the layers of a pyramid. The number of layers can vary, but roughly speaking (see Fig. 9.1).

- the base is meant to satisfy basic needs, and thus the funds allocated therein cannot be exposed to any risk; hence, the base portfolio contains only risk-free assets.
- the intermediate layer incorporates income-generating assets.
- the (risky) top layer holds lottery-like speculative assets that can potentially perform in a life-changing fashion.

Through several empirical tests, it has been clearly shown that behavioral finance describes reality much better than conventional finance does. In particular, the following are now clear:

(A) For most individuals the pain for a loss is greater than the pleasure of an equivalent profit. In other words, the disutility of one-unit loss is significantly larger than the utility of one-unit gain. The concept of loss aversion was already present inside the prospect theory proposed by Kahneman and Tversky in 1979. In particular, they showed that losses are weighted about twice as heavily as gains and that subjects are risk lovers in the region of losses. Loss aversion could thus lead investors to make opposite choices if alternatives are presented as a loss rather than as lower profits. It makes individuals less prone to invest in equity (Barberis et al. 2006), because subjects require a higher risk premium for investing in stocks. Loss aversion is a powerful driver, because it is innate in the human nature. In fact, it is a common feeling not only among investors, but also among primates. In 2006, Chen et al. (2006) made an experiment with monkeys. They gave one apple in one of these two ways: (i) they just got one apple, or (ii) they got two apples and then one was taken away. In the second case, where an apple was taken away, monkeys showed hate with respect to the server. They were thus loss-averse; it derives that emotionally one apple is not equal to two apples minus one. Money is not fungible.

(B) If loss aversion is the tendency to weigh more losses than gains, mental accounting is the individuals' tendency to divide their investments (and their expenses) in several portfolios and manage those accounts separately, depending, for example, on the function of each account (among others, Thaler 1999). According to Benartzi and Thaler (1995), under the mental accounting assumptions, investors also tend to evaluate the performance of their investments over a short time horizon. Therefore, mental accounting makes investors myopic, in contrast to the traditional theory, which targets maximization of returns over a long-term period. Since this first study, other researchers have confirmed the presence of myopic loss aversion among investors.

But are there immediate implications of (A) and (B) for portfolio allocation techniques vis-à-vis portfolio allocation as predicted by conventional finance? Surprisingly enough, for some behavioral theorists, the answer to this question has been, on occasion, negative.

9.2 Mean Variance Optimization Strikes Again?

In 2011, S. Das, H. Markowitz, J. Scheid, and M. Statman (DMSS) published an important paper in *The Journal of Wealth Management*. The paper was entitled "Portfolios for Investors Who Want to Reach Their Goals While Staying on the Mean–Variance Efficient Frontier". One of the reasons for the importance of the paper was, of course, the very influential profile of the authors. In particular, Markowitz "invented" mean-variance portfolio allocation, whereas Statman (together with Shefrin) is considered the father of behavioral portfolio theory.

The opening of the paper is already revealing. DMSS present a world populated by two distinct categories of investors: mean variance investors (MVI) and behavioral investors (BI).

MVI invest in a single portfolio, trying to maximize its overall returns for a given level of risk aversion (where risk is equated to volatility as measured by variance around the mean return). In contrast, BI invest in a number of portfolios, each targeted to finance a specific aim (ranging from the fulfillment of basic needs to the participation to lotteries that can change your life). It is remarkable that DMSS do not explain why both MVI and BI exist, and in what circumstances a prospective investor ends up belonging to MVI rather than to BI, or the other way around.

Then DMSS proceed in the attempt to reconcile the two categories of investors by creating a third category: that of investors who apply mean-variance optimization to EACH of the portfolios created by mental accounting. In practice, what the investors imagined by DMSS do are the following:

First, as behavioral finance would predict, they create three different portfolios, each for a different purpose. In descending order of size, they are:

- Retirement, with a low target return and a high aversion to losses
- Education, with an intermediate target return and aversion to losses
- Bequest, with a high target return and a low aversion to losses

Second, they choose assets for each portfolio in such a way that the probability of loss is limited to a given percentage. For example, allocations for the retirement portfolio are such that the probability of losing more than 10% is limited to 6.28%.

On the surface, it seems like the best of both worlds: investors with a set of different portfolios dictated by mental accounting manage to optimize them in compliance of mean-variance prescriptions!

There are, however, a couple of problems with the framework developed by DMSS.

The first one is that by definition BI do NOT identify risk with volatility (as represented by the standard deviation measure used by DMSS) but with potential losses. Therefore, as in the paper, the probability of losing X% in one of the portfolios is actually a function of the standard deviation of the portfolio itself, BI investors would not make recourse to such kind of probability estimation.

The second one (and related) stands in the very rationale of the DMSS idea. Why should BI care about being compliant with the predictions of a theory (mean variance) which has been proven unfit to explain real-world investor behavior? Once again, the impression is that some behavioral economists have a sort of inferiority complex toward conventional economics and finance, and hence they try to show that behavioral theories can be compliant with conventional finance, as if this fact could give a more legitimate status to behavioral research. That's not really the path to follow for behavioral economics and finance to stand up as a self-contained discipline.

9.3 Asset Allocation and Loss Indicator Issues: Problems and Research Perspectives

Even leaving aside the "identity problems" just highlighted, behavioral finance still suffers from the absence of consensus on some important issues.

One of these issues has to do with the layers of the portfolio pyramid investors with mental account use for asset allocation. In particular, the base layer(s) of the pyramid should hold all the funds which, invested at the risk-free rate, guarantee the satisfaction of the investor's basic needs. But what is the definition of "basic needs"? And for how long should the protection be ensured? And how sensitive is this approach to crucial variables like interest rate levels?

Let's make an example. Assume there is an investor who assigns the base layer of her pyramid to retirement needs (i.e. an integration to pension treatment which can also cover at least part of unexpected expenses, e.g. healthcare-related expenses). Say that with retirement occurring at 65 years of age and a life expectancy of 85 years, the target would be to have a yearly sum of $50,000 (1,000,000 over 20 years). The last assumption we have to make is about the expected return of assets allocated to the base layer portfolio. Given the absolute need to minimize losses for a portfolio targeted to retirement, it is likely that only risk-free assets are selected, and such assets typically yield a very low return. Say that this return is not higher than 1%. Then if the investor builds her portfolio when she is 50 years old (15 years before retirement), the initial allocation to the retirement portfolio will need to be of about $861,000. But what happens if portfolio building begins much earlier? With such low returns, if the investor builds her portfolio when she is 35 years old (30 years before retirement), the initial allocation to the retirement portfolio will need just as substantial ($742,000). Is it realistic that with such a big allocation to the retirement portfolio, our 35-year-old average investor can also have additional funds to allocate to upper layers of the pyramid? It seems that the existence of a multiple-layer pyramid is especially likely whenever risk-free returns are high and/or the investor is old enough to have accumulated substantial wealth. Otherwise, in most cases (that is, net of millionaires), the base layer could absorb almost totally available resources.

Another unsolved issue relates to the definition of loss. As highlighted earlier, influential researchers like DMSS have used a definition ("probability of falling short of targeted return") which is unsatisfactory, as it is contaminated by the mean-variance framework, in which volatility plays a big role.

But volatility (i.e. dispersion around the mean) in itself has to do mostly with risk aversion, rather than with loss aversion.

In order to properly understand the difference, it is important to recall the concept of reference point first introduced by Kahneman and Tversky's prospect theory in 1979. According to this concept, utility is NOT a function of levels of wealth, but rather a function of the increase in wealth with respect to some initial level. Accordingly, the concept of loss is to be defined in an analogous way. So, an asset could be thought of as generating losses whenever its current price is below the initial purchase price.

In order to better highlight the difference in asset selection that can arise if the investor uses loss rather than volatility indicators, consider two assets A and B. Figure 9.2 visualizes their price performance in the last 10 months. At the beginning of the period considered, A and B had the same price (100), but later on their price performance diverged considerably.

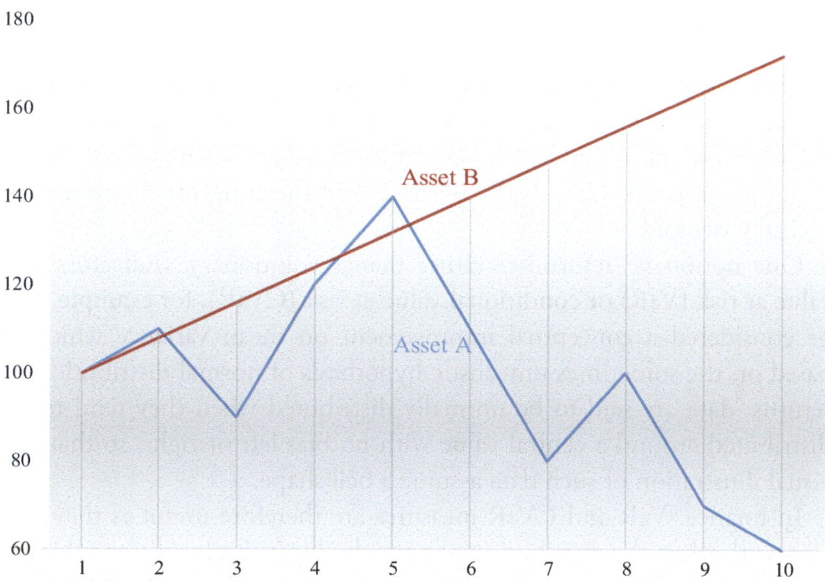

Fig. 9.2 Asset A and Asset B: Price Dynamics

If you were a mean-variance investor you would think of the two assets as equally risky, as they feature the same standard deviation (dispersion around the mean) in price, so from a risk perspective you would be indifferent between them.

However, if you were a behavioral investor you would definitely prefer A to B, as the price of A in the last 10 months has always been higher than the initial price, that is, no losses were recorded.

Obviously, this definition of loss is perhaps exceedingly crude, and is best applied to historical data. So the point is: how do we define expected losses?

Of course, the answer to the question is first of all crucially dependent on the hypotheses that are associated with expectation formation (cf. Chap. 6). Are expectations of behavioral investors rational?

Or adaptive? Or … something else?

For the time being, assume that expectations are rational in their broadest sense; that is, people use what they think is the best in available information (Barro 1986). Therefore, no perfect knowledge is assumed: investors do not know the "true" model, they don't have in real time all the knowledge and information that are pertinent to future events, and so forth. They just do what THEY think is best with whatever information they can gather.

The choice of a specific expectation scheme is not enough, however. We also need a consensus view on the indicator to be used, and so far behavioral economics research has not provided any such view.

So, progress on this is badly needed. And the conceptual options are basically twofold.

One option is "reformist" rather than revolutionary. Indicators like value at risk (VaR) or conditional value at risk (CVaR), for example, can be considered a conceptual improvement on mean variance which is based on the sometimes unrealistic hypothesis of normal distribution of returns: data are said to be normally distributed when they tend to be distributed around a central value with no bias left or right, so that the visual illustration of such data assume a bell shape.

In finance, VaR and CVaR measures are therefore useful as they can also work when the distribution of portfolio logarithmic returns substantially deviates from normal. Such techniques are used to determine the extent and occurrence ratio of potential losses in portfolios.

Still, VaR and CVaR do not escape a couple of major problems. The first is conceptual, as losses are modeled as they were random variables, that is, outcomes from some chance process, like how many heads will occur in a series of 20 flips. Are we sure that this assumption fits real-world losses?

The second problem in a BEF context is even more fundamental. As it has been repeatedly highlighted, behavioral finance has to do with the way in which investors behave in the real world. Keeping this in mind, let's have a look at the mathematical definition of these indicators:

- Portfolio VaR is defined as a maximum portfolio loss (measured in % of initial wealth) over a given time interval at a given level of statistical confidence.
- *Definition.* VaR_α^T is implicitly defined by the following expression (for simplicity, we assume that portfolio returns have continuous distribution):

$$P\left(p_{[0,T]}^e < -\mathrm{VaR}_\alpha^T\right) = 1 - \alpha,$$

where $p_{[0,T]}^e$ is portfolio excess simple return over [0, *T*] period.

To put it more formally, $-\mathrm{VaR}_\alpha^T$ corresponds to the $(1 - \alpha)$ -quantile of the distribution of portfolio excess simple return over [0, *T*] period.

- Portfolio CVaR is conditional expectation of losses beyond VaR.
- *Definition.* CVaR_α^T is an expected value (with opposite sign) of portfolio excess simple return $p_{[0,\mathrm{T}]}^e$ under the condition $\mathrm{P}\left(p_{[0,\mathrm{T}]}^e \le -\mathrm{VaR}_\alpha^\mathrm{T}\right)$:

$$\mathrm{CVaR}_\alpha^T = -E\left(p_{[0,T]}^e \mid p_{[0,T]}^e \le -\mathrm{VaR}_\alpha^T\right)$$

In other words, $-\mathrm{CVaR}_\alpha^T$ is an average value of $(1 - \alpha) \times 100\%$ of highest losses. Common values for α are 0.9, 0.95, 0.975, and 0.99. The time horizon *T* corresponds to a period required for complete liquidation of all portfolio positions.

Source: *http://www.smartfolio.com/theory/details/risk_tools/definitions/*

Are we sure that real-world investors setting up a retirement portfolio as the base of their investment pyramid would use THAT? Perhaps it is not the case that VaR and CVaR are most commonly used by investment and commercial banks!

The second option (more "revolutionary") would be to forget everything about density functions and probability distributions, and just think of what indicator a real-world prospective pensioner would use when trying to estimate future losses on different assets.

It may well be that if the investor (the prospective pensioner) has to evaluate the outlook for a specific asset, she will be especially interested to estimate, together with expected returns, how much she can lose each time that a loss occurs and how frequently losses can be recorded.

An example: assume that the assets available for investment are the following:

1. Cash and bank deposits
2. Government bonds
3. Corporate bonds
4. Small and Medium enterprise (SME) shares
5. Large enterprise shares

Expectations are formed on the basis of quarterly data for the last five years.[1]

Out of an overall wealth to be invested of about \$100,000, the investor builds a three-layered pyramid. Above the base layer of \$46,000 (Safety) holding only cash and deposits, there are the middle layer (Income) of \$36,000 and the top layer (Growth) of \$18,000.[2]

Table 9.1 highlights average returns.

Now the loss component. From this point of view, the SME shares sector is the one in which not only average losses[3] are the greatest (1.6%), but losses are also more frequent (6).

For each asset, the product of average size and frequency of losses becomes the denominator of a ratio which has average return as its numerator. So, for a given return, a bigger (and/or more frequent) loss reduces the ratio, which measures the overall appeal of a specific asset for a loss-averse investor (see Table 9.2).

Table 9.1 Average Returns

	Government Bonds (%)	Corporate Bonds (%)	SME Shares (%)	Large Enterprise Shares (%)
Average Quarterly Return	0.63	0.64	1.87	1.5

Table 9.2 Calculating Expected Losses

	Government Bonds (%)	Corporate Bonds (%)	SME Shares (%)	Large Enterprise Shares (%)
Average Loss	1.00	1.00	1.6	1.2
Number of Recorded Loss	5	3	6	5
Average Return/(1 + number of losses × average loss)	10.5	16	17.6	21.4

But how would our investor use this "loss weighted return indicator" (LWR) in practice?

If, for example, the investor has to cover 100% of the "Income" layer with the two types of bonds, by using the values of LWR she would allocate 42% of the total to government bonds and 58% to corporate bonds. Similarly, in the "Growth" layer, 34% of the total would be invested in SME shares and 66% in large enterprise shares.

It turns out that LWR allocation is more prudent than a mean-variance allocation (in particular a bigger share is given to government bonds).

Of course, this example is merely illustrative, as LWR allocation is very crude, as opposed to the sophisticated setup of techniques (like CVaR) relying on high-level mathematics.

However, the progress to be made by behavioral finance is precisely that of bridging the gap between complex (but unrealistic) expected loss indicators and the "rule of thumb" approach just explained.

Notes

1. In order not to introduce spurious elements that could make results less legible, in this example we assume adaptive expectations, the simplest expectation scheme.

2. To avoid "corner solutions" (all the investment in a single asset) in the example, we impose the constraint that each asset represents at least 10% of total investments.
3. A loss is defined as: 100 minus the percentage ratio of current asset market price to initial market price, whenever current market price is lower.

References

Barberis, N., M. Huang, and R. Thaler. 2006. Individual Preferences, Monetary Gambles, and Stock Market Participation: A Case for Narrow Framing. *American Economic Review 96* (4): 1069–1090.

Barro, R.J. 1986. Reputation in a Model of Monetary Policy with Incomplete Information. *Journal of Monetary Economics 17* (1): 3–20.

Benartzi, S., and R.H. Thaler. 1995. Myopic Loss-Aversion and the Equity Premium Puzzle. *Quarterly Journal of Economics 110* (1): 73–92.

Chen, M.K., V. Lakshminarayanan, and L.R. Santos. 2006. How Basic are Behavioral Biases? Evidence from Capuchin Monkey Trading Behavior. *Journal of Political Economy 114* (3): 517–537.

Friedman, M., and L.J. Savage. 1948. The Utility Analysis of Choices Involving Risk. *Journal of Political Economy 56* (4): 279–304.

Lopes, L. 1987. Between Hope and Fear: The Psychology of Risk. In *Advances in Experimental Social Psychology*, ed. L. Berkowitz, vol. 20, 255–295. San Diego: Academic Press.

Markowitz, H.M. 1952. Portfolio Selection. *The Journal of Finance 7* (1): 77–91.

Shefrin, H., and M. Statman. 2000. Behavioral Portfolio Theory. *The Journal of Financial and Quantitative Analysis 35* (2): 127–151.

Thaler, R.H. 1999. Mental Accounting Matters. *Journal of Behavioral Decision Making 12* (3): 183.

10

Should Biased Nudgers Nudge Us?

10.1 What Is Nudging? Flies and Toilets

What's that? A fly in the urinal? And what does a fly in the urinal have to do with behavioral economics? (See Fig. 10.1)

Fig. 10.1 Should I Aim at It?

F. Ghisellini, B. Y. Chang, *Behavioral Economics*,
https://doi.org/10.1007/978-3-319-75205-1_10

Apparently, the story is as follows. Management at Amsterdam Airport Schiphol was concerned about excess spillage on men's toilet floor. So they called to the rescue Aad Kieboom, an economist, in order to have suggestions on how to help users to be more "precise", although he says the final idea wasn't his. Whoever the inventors were, Schiphol urinals in men's toilets were promptly equipped with fly etchings.

And theories on why flies should do the trick vary. According to Klaus Reichardt, who invented the waterless urinal, "*Guys are simple-minded and love to play with their urine stream, so you put something in the toilet bowl and they'll aim at that*".

The analysis of Mike Friedberger, product director for chinaware at American Standard, which supplies fly-engraved urinals to JFK Terminal 4, is more sophisticated:

> "*If it's something that you consciously don't like, you're more likely to pee on it,*" he says. "*If they had put a pretty butterfly or ladybug there, men might not aim directly at it. On the other hand, if you used an ugly-looking spider or a cockroach, people might be afraid of it and not even stand there. A fly seems to be a compromise: something that is universally disliked, but that doesn't elicit fear and make people not want to stand there.*"

Is the initiative politically correct? In public women's toilets, some girls actually engage in awkward squatting poses so as to avoid contact with the unclean seat and in doing so they often leave an even more unclean seat for the next user. But, of course, that doesn't imply higher cleaning costs for the management.

Has it been effective? Sphinx, the urinal manufacturer that provides the toilets for Schiphol, says that having the fly in the toilet represents savings in cleaning costs of 20% or more.

If Friedberger's analysis is correct, however, savings have probably been even higher in Iceland in 2008, shortly after the country's three main commercial banks had collapsed. Rather than flies, the targets in the urinals were pictures of Icelandic bankers.

10.1.1 Definition of the Perfect Nudge

The fathers of the term "nudge", Richard Thaler and Cass Sunstein, describe a nudge as "*any aspect of the choice architecture that alters people's behavior in a predictable way without forbidding any options or significantly changing their economic incentives. To count as a mere nudge, the intervention must be easy and cheap to avoid. Nudges are not mandates. Putting the fruit at eye level counts as a nudge. Banning junk food does not*" (Thaler and Sunstein 2008: 6).[1] As a matter of fact, nudge theorists hold that the assumption that people always make optimal decisions for themselves when provided with accurate information is not true, as decisions are often influenced by the context in which they are made.

> *It is legitimate … to try to influence people's behavior in order to make their lives longer, healthier, and better. In other words, we argue for self-conscious efforts, by institutions in the private sector and also by government, to steer people's choices in directions that will improve their lives.*

So nudges can be used to help people to "do the right thing" (save more, eat healthier food, pollute less, etc.). This is why—according to nudge supporters—nudges are the best of both worlds: they are paternalistic in that they help people to make decisions that are in their true best interest, but at the same time, nudges are also libertarian, in that they preserve freedom of choice. Hence, the term "libertarian paternalism" is used to describe this school of thought.

The key word here is architecture, that is, the way/order in which alternative choices are presented.

And the most important concept in choice architecture is framing. A very simple example of framing is the following. Imagine that you run a telephone company, and for budgetary reasons, you know that in one-year time you will be forced to raise subscription charges, which could make the number of customers shrink. The optimal advertisement to launch today in order to set up in advance a "cushion" of new customers will be that for new customers charges are guaranteed to be locked for one year! It is almost a lie, but it is called framing.

In a subtle way, defaults can be considered as a special type of framing. Defaults denote a predefined (standard) choice which is then presented as the "normative choice". So "opting out" and choosing a different option requires an active behavior, which in turn implies the existence of preferences that are strong enough to make you take a position against the default option on which you have been automatically enrolled. Given that in many cases preferences are not so strong, you remain passive and go along with the default choice. Sometimes the compliance with defaults is generated by other "environmental" considerations. For example, if you have been automatically enrolled in an organ donation program, you may not want to appear as someone who is against the spirit of the program, even though you wouldn't have enrolled if you had been free to choose!

Generally speaking, Thaler and Sunstein equate heuristics with nudges. For example, by the availability heuristic, people tend to draw general inferences from a fact that is highly visible and/or perceived (e.g. via news coverage) to materialize often. So, in Thaler and Sunstein words,

> *A good way to increase people's fear of a bad outcome is to remind them of a related incident in which things went wrong; a good way to increase people's confidence is to remind them of a similar situation in which everything worked out for the best.*

Next, the purpose of nudges. Of course, broadly defined, nudges could be used for whatever purpose, and many times they are indeed projected to serve the interest of nudgers (cf. the example of the telephone company introduced earlier). According to Thaler and Sunstein, however, "*choice architectures can make major improvements to the lives of others by designing environments which promote choices in individuals' best interest*". So, is the "urinal fly" story we just told a nudge? Well, the answer should be negative, as the scheme was conceived just for the management (the "nudgers") in order to save money for cleaning the toilets.

So, a proper nudge shouldn't aim at favoring the nudgers. But then, what is a proper nudge?

As just mentioned, proper nudges should be oriented to the best interest of the nudgee (LPNs, "libertarian paternalistic nudges").[2] To recapitulate, a visual illustration of what the prerequisites are for a true LPN is given by the following flowchart (see Fig. 10.2).

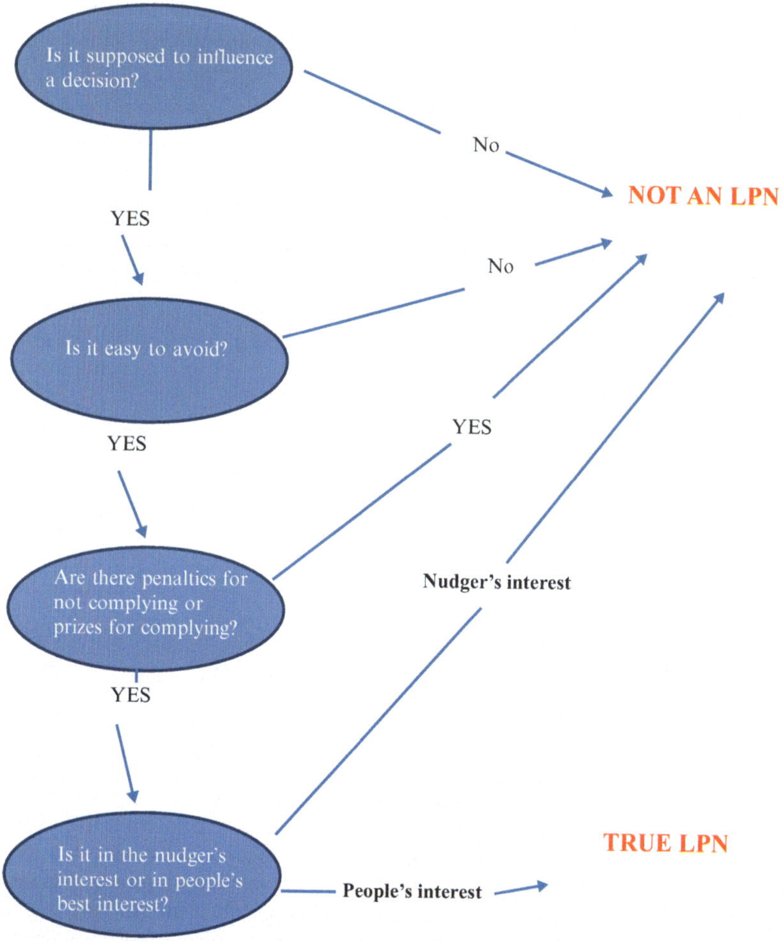

Fig. 10.2 Identification of an LPN

10.2 Public and Private Nudges

In 2010, the UK Institute for Government (reporting to the Cabinet Office) published a comprehensive study highlighting the case for the application of behavioral theory to public policies (Halpern et al. 2010). Basically, according to the study, the case rests on the following considerations:

> *Tools such as incentives and information are intended to change behaviour by "changing minds". If we provide the carrots and sticks, alongside accurate information, people will weigh up the revised costs and benefits of their actions and respond accordingly. Unfortunately, evidence suggests that people do not always respond in this "perfectly rational" way. In contrast, approaches based on "changing contexts"—the environment within which we make decisions and respond to cues—have the potential to bring about significant changes in behaviour at relatively low cost. Shaping policy more closely around our inbuilt responses to the world offers a potentially powerful way to improve individual wellbeing and social welfare. With this in mind, we set out nine of the most robust (non-coercive) influences on our behaviour, captured in a simple mnemonic—MINDSPACE—which can be used as a quick checklist when making policy.*

This is the checklist (see Table 10.1).

Since 2010, the so-called nudge units, which are based on the already mentioned Thaler-Sunstein book, have been created by many governments all around the world.

Table 10.1 The MINDSPACE

Messenger	We are heavily influenced by who communicates information
Incentives	Our responses to incentives are shaped by predictable mental shortcuts such as strongly avoiding losses
Norms	We are strongly influenced by what others do
Defaults	We "go with the flow" of preset options
Salience	Our attention is drawn to what is novel and seems relevant to us
Priming	Our acts are often influenced by subconscious cues
Affect	Our emotional associations can powerfully shape our actions
Commitments	We seek to be consistent with our public promises, and reciprocate acts
Ego	We act in ways that make us feel better about ourselves

The UK's Behavioural Insights Team (BIT) was the first, while the White House–based Social and Behavioral Sciences Team was introduced by the Obama administration in 2014.

Governments in Australia, Canada, the Netherlands, and Greece are all now converting to the cause.

The BIT in the UK, spun out of the government in February 2014 and whose Advisory Panel includes Richard Thaler, coauthor of *Nudge*, has been by far the most active nudge team around.

Following the MINDSPACE philosophy, BIT focused on three broad policy areas:

1. "Safer Communities": Challenges include preventing crime, reducing antisocial behavior, preventing degradation of surroundings
2. "The Good Society": Challenges include promoting pro-environmental behavior, increasing voting, encouraging responsible parenting
3. "Healthy and Prosperous Lives": Challenges include stopping smoking, reducing obesity, promoting responsible personal finances, encouraging take-up of education and training

Truth be told, some of the many BIT trials have little to do with behavioral economics. Consider the one aimed at reducing the consumption of sugar-sweetened beverages in hospitals. They "discovered" that raising by 20% the price of high-calorie red drinks in vending machines, people would reduce their consumption in favor of healthier drinks!

If we focus on proper nudges, one of the instruments most used was the normative/personalized letter/email.

One interesting experiment was the one aimed at increasing tax compliance in 2011. The control group (i.e. the group not targeted by BIT initiative) received standard tax letters. The treatment groups received the letters with an added normative message (e.g. *"Did you know that 90% people in your area pay taxes in due time?"* or *"Not paying tax means we all lose out on vital public services like the NHS, roads and schools"*).

The tax communication program is considered a nudge, but it is questionable whether it is in the best self-interest of those nudged. You could argue that paying your taxes timely should be in people's interest, but is it? Try asking someone whether they prefer to pay sooner rather than later! But more importantly, it is also debatable whether a letter from government exerting pressure on you to pay your debts can be considered a true nudge or can controlled trial schemes that use lotteries to encourage weight loss (cf. the prerequisites of a nudge in the flowchart). As a matter of fact, a great number of alleged nudge schemes incorporate explicit or implicit compensation/punishment elements.

If we further shrink the analysis to more unquestionable LPN initiatives in the BIT experience (i.e. initiatives that fulfill all the prerequisites introduced in the flowchart above), they are a minority.

Among them is the text message-based Manchester College project to reduce the dropout rate of adult literacy classes. The same project—which reduced dropout rates by more than 35%—consisted of a very simple text sent to students on Sunday evenings, reading "*I hope you had a good break, we look forward to seeing you next week. Remember to plan how you will get to your class*".

Another interesting trial run in 2013 had to do with organ donation associated with car tax renewal. In particular, when people renewed their car tax online, they received different messages inviting them to join the organ donation registry. One of these messages, "*If you needed an organ transplant, would you have one? If so, please help other*", has been estimated to add around 100,000 extra organ donors per year relative to the control.

Long before Thaler and Sunstein wrote about nudges, private firms made ample recourse to framing in order to influence customers' behavior in a way that could be conducive to the success of marketing strategies and to higher profits. Experts who design the floor plans for supermarkets strategically place what "must" be bought at eye level on the shelves and cheap impulse items near the checkout line.

As a result, the interpretation of nudging policies in the private sector is even trickier than that of public nudges, as private nudges have to satisfy an additional conceptual constraint; that is, they are bound to have a positive impact on firms' profitability.

In some cases, however, the quest for profitability can be compatible with the pursuit of consumers' best interests. In such cases, nudges are called by some "Pareto nudges" (even though in conventional economics, Pareto optima describe situations in which one of the two parties maximizes welfare without causing harm to the other party).

Consider the example of healthy foods, which are very fashionable these days. In terms of price, it comes at a nice (sometimes unduly) premium over traditional food. Given that the sale of healthy food generates higher profit margins for retailers, leading people to buy it (via catchy showcases, temporary discount initiatives, etc.) represents a true "Pareto nudge".

The same could be said for default enrollment in preset retirement schemes. In the US, an important field study showed that simply by enrolling employees in the retirement program by default (they can still opt out quite easily, while previously they had to opt in), participation rates increased dramatically.

10.3 Case Studies: Do Nudges Work?

The BIT initiative to increase tax compliance mentioned earlier yielded a difference in compliance rates between the control and the treatment group that was in the order of 5%. Not a lot. And, as it has been noted, it is dubious that the initiative can be considered a legitimate nudge (i.e. targeted only to the explicit best interest of those nudged).

So let's focus instead on the record of type I nudges. It seems that the most effective schemes rely on default choices.

Consider first the organ donation program. It has been undoubtedly successful, as shown in the following chart, which compares consent percentages across countries with different regimes ("nudged" countries are in the "opt out" bracket) (see Fig. 10.3).

In the same vein, one should mention the success of the default "Save More Tomorrow" (SMarT) program (Benartzi and Thaler 2004). The idea (automatically increasing the percentage of employees' wage devoted to saving) worked very well, as average saving rates for program participants increased from 3.5% to 13.6% over the course of observation period.

The success of the default programs is commonly ascribed mainly to the action of loss aversion combined with two mental processes:

- the first one is generally referred to as the status quo bias. In the absence of strong enough reasons to choose otherwise, people tend to stick to the existing situation (in this case, the default option)

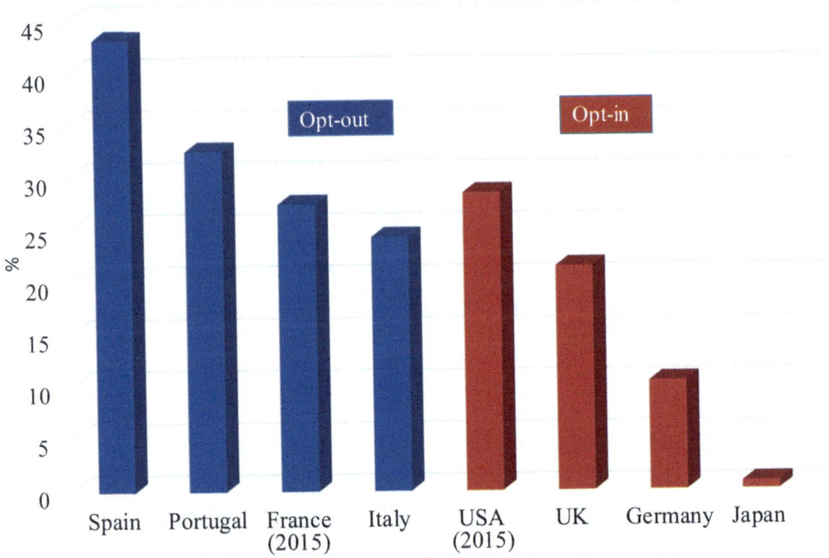

Fig. 10.3 Actual Deceased Organ Donors 2016 (%) in Selected Countries. Source: International Registry on Organ donation and Transplantation Database

- the second has to do with the so-called "Paradox of Choice", by which the very fact of being forced to choose among different alternatives (which implies devoting time to read and to understand the implications of each choice) is in itself a painful and frustrating experience

Measurement of the success rate of nudge schemes different from the organ donation and the default saving/retirement programs is in many cases difficult, and prone to controversy.

One tricky aspect of evaluation has to do with time, and the implications of passing time.

Consider the case of the fly etchings in men's urinals at the airport we presented at the beginning of this section. Initially, they were introduced at Amsterdam Airport Schiphol and apparently did the trick. In the first few months, spillage in the toilets went down dramatically, and with it cleaning costs. Given this performance, many other airports decided to follow suit and installed fly etchings.

How would evaluation results change if measured after a longer time, say, one year? Apparently the degree of success of the initiative has not been measured over a longer term, but a few plausible considerations can point to a much lower success rate.

First, the novelty effect disappears. Once you understand that the fly in the urinal is of course a fake and you get accustomed to its presence, it is highly implausible that the nudge can work as it did the first time. You wouldn't continue to aim at it, would you?

Second, and related, if a nudge is too strong or too overt, it can easily make people immune or even backfire, in particular if a message is perceived to challenge our dignity. In that case, spillage in toilets could actually increase beyond prenudge levels.

Finally, the impact of nudges can vary depending on the receiver's profile. On the occasion of a forthcoming economics conference in Nottingham, Gächter et al. sent letters to economists who submitted papers, with a sentence varying between discount—and penalty—framings.

> *We take this opportunity to remind you that [(1) the discounted conference fee for early registration is available until/ (2) the conference fee will include a penalty for late registration after] 10 July 2006.*

They found that only the behavior of junior economists was affected by the framing. For your information, the authors of this book are senior economists.

10.4 Is Nudging Right?

Nudges can be well designed or badly designed, and can have success or failure, but the most important question that remains is whether they are desirable and/or admissible from different, but sometimes overlapping, points of view.

First, there is an epistemic problem, that is, a problem relating to knowledge.

In theory, nudges "influence choices in a way that will make the chooser better off" and facilitate decisions that people would have chosen if they were not affected by cognitive biases and lack of self-control or information.

But do nudgers know the real preferences of people to be nudged? Take the classical example of nudging toward healthy food in cafeterias. Signs and shelves can be arranged in a way that favors explicitly the consumption of green vegetables and fruit over fish and chips or sausages, for instance. There can be a wider choice of vegetables, and sausage trays can be few and half-hidden. So if you, nonetheless, go for sausage, then in the checkout line you can as well perceive the stigma others place on your vicious choices.

Is this right? This is questionable, as individuals may have multiple interests that combine differently according to their specific personal context. For example, I can follow a diet by which vegetable consumption is planned for dinners, so at lunch in the office cafeteria I would like to opt for tastier choices without being stared at as if I were a dirty fat eater. Or I am in a negative phase of my life that pushes me toward depression, so I do need to eat comfort food that can compensate for that, and that food cannot really be tofu or soy sprouts.

Therefore, the fact that people's behavior does not seem to comply with the commandments of what you think should be their best interest should not lead you to draw conclusions on the desirability of introducing nudges.

White (2013) uses the example of Patrick, a corpulent man, who, every Sunday morning, sits at a café and orders a very rich muffin. That's bad for health and hence irrational, the "choice architect" would comment, and—presto—you would rearrange the café's shelves to make muffins less visible. However, the architect in this case could completely miss the point. Patrick knows perfectly that muffins are bad for health, but has decided to have one on Sunday and in that café in remembrance of when he was a kid and his grandfather took him there to buy him a muffin. Therefore, he will stick to his habit even in a nudged context.

Also, even nudges with the right core content may impact adversely on other interests pursued by individuals. Nudges increasing savings can lead, for example, to a cut of cultural consumption (books, concerts, etc.), so the net effect can turn negative.

Finally, there is an issue with the knowledge of short-term preferences vs. the knowledge of longer-term preferences. In the short term, people can have preferences which are different from those applicable to longer-term time horizons (which are those typically targeted by nudges). Therefore, I can be perfectly aware that increasing my saving rate is in the long run desirable, and I plan to do it ten years from now, but I do not want to do it already today. And I am not irrational either, as my actions are fully representative of my individual goals and values. I can intentionally act in a "negative" way and accept the future consequences.

As a result, being nudged to save more today is completely out of line with my true preferences at the moment and therefore makes me irrational.

However, nudge advocates argue that even if the epistemic critique were correct, nudging could simply be ignored, as the implied alteration to choice architecture, such as changing arrangement of options or default choices, does not foreclose alternative choices. But here comes the second problem, which is a method problem.

To start with, the secret of any successful nudges lies exactly in the exploitation of the same cognitive distortions whose impact the nudge is supposed to reduce. Default retirement schemes based on the opt-out mechanism do not reduce laziness; they use laziness to obtain the result that the nudger wants. As nudges rely on distortions to achieve the desired outcome, they reinforce rather than lessen the impact of cognitive/emotional biases. And this of course implies for people on the one hand the impossibility of learning from their own mistakes and on the other hand the continuing/growing need for additional nudges.

And the alleged freedom of choosing different options is hardly there, given the psychological pressure and the subtle methods by which nudges operate. As a matter of fact, if it were true that the substance of freedom to choose is preserved, nudges would be ineffective in the first place. So, paradoxically, in order to be effective, nudges are required to reduce freedom of choice.

Finally, consider the ethical problem. Is nudging on the part of governments ethically legitimate? Of course you can think of extreme cases in which the usage of classical nudge tools such as default options are clearly not admissible (e.g. a rule according to which you are automatically enrolled in the incumbent party in power, unless you explicitly state otherwise). But what about softer approaches, like the one called "libertarian paternalism" (Thaler and Sunstein 2003), by which we should all remain truly free to choose, while the government nudges us in the "right" direction?

The case for libertarian paternalism rests on a well-defined set of propositions, and each of them is necessary. Some have to do with knowledge (e.g. the existence of a universal definition for welfare increasing behavior, the measurement of the gap between such behavior and real-world behavior), some with supply side requirements (government's ability to effectively nudge people toward "good choices"), and still others have to do with politics and philosophy: nudge policies can only be considered if they do not alter the most relevant parts of the social contract between government and citizens. And what are those most relevant parts?

One is that government is there just to represent the interests of citizens and should not think of itself as it were an entity with superior knowledge.

Many political theorists would argue that nudging is an intrinsically elitist practice, as it enables governments to impose on citizens their conception of what constitutes "the right life". According to White (2013), libertarian paternalism therefore executes a value substitution which replaces the decision-maker's interest with the policymaker's interest.

As philosopher Dan Brock (1988) wrote,

> *paternalistic interference involves the claim of one person to know better what is good for another person than that other person him- or herself does. It involves the substitution by the paternalistic interferer of his or her conception of what is good for another for that other's own conception of his or her good. If this involves a claim to know the objectively correct conception of another's good—what ultimate values and aims define another competent individual's good, independent of whether that other accepts them—then it is ethically problematic.*

Another refers to transparency in accountability and responsibility.

Thaler and Sunstein (2008) hold and stress many times that nudges are unavoidable, they are everywhere in life, and they are never neutral. So, given how pervasive nudges are, there is little reason to take issue with them on ethical grounds. However, the fathers of nudge forget a minor detail. In a democracy, governments must take decisions and assume full political responsibility for such decisions, so that when election time comes they can be judged by voters. In contrast, the use of nudges waters down responsibilities, as governments just create the choice architectures that lead other subjects (the citizens) to select specific options, and therefore reduces accountability.

Finally, there is the question of preserving as much freedom as possible for citizens.

Radical libertarians would no doubt consider nudges as unduly forms of intervention that reduces personal autonomy only marginally less than do flat bans. Faced by nudges, people have to fight, and are often exposed to a social stigma, in order to reaffirm their choices. As Heidi Fudging (2016) puts it,

> *one may not have a right to ride a motorcycle without a helmet, but one has a right not to be told to wear a helmet because it is in one's own best interests.*

According to this view, paternalism of any type violates the personal autonomy of people and discourages people from engaging in active choice. Schubert (2016) produces an enlightening example:

> *Consider a world with widespread adoption of public nudging. There, I, the consumer, don't need to worry about my retirement savings, nor about mustering the little self-control that I have to avoid the chocolate bars in the cafeteria, nor about being wary about the tricks of door-to-door salespersons. In all these cases, some choice architect, somewhere behind the scenes, subtly steers me into the "right" direction—by changing defaults and frames, and by implementing cooling-off periods. In other words, I'm outsourcing my choices to some external body.*

In John Stuart Mill's (1869) words,

> *the strongest of all the arguments against the interference of the public with purely personal conduct is that, when it does interfere, the odds are that it interferes wrongly, and in the wrong place. On questions of social morality, of duty to others, the opinion of the public, that is, of an overruling majority, though often wrong, is likely to be still oftener right; because on such questions they are only required to judge of their own interests; of the manner in which some mode*

> *of conduct, if allowed to be practiced, would affect themselves. But the opinion of a similar majority, imposed as a law on the minority, on questions of self-regarding conduct, is quite as likely to be wrong as right; for in these cases public opinion means, at the best, some people's opinion of what is good or bad for other people.*

And then there is a final paradox, which arises precisely as a result of the logical premise of nudge activity, that is, the existence of biases.

On the one hand, a potential problem exists on the nudgees' side. We reported that according to Thaler and Sunstein, the only acceptable type of nudge is the one which "*influence choices in a way that will make the choosers better off as judged by themselves*". But if people are indeed biased, how likely is it that, when called to state whether nudges make them better-off, their feedback also incorporates the effect of cognitive distortions?

On the other hand, aren't nudge advocates forgetting the minor detail that, given that governments (and nudge units) are made of people, they, very much as the people they want to nudge, are not immune to biases in the first place? Who will nudge the nudgers?

But then, in light of these considerations, is there a solution which defines at least some optimal/legitimate nudge policies? According to many, the answer is to a large extent negative, as governments should always respect the choices made by people and simply hold them accountable and responsible for the consequences of those choices.

The very limited space left for quasi-nudge activities is then defined by White (2013) when he concedes that all that policymakers could do is to "*make sure they are not doing anything that would discourage good decision-making, and possibly take careful and neutral actions to promote it*". However, the conceptual definition of the correct and freedom-preserving "neutral actions" is something that in itself would require far more pages than this book can contain. A possible way would be that if the government used nudges NOT to impose its specific preferences on citizens, but to make up for "information market failures". As a matter of fact, there could be situations in which, for example as a result of inadequate media coverage, people do not know all the available options to choose from. For instance, in Italy, financial education is lagging behind. Therefore, people think that when it comes to investments, they can either buy bonds or stocks.

In fact, there are other options, like ETFs (Exchange Traded Funds), which are potentially superior under many respects (transparency, risk diversification, cost saving, etc.) but—for dubious reasons— do not receive adequate media coverage. The government could launch a proper information strategy for households, in which the pros and cons of ETFs vs. bonds/stocks would be adequately covered.

In any case, it should be imperative that governments' nudging aims at contrasting biases, rather than leveraging on them. An example could be that of saving decisions. As reported, so far default schemes of the opt-out type have worked with noticeable success, leveraging on inertia on the part of employees. But the original sin remains: you, as government, are pushing people to do what YOU think is best. Is there a way to nudge people into being more active, at the same time safeguarding their autonomy? A way to be explored could be that of making people face more concretely the potential consequences of their choices. At the moment, the choice save/not save is structured very much as what in finance is called an "American option", by which at any moment in time you can decide whether to save or not, so people are prey of laziness ("I'll decide tomorrow"). How would the problem change with the introduction of a provision by which the option you are bound to select today cannot be changed before a specific date (X years)? Isn't that feature (which in finance would be called an "European option") likely to help people out of their inertia?

But this is just an example, as there are many areas to be explored to make nudging more democratic. In all cases, however, choice architecture should try to widen, rather than reduce, the menu of available options, and with that people's freedom.

Notes

1. Cf. Soman et al. (2005).
2. If one wants to be precise, that's not the end of the story. What is exactly the "best interest" of the nudge, and *who* is entitled to define it? Many would say that proper LPNs should NOT include what nudge supporters call "type 2" nudges, i.e. those changing actors' choice architectures to achieve desired collective ends AS DEFINED by nudgers (e.g. paying taxes).

References

Benartzi, S., and R. Thaler. 2004. Save More Tomorrow. *Journal of Political Economy 112* (S1): S164–S187.

Brock, D. 1988. Paternalism and Autonomy. *Ethics*: 550–565.

Fudging, H.M. 2016. Nudging: Why 'Libertarian Paternalism' is the Contradiction It Claims It's Not. *Georgetown Journal of Law and Public Policy 14*: 703.

Halpern, D., D. King, I. Vlaev, and M. Hallsworth. 2010. *Mindspace*. Institute for Government.

Mill, J.S. 1869. *On Liberty*.

Schubert, C. 2016. A Note On the Ethics of Nudges. http://voxeu.org/article/note-ethics-nudges

Soman, D., et al. 2005. The Psychology of Intertemporal Discounting: Why are Distant Events Valued Differently from Proximal Ones? *Marketing Letters Springer 16* (3–4): 347–360.

Thaler, R., and C. Sunstein. 2003. Libertarian Paternalism. *The American Economic Review 93* (2): 175–179.

Thaler, Richard H., and Cass R. Sunstein. 2008. *Nudge: Improving Decisions about Health, Wealth, and Happiness*. Penguin Books.

White, M. 2013. *The Manipulation of Choice: Ethics and Libertarian Paternalism*. Hampshire: Palgrave Macmillan.

11

What We Talk About When We Talk About Behavioral Economics

In CE books, conclusions often:

1. begin by referring back to the Introduction, thus creating a nice circular effect and a sense of unity.
2. wrap up the contents of the book, restating the main points and arguments made, so that they remain stuck in the mind of the reader.
3. conclude with a "call to action", for example, present the book as a bridge between what was the state of the art before the book was published and what should presumably be done in the future given the new insights provided by the book.

So what follows is not the typical conclusion, as it only (partially) retains the "call to action" component mentioned in point 3. In fact, this conclusion is rather a full member of the "unfinished businesses" club. The main difference is that, while the six unfinished businesses identified previously referred to specific issues, the seventh unfinished business we are about to introduce is much more general (though perhaps not less important), as it relates to *how* research is formulated and to *what* behavioral economics really is (or should be).

F. Ghisellini, B. Y. Chang, *Behavioral Economics*,
https://doi.org/10.1007/978-3-319-75205-1_11

As to the former aspect, we'll begin with one preliminary brief thought about the language in economics, and in particular about the use of the language of mathematics.

As exemplified by the (admittedly extreme) excerpt presented in Chap. 3, economics (especially in the last 30 years of the past century) has been often reduced to a province of mathematics, more than it was the case for any other subject except mathematics itself. And perhaps the most shocking aspect of this phenomenon was, of course, that the absolute majority of the mathematical models used to explain issues like cash preference or wage dynamics were found to have no matching at all with reality. But that didn't seem to matter, as long as these models continued to be formally beautiful! Mainstream economists "*have adopted the view that formal, or mathematical, proofs are entirely sufficient to establish the validity of a theory rather than being just necessary*" (Eichner 1983: 229–230). Further, "*the position of the 'pure' mathematician among economic theorists has become the dominant one, especially at the leading graduate schools where, as the teachers in the required core courses, they are able to exert a particularly strong influence on the profession. The result is that, in economics, the imperatives of mathematics—with the emphasis on formal rather than on empirical proofs and on elegance rather than on relevance—have replaced the norms of science*" (p. 231). And the absence of empirical proof was indeed a serious handicap for the credibility of the exercise. As Ackoff put it, "No real problem worth solving can be solved without some basic research. Therefore the engagement of faculty and students on real problems yields basic research problems whose solutions are of practical significance. Furthermore, the validity of these solutions can be tested in the most effective way known: in application. This avoids one's confusing mathematical masturbation with intercourse between research and reality" (Ackoff 1970).

There was a moment in which the most influential "economists" were actually engineers by trade, and they still form a sort of closed caste.[1] In an interview, Richard Thaler describes the caste situation well:

> *If you criticize it, they suspect, and rightly so in my case, that it's because you're not as good at math as them. You know, most economists are failed mathematicians or physicists. We have lots of MIT and Caltech undergrads that are now famous economists.*[2]

In a 2015 paper, even Paul Romer (2015)—one of the most influential growth economists around—criticizes important Neoclassical economists like Robert Lucas for producing research with a lot of math but with very little realism. And it seems that Romer's input is already producing its effects, as the importance of math-based theoretical research in conventional economics seems today less pronounced than it was only a few years ago.

There is more reason why behavioral economics should consider the same issue. If we try, for example, to describe the decisional process of a real-world investor, can he really do that through the usage of advanced calculus and differential equations? Wouldn't that be a contradiction for a discipline whose distinctive feature lies in the adherence to real-world situations?

More generally, in order to become the "normal" economics, behavioral economics theories should outperform conventional economics theories, and in order to do so, behavioral economics theories will need to fulfill all the three preconditions (accuracy of predictions, generality, and tractability) identified by Stigler (1965) at a higher degree.

But in order to arrive at a "consensus" model that is compact, parsimonious, empirically testable, AND representative of behavioral economics, there is a minor detail to clarify, which is the definition of behavioral economics.

In an email exchange published in *Forbes* in February 2015, Richard Thaler states that "*the definition of behavioral economics has been abused*". As he is considered one of the founders of behavioral economics, Thaler is to an extent entitled to defend his own definition of behavioral economics. His definition is only implicit, however, as it only describes what behavioral economics does, rather than what it is. As a matter of fact, the definition Mullainathan and Thaler give (cf. 6.3.1) seems to imply that behavioral economics is just a "correction factor" for conventional economics.

So Thaler thinks that different definitions represent an abuse. And there are many abuses around. Just a couple of examples.

For instance, Erik Angner remarked that the definition he and George Lowenstein share, which was the basis for their 2007 paper, is "behavioral economics" refers to

> *the attempt to increase the explanatory and predictive power of economic theory by providing it with more psychologically plausible foundations. By "psychologically plausible" we mean consistent with the best available psychology.* (Angner and Lowenstein 2007)

In the same year, the BIT set up by the UK prime minister in 2008 states that

> *we coined the term "behavioural insights" in 2010 to help bring together ideas from a range of inter-related academic disciplines (behavioural economics, psychology, and social anthropology). These fields seek to understand how individuals take decisions in practice and how they are likely to respond to options.*

The main difference separating the three definitions stands in their degree of narrowness. Thaler's definition is the narrowest, as it reduces the contribution of behavioral economics to relaxing a few specific assumptions of conventional theory.

But can that work? Fudenberg (2006) raises a very valid point when he remarks that "this approach overlooks the fact that the factors that support one modification of the standard model may be correlated with factors that argue for further modifications. Thus, modifying one or two assumptions and leaving the rest unchanged may lead to a logically consistent alternative model, but one whose domain of application is unclear or non-existent".

This is one of the reasons why we consider the BIT's general definition more functional and appropriate. But there is, of course, a trade-off (there is always a trade-off). The wider the definition, the more serious the problems encountered by behavioral economics in the last decade can become. What problems?

As a matter of fact in the literature, there are now countless behavioral factors, each of which has been studied in isolation. Therefore, in the last few years, we can argue that behavioral economics has been growing "horizontally", and the main product of this has been that behavioral economics is plagued with confusing definitions, unanswered questions, and conceptual gaps. It is reminiscent of a person who needs a diet for both a detox and a weight loss. Paradoxically, behavioral economics suffers from an "information overload", with little or no guidance on what model is to be used in specific contexts.

It is therefore an absolute priority that going forward behavioral economics is capable of generating a tractable "reduced form" for theoretical models. The hundreds of different behavioral factors should eventually be translated into results of a combination of a smaller set of primitive factors.

We hardly need the discovery of yet another behavioral bias to be added to Wikipedia list of 180 (as of September 2017). What we really need at this stage is parsimony, and an effort to synthesize what already exists in a general mainstream model that can represent a full-fledged alternative to conventional models.

Just as an example of the kind of work that should (and could) be done, consider the unrealistic traits of conventional economics (unbounded rationality, unbounded willpower, and unbounded selfishness) highlighted by Mullainathan and Thaler (cf. 6.3.1). These three unrealistic traits have typically been dealt with by behavioral economics one at a time, each in isolation from the others, generating myriad of subproblems for each of the three traits concerned and having as a conceptual reference utility as defined in conventional economics (i.e. wealth maximization).

If, however, we subscribe to Herbert Simon's (1945) definition of rationality, by which "*behavior is rational in so far as it selects alternatives which are conducive to the achievement of the previously selected goals*", the statement by Mullainathan and Thaler could be simply reformulated as: "*The economic model of human behavior is based on a definition of rationality which is based on consistency between actions and goals*". This definition is much more compact and much more tractable: instead of testing separately for rationality, willpower, and selfishness, you just check consistency between decisions and purposes.

There may be a long way to go, but the destination is clear. In order to get rid of its semantic specificity (the adjective "behavioral"), the effort should be that of synthetizing models, so that more general as well as more specific ones can be developed. Of course, that can only be achieved through reaching some level of consensus among economists. So, maybe even a more explicit fracture between those who think that people are stupid and those who don't might be desirable after all; it would make the picture clearer and in any case better than the current equivocal configuration.

* * *

Did we miss anything? That is likely, and you as a reader might have in mind your personal list of priority "unfinished businesses". But after all, this is not as important as it may seem. In our view, what is important is shaking things up. For years now, behavioral economics has been resting on its laurels, with much of related research just restating how stupid and irrational we are and/or adding still another bias to the ever expanding list of alleged cognitive distortions. We think that behavioral economics deserves a better fate and still has the opportunity to come of age and become a full-fledged alternative to conventional economics, rather than "a collection of quirks". But in order to do that, what is needed is to regain momentum and courage. With this book, we try to contribute to this effort—by providing the indication of avenues for further research for each of the seven unfinished businesses we focus on. Obviously, there is more work to be developed and we need actions. Soon. As House (2014) writes:

> *I would think that if behavioral is to somehow fulfill its earlier promise then there has to be some transcendent principle or insight which comes from behavioral economics that we can use to understand the world. In any case, if behavioral is to continue to develop, it will need some very smart, energetic young researchers to pick up where Laibson and the others left off. If not, behavioral economics gets a goodbye kiss from Heidi Klum and it's "Auf Wiedersehen".*[3]

The readers will judge how good this book is, but for certain the book is not "yet another book on behavioral economics". Because it carries a special message. And the message is that behavioral economics is not ready to say that "*Auf Wiedersehen*".

Notes

1. Personal experience of one of the authors: during the mid-1980s, most people in the Economics department of the Imperial College in London actually went around in lab coats.
2. https://qz.com/414616/richard-thaler-on-misbehavior-tipping-and-economists-as-failed-mathematicians/, 2015.
3. Cf. House (2014).

References

Ackoff, R. 1970. Some Ideas on Education in the Management Sciences. *Management Science* 17 (2): B-2.

Angner, E., and G. Loewenstein. 2007. Behavioral Economics. In *Handbook of the Philosophy of Science*, ed. J. Woods. Elsevier.

Chris House. 2014. Is Behavioral Economics the Past or the Future? *Orderstatistic*, February 28. <https://orderstatistic.wordpress.com/2014/02/28/is-behavioral-economics-the-past-or-the-future/>.

Eichner, A.S. 1983. Why Economics is Not Yet a Science. *The Quarterly Journal of Economics 17* (2): 507–520.

Fudenberg, D. 2006. Advancing beyond "Advances in Behavioral Economics". *Journal of Economic Literature* 44 (3): 694–711.

Romer, P. 2015. Mathiness in the Theory of Economic Growth. *American Economic Review Papers and Proceedings 105* (5): 89–93.

Simon, H.S. 1945. *Administrative Behavior, A Study of Decision-Making Processes in Administrative Organization*. New York: The Free Press.

Stigler, G. 1965. The Development of Utility Theory. In *Essays in the History of Economics*, ed. G. Stigler. Chicago, IL: Chicago University Press.

Index[1]

[1] Note: Page numbers followed by 'n' refer to notes.

F. Ghisellini, B. Y. Chang, *Behavioral Economics*,
https://doi.org/10.1007/978-3-319-75205-1

The manufacturer's authorised representative in the EU is Springer Nature Customer Service Centre GmbH, Europaplatz 3, 69115 Heidelberg, Germany. If you have any concerns regarding our products, please contact ProductSafety@springernature.com

Printed and bound by CPI Group (UK) Ltd, Croydon, CR0 4YY
22/09/2026
02220990-0003